Walter Savage Landor

Pericles and Aspasia

Walter Savage Landor

Pericles and Aspasia

ISBN/EAN: 9783744760812

Printed in Europe, USA, Canada, Australia, Japan

Cover: Foto ©ninafisch / pixelio.de

More available books at **www.hansebooks.com**

PERICLES AND ASPASIA.

BY

WALTER SAVAGE LANDOR.

BOSTON:
ROBERTS BROTHERS.
1894.

PERICLES AND ASPASIA.

I. ASPASIA TO CLEONE.

CLEONE! I write from Athens. I hasten to meet your reproaches, and to stifle them in my embrace. It was wrong to have left Miletus at all: it was wrong to have parted from you without intrusting you with my secret. No, no, neither was wrong. I have withstood many tears, my sweet Cleone, but never yours; you could always do what you would with me; and I should have been wind-bound by you on the Mæander, as surely and inexorably as the fleet at Aulis by Diana.

Ionia is far more beautiful than Attica, Miletus than Athens; for about Athens there is no verdure, no spacious and full and flowing river, few gardens, many olive-trees, so many, indeed, that we seem to be in an eternal cloud of dust. However, when the sea-breezes blow, this tree itself looks beautiful; it looks, in its pliable and undulating branches, irresolute as Ariadne when she was urged to fly, and pale as Orithyia when she was borne away.

II. CLEONE TO ASPASIA.

Come out, Aspasia, from among those olives. You would never have said a word about any such things, at such a time, unless you had met with an adventure. When you want to hide somewhat, you always run into the thickets of poetry. Pray leave Ariadne with Bacchus, she cannot be safer; and Orithyia with Boreas, if you have any reverence for the mysteries of the gods. Now I have almost a mind to say, tell me nothing at all

(5)

of what has happened to you since you left us. This would punish you as you deserve, for you know that you are dying to tell it. The venerable and good-natured old widow, Epimedea, will have trouble enough, I foresee, with her visitor from Asia. The Milesian kid will over-leap her garden-wall, and browse and butt everywhere. I take it as a matter of certainty that you are with her, for I never heard you mention any other relative in Athens, and she was, I remember, the guest of your house. How she loved you, dear good woman! She would have given your father Axiochus all her wealth for you. But when you were seven years old you were worth seven times over what you are now. I loved you then myself. Well, I am resolved to relieve you of your secret.

Prodigal scatterer of precious hopes, and of smiles that seem to rise from the interest you feel, and not from the interest you excite, what victim have you crowned with flowers, and selected to fall at your altar?

III. ASPASIA TO CLEONE.

Spirit of divination! how dared you find me out? And how dared you accuse me of poetizing? You who poetize more extravagantly yourself. Mine, I do insist upon it, is no worse than we girls in general are apt to write; "and no better," you will reply, "than we now and then are condemned to listen to, or disposed to read."

Poetry is the weightless integument that our butterflies always shed in our path, ere they wing their way toward us. It is precisely of the same form, color, and sub-stance, for the whole generation. Are all mine well? and all yours? I shall be very angry to hear that mine are. If they do not weep, and look wan, and sicken, why then I must, out of very spite. But may the gods in their wisdom keep not only their hearts, but their persons too, just where they are! I intend to be in love here at Athens. It is true, I do assure you, when I have time, and idleness, and courage for it.

Ay, ay, now your eyes are running over all the rest of

the letter. Well, what have you found? where is the
place? I will keep you in suspense no longer.

As soon as there was any light at all, we discovered, on
the hill above the city, crowds of people and busy preparations. You are come to it.

IV. ASPASIA TO CLEONE.

I was determined to close my letter when your curiosity was at the highest, that you might flutter and fall
from the clouds like Icarus. I wanted two things : first,
that you should bite your lip, an attitude in which you
alone look pretty ; and secondly, that you should say
half-angrily, " This now is exactly like Aspasia." I will
be remembered ; and I will make you look just as I would
have you.

How fortunate ! to have arrived at Athens at dawn on
the twelfth of Elaphebolion. On this day begin the festivals of Bacchus, and the theatre is thrown open at
sunrise.

What a theatre ! what an elevation ! what a prospect
of city and port, of land and water, of porticos and
temples, of men and heroes, of demi-gods and gods !

It was indeed my wish and intention, when I left
Ionia, to be present at the first of the Dyonysiacs ; but
how rarely are wishes and intentions so accomplished,
even when winds and waters do not interfere !

I will now tell you all. No time was to be lost : so I
hastened on shore in the dress of an Athenian boy who
came over with his mother from Lemnos. In the giddiness of youth he forgot to tell me that, not being yet
eighteen years old, he could not be admitted ; and he
left me on the steps. My heart sank within me ; so
many young men stared and whispered ; yet never was
stranger treated with more civility. Crowded as the
theatre was (for the tragedy had begun) every one made
room for me. When they were seated, and I too, I
looked toward the stage ; and behold there lay before
me, but afar off, bound upon a rock, a more majestic

form, and bearing a countenance more heroic, I should rather say more divine, than ever my imagination had conceived! I know not how long it was before I discovered that as many eyes were directed toward me as toward the competitor of the gods. I was neither flattered by it nor abashed. Every wish, hope, sigh, sensation, was successively with the champion of the human race, with his antagonist Zeus, and his creator Æschylus. How often, O Cleone, have we throbbed with his injuries! how often hath his vulture torn our breasts! how often have we thrown our arms around each other's neck, and half renounced the religion of our fathers! Even your image, inseparable at other times, came not across me then; Prometheus stood between us. He had resisted in silence and disdain the cruellest tortures that Almightiness could inflict; and now arose the Nymphs of ocean, which heaved its vast waves before us; and now they descended with open arms and sweet benign countenances, and spake with pity; and the insurgent heart was mollified and quelled.

I sobbed; I dropt.

V. CLEONE TO ASPASIA.

Is this telling me all? you faithless creature! There is much to be told when Aspasia faints in a theatre : and Aspasia in disguise!

My sweet and dear Aspasia! with all your beauty, of which you cannot but be conscious, how is it possible you could have hoped to be undetected? Certainly there never was any woman, or even any man, so little vain as you are. Formerly you were rather so about your poetry; but now you really write it well, you have overcome this weakness; nay, you doubt whether your best verses are tolerable. You have told me this several times; and you always say what you think, unless when any one might be hurt or displeased. I am glad the observation comes across me, for I must warn you upon it.

Take care then, Aspasia! do not leave off entirely all

dissimulation. It is as feminine a virtue, and as necessary to a woman, as religion. If you are without it, you
will have a grace the less, and (what you could worse
spare) a sigh the more.

VI. ASPASIA TO CLEONE.

I was not quite well when I wrote to you. When I
am not quite well I must always write to you ; I am better after it.

Where did I leave off ?

Ah Cleone ! Cleone ! I have learnt your lesson ; I am
dissembling ; it must not be with you. My tears are
falling. I acted unworthily. And are these tears indeed
for my fault against you? I cannot tell; if I could, I
would candidly. Everything that has happened, everything that shall happen hereafter, I will lay upon your
knees. Counsel me ; direct me. Even were I as sensible as you are, I should not be able to discover my own
faults. The clearest eyes do not see the cheeks below,
nor the brow above them.

To proceed, then, in my narrative. Everything appeared to me an illusion but the tragedy. What was
divine seemed human, and what was human seemed divine.

An apparition of resplendent and unearthly beauty
threw aside, with his slender arms, the youths, philosophers, magistrates, and generals, that surrounded me,
with a countenance as confident, a motion as rapid, and
a command as unresisted as a god.

" Stranger !" said he, " I come from Pericles, to offer
you my assistance."

I looked in his face ; it was a child's.

" We have attendants here who shall conduct you from
the crowd," said he.

" Venus and Cupid !" cried one.

" We are dogs ! " growled another.

" Worse !" rejoined a third, " we are slaves."

" Happy man ! happy man ! if thou art theirs," whispered the next in his ear, and followed us close behind.

I have since been informed that Pericles, who sate below us on the first seat, was the only man who did not rise. No matter; why should he? why did the rest? But it was very kind in him to send his cousin; I mean it was very kind for so proud a man.

Epimedea wept over me when I entered her house, and burnt incense before the gods, and led me into my chamber.

" I have a great deal to say to you, my dear Aspasia; but you must go to sleep: your bath shall be ready at noon; but be sure you sleep till then," said she.

I did indeed sleep, and (will you believe it?) instantly and soundly. Never was bath more refreshing, never was reproof more gentle, than Epimedea's.

I found her at my pillow when I awoke, and she led me to the marble couch.

" Dear child!" said she, when I had stept in, " you do not know our customs. You should have come at once to my house; you never should have worn men's clothes: indeed you should not have gone to the theatre at all; but, being there, and moreover in men's habiliments, you should have taken care not to have fainted, as they say you did. My husband Thessalus would never hear of fainting; he used to tell me it was a bad example. But he fainted at last, poor man! and . . I minded his admonition. Why! what a lovely child you are grown, my little Aspasia! is the bath too hot? Aspasia! can it be? why, you are no child at all!"

I really do believe that this idle discourse of Epimedea, which will tire you, perhaps, was the only one that would not have wearied out my spirits. It neither made me think nor answer. What a privilege! what a blessing! how seldom to be enjoyed in our conferences with the silly! Ah! do not let me wrong the kind Epimedea! Those are not silly who have found the way to our hearts; and far other names do they deserve who open to us theirs.

VII. ASPASIA TO CLEONE.

The boy about whom I wrote to you in my letter of yesterday, is called Alcibiades.* He lisps and blushes at it. His cousin Pericles, you may have heard, enjoys the greatest power and reputation, both as an orator and a general, of any man in Athens. Early this morning the beautiful child came to visit me, and told me that, when his cousin had finished his studies, which he usually had done about three hours after sunrise, he would desire him to come also.

I replied, " By no means do it, my beautiful and brave protector! Surely, on considering the matter, you will think you are taking too great a liberty with a person so distinguished."

" I take no liberties with any other," said he.

When I expressed in my countenance a little surprise at his impetuosity, he came forward and kissed my brow. Then said he, more submissively, " Pardon my rudeness. I like very well to be told what to do by those who are fond of me ; but never to be told what not to do ; and the more fond they are of me the less I like it. Because when they tell me what to do, they give me an opportunity of pleasing them ; but when they tell me what not to do, it is a sign that I have displeased, or am likely to displease them. Beside . . I believe there are some other reasons, but they have quite escaped me.

" It is time I should return," said he, " or I shall forget all about the hour of his studies (I mean Pericles) and mine too."

I would not let him go, however, but inquired who were his teachers, and repeated to him many things from Sap-

---

* He had no right to be at the theatre; but he might have taken the liberty, for there was nobody in Athens whom he feared, even in his childhood. Thucydides calls him *a youth* in the twelfth year of the Peloponnesian war. He was, on the mother's side, grandson of Megacles, whose granddaughter Isodoce married Cimon : her father Euryptolemus was cousin-german to Pericles.

pho and Alcæus and Pindar and Simonides. He was amazed, and told me he preferred them to Fate and Necessity, Pytho and Pythonissa.

I would now have kissed him in my turn, but he drew back, thinking (no doubt) that I was treating him like a child; that a kiss is never given but as the price of pardon; and that I had pardoned him before for his captiousness.

VIII. CLEONE TO ASPASIA.

Aspasia! I foresee that henceforward you will admire the tragedy of Prometheus more than ever. But do not tell any one, excepting so fond a friend as Cleone, that you prefer the author to Homer. I agree with you that the conception of such a drama is in itself a stupendous effort of genius; that the execution is equal to the conception; that the character of Prometheus is more heroic than any in heroic poetry; and that no production of the same extent is so magnificent and so exalted. But the Iliad is not a region: it is a continent; and you might as well compare this prodigy to it as the cataract of the Nile to the Ocean. In the one we are overpowered by the compression and burst of the element; in the other we are carried over an immensity of space, bounding the earth, not bounded by her, and having nothing above but the heavens.

Let us enjoy, whenever we have an opportunity, the delight of admiration, and perform the duties of reverence. May others hate what is admirable! We will hate likewise, O my Aspasia! when we can do no better. I am unable to foretell the time when this shall happen; it lies, I think, beyond the calculations of Meton.

I am happy to understand that the Athenians have such a philosopher among them. Hitherto we have been inclined to suppose that philosophy, at Athens, is partly an intricate tissue of subtile questions and illusory theories, knotted with syllogisms, and partly an indigested mass of unexamined assertions and conflicting dogmas. The Ionians are more silent, contemplative, and recluse. Knowing that Nature will not deliver her oracles in the crowd nor by sound of trumpet, they open their breasts to her in solitude with the simplicity of children, and look earnestly in her face for a reply. Meton and Democritus and Anaxagoras may perhaps lay their hands upon the leapings of your tettinxes, and moderate their chirping, but I apprehend that the genius of the people will always repose upon the wind-skins of the sophists. Comedy might be their corrector; but Comedy seems to think she has two offices to perform; from one side of the stage to explode absurdity, and from the other to introduce indecency. She might, under wise regulations (and these she should impose upon herself), render more service to a state than Philosophy could, in whatsover other character. And I wonder that Aristophanes, strong in the poetical faculty, and unrivalled in critical acuteness, should not perceive that a dominion is within his reach which is within the reach of no mortal beside; a dominion whereby he may reform the manners, dictate the pursuits, and regulate the affections of his countrymen. Perhaps he never could have done it so effectually, had he been better and begun otherwise; but having, however unworthy might have been the means and methods, seized upon their humors, they now are as pliable to him as waxen images to Thessalian witches. He keeps them before the fire he has kindled, and he has only to sing the right song.

Beware, my dear Aspasia, never to offend him; for he holds more terrors at his command than Æschylus. The tragic poet rolls the thunder that frightens, the comic wields the lightning that kills. Aristophanes has the power of tossing you among the populace of a thousand cities for a thousand years.

A great poet is more powerful than Sesostris, and a wicked one more formidable than Phalaris.

IX. ASPASIA TO CLEONE.

Epimedea has been with me in my chamber. She asked me whether the women of Ionia had left off wearing ear-rings. I answered that I believe they always had worn them, and that they were introduced by the Persians, who received them from nations more remote.

"And do you think yourself too young," said she, "for such an ornament?" producing at the same instant a massy pair, inlaid with the largest emeralds. "Alas! alas!" said she, "your mother neglected you strangely. There is no hole in the ear, right or left! We can mend that, however; I know a woman who will bring us the prettiest little pan of charcoal, with the prettiest little steel rod in it; and, before you can cry out, one ear lets light through. These are yours," said she, "and so shall everything be when I am gone . . house, garden, quails, leveret."

"Generous Epimedea!" said I, "do not say things that pain me. I will accept a part of the present; I will wear these beautiful emeralds on one arm. Thinking of nailing them in my ears, you resolve to make me steady; but I am unwilling they should become dependencies of Attica."

"All our young women wear them; the goddesses too."

"The goddesses are in the right," said I; "their ears are marble; but I do not believe any one of them would tell us that women were made to be the settings of pearls and emeralds."

I had taken one, and was about to kiss her, when she said, "Do not leave me an odd ear-ring; put the other in the hair."

"Epimedea," said I, "I have made a vow never to wear on the head anything but one single flower, a single wheat-ear, green or yellow, and ivy or vine leaves: the number of these are not mentioned in the vow."

"Rash child!" said Epimedea, shaking her head; "I never made but two vows; one was when I took a husband."

"And the other? Epimedea!"

"No matter," said she, "it might be, for what I know, never to do the like again."

X. ASPASIA TO CLEONE.

Pericles has visited me. After many grave and gentle inquiries, often suspended, all relating to my health; and after praises of Miletus, and pity for my friends left behind, he told me that, when he was quite assured of my recovery from the fatigues of the voyage, he hoped I would allow him to collect from me, at my leisure hours, the information he wanted on the literature of Ionia. Simple-hearted man! in praising the authors of our country, he showed me that he knew them perfectly, from first to last. And now indeed his energy was displayed: I thought he had none at all. With how sonorous and modulated a voice did he repeat the more poetical passages of our elder historians! and how his whole soul did lean upon Herodotus! Happily for me, he observed not my enthusiasm. And now he brought me into the presence of Homer. "We claim him," said he, "but he is yours. Observe with what partiality he always dwells on Asia. How infinitely more civilized are Glaucus and Sarpedon than any of the Grecians he was called upon to celebrate! Priam, Paris, Hector, what polished men! Civilization has never made a step in advance, and never will, on those countries; she had gone so far in the days of Homer. He keeps Helen pretty rigorously out of sight, but he opens his heart to the virtues of Andromache. What a barbarian is the son of a goddess! Pallas must seize him by the hair to avert the murder of his leader; but at the eloquence of the Phrygian king the storm of the intractable homicide bursts in tears."

"And Æschylus," said I, but could not continue: blushes rose into my cheek, and pained me at the recollection of my weakness.

"He has left us," said Pericles, who pretended not to have perceived it; "I am grieved that my prayers were inadequate to detain him. But what prayers or what expostulations can influence the lofty mind, laboring and heaving under injustice and indignity? Æschylus knew he merited, by his genius and his services, the gratitude and admiration of the Athenians. He saw others preferred before him, and hoisted sail. At the rumor of his departure such was the consternation as if the shield of Pallas in the Parthenon had dropt from her breast upon the pavement. That glory shines now upon the crown of Hiero, which has sunk for Athens."

"You have still great treasures left," said I; for he was moved.

"True," replied he, "but will not every one remark, who hears the observation, that we know not how to keep them, and have never weighed them?"

I sate silent; he resumed his serenity.

"We ought to change places," said he, "at the feet of the poets. Æschylus, I see, is yours; Homer is mine. Aspasia should be a Pallas to Achilles; and Pericles a subordinate power, comforting and consoling the afflicted demi-god. Impetuosity, impatience, resentment, revenge itself, are pardonable sins in the very softest of your sex; on brave endurance rises *our* admiration."

"I love those better who endure with constancy," said I.

"Happy!" replied he, "thrice happy! O Aspasia, the constancy thus tried and thus rewarded!"

He spoke with tenderness; he rose with majesty; bowed to Epimedea: touched gently, scarcely at all, the hand I presented to him, bent over it, and departed.

XI. ASPASIA TO CLEONE.

I told you I would love, O Cleone! but I am so near it that I dare not.

Tell me what I am to do; I can do anything but write and think.

Pericles has not returned.

I am nothing here in Athens.

Five days are over; six almost.

O what long days are these of Elaphebolion!

XII. CLEONE TO ASPASIA.

Take heed, Aspasia! All orators are deceivers; and Pericles is the greatest of orators.

I will write nothing more, lest you should attend in preference to any other part of my letter.

Yes; I must repeat my admonition: I must speak out plainly; I must try other words . . stronger . . more frightful. Love of supremacy, miscalled political glory, finds most, and leaves all, dishonest.

The gods and goddesses watch over and preserve you, and send you safe home again!

XIII. ASPASIA TO CLEONE.

Fear not for me, Cleone! Pericles has attained the summit of glory; and the wisdom and virtue that acquired it for him are my sureties.

A great man knows the value of greatness: he dares not hazard it, he will not squander it. Imagine you that the confidence and affection of a people, so acute, so vigilant, so jealous, as the Athenians, would have rested firmly and constantly on one inconstant and infirm.

If he loves me the merit is not mine; the fault will be if he ceases.

XIV. CLEONE TO ASPASIA.

I must and will fear for you, and the more because I perceive you are attracted as the bees are, by an empty sound, the fame of your admirer. You love Pericles for that very quality which ought to have set you on your guard against him. In contentions for power, the philosophy and the poetry of life are dropt and trodden down. Domestic affections can no more bloom and flourish in the hardened race-course of politics, than flowers can find nourishment in the pavement of the streets. In the poli-

2

tician the whole creature is factitious; if ever he speaks as before, he speaks either from memory or invention.

But such is your beauty, such your genius, it may alter the nature of things.   Endowed with the power of Circe, you will exert it oppositely, and restore to the most selfish and most voracious of animals the uprightness and dignity of man.

XV. PERICLES TO ASPASIA.

It is not wisdom in itself, O Aspasia! it is the manner of imparting it that affects the soul, and alone deserves the name of eloquence. ⟩ I have never been moved by any but yours.

Is it the beauty that shines over it, is it the voice that ripeus it, giving it those lovely colors, that delicious freshness; is it the modesty and diffidence with which you present it to us, looking for nothing but support?   Sufficient were any one of them singly; but all united have come forward to subdue me, and have deprived me of my courage, my self-possession, and my repose.

I dare not hope to be beloved, Aspasia!   I did hope it once in my life, and have been disappointed.   Where I sought for happiness none is offered to me : I have neither the sunshine nor the shade.

So unfortunate in earlier days, ought I, ten years later, to believe that she, to whom the earth, with whatever is beautiful and graceful in it, bows prostrate, will listen to me as her lover?   I dare not; too much have I dared already.   But if, O Aspasia! I should sometimes seem heavy and dull in conversation, when happier men surround you, pardon my infirmity.

I have only one wish; I may not utter it: I have only one fear; this at least is not irrational, and I will own it; the fear that Aspasia could never be sufficiently happy with me.

XVI. ASPASIA TO PERICLES.

Do you doubt, O Pericles, that I shall be sufficiently happy with you? This doubt of yours assures me that I shall be.

I throw aside my pen to crown the gods. And I worship thee first, O Pallas! who protectest the life, enlightenest the mind, establishest the power, and exaltest the glory, of Pericles.

XVII. CLEONE TO ASPASIA.

I tremble both for you and your lover. The people of Athens may applaud at first the homage paid to beauty and genius; nevertheless there are many whose joy will spring from malignity, and who will exult at what they think (I know not whether quite unjustly) a weakness in Pericles.

I shall always be restless about you. Let me confess to you, I do not like your sheer democracies. What are they good for? Why, yes, they have indeed their use; the filth and ferment of the compost are necessary for raising rare plants.

O how I wish we were again together in that island on our river which we call the *Fortunate!* It was almost an island when your father cut across the isthmus of about ten paces, to preserve the swan-nest.

Xeniades has left Miletus. We know not whither he is gone, but we presume to his mines in Lemnos. It was always with difficulty he could be persuaded to look after his affairs. He is too rich, too young, too thoughtless. But since you left Miletus, we have nothing here to detain him.

I wish I could trifle with you about your Pericles. Any wager, he is the only lover who never wrote verses upon you.

In a politician a verse is an ostracism.

XVIII. ASPASIA TO CLEONE.

My Pericles (mine, mine he is) *has* written verses upon me ; not many, nor worth his prose, even the shortest sentence of it.   But you will read them with pleasure for their praises of Miletus.

No longer ago than yesterday an ugly young philosopher declared his passion for me, as you shall see.   I did not write anything back to Pericles : I did to the other. I will not run the risk of having half my letter left unread by you, in your hurry to come into the poetry.

Here it all is :

PERICLES TO ASPASIA.

Flower of Ionia's fertile plains,
Where Pleasure leagued with Virtue reigns,
Where the Pierian Maids of old,
Yea, long ere Ilion's tale was told,
Too pure, too sacred for our sight,
Descended with the silent night
To young Arctinus, and Mæander
Delay'd his course for Melesander !
If there be city on the earth
Proud in the children of her birth,
Wealth, science, beauty, story, song,
These to Miletus all belong.
To fix the diadem on his brow
For ever, one was wanting . . thou.

I could not be cruel to such a suitor, even if he asked me for pity. (Love makes one-half of every man foolish, aud the other half cunning.) Pericles touched me on the side of Miletus, and Socrates came up to me straightforward from Prometheus :

SOCRATES TO ASPASIA.

He who stole fire from heaven,
Long heav'd his bold and patient breast ; 'twas riven
By the Caucasian bird and bolts of Jove.
Stolen that fire have I,
And am enchain'd to die
By every jealous Power that frowns above.

I call not upon thee again
To hear my vows and calm my pain,
   Who sittest high enthron'd
Where Venus rolls her gladsome star,
   Propitious Love! But thou disown'd
By sire and mother, whosoe'er they are,
Unblest in form and name, Despair!
Why dost thou follow that bright demon? why
His purest altar art thou always nigh?

I was sorry that Socrates should suffer so much for me.
Pardon the fib, Cleone! let it pass: I was sorry just
as we all are upon such occasions, and wrote him this
consolation:

O thou who sittest with the wise,
   And searchest higher lore,
And openest regions to their eyes
   Unvisited before!
I'd run to loose thee if I could,
Nor let the vulture taste thy blood.
But, pity! pity! Attic bee!
'Tis happiness forbidden me.

Despair is not for good or wise,
   And should not be for love;
We all must bear our destinies
   And bend to those above.
Birds flying o'er the stormy seas
Alight upon their proper trees,
Yet wisest men not always know
Where they should stop or whither go.

XIX. ASPASIA TO CLEONE.

I am quite ashamed of Alcibiades, quite angry with
him. What do you imagine he has been doing? He
listened to my conversation with Pericles, on the declaration of love from the *Philosopher Bound*, and afterward
to the verses I repeated in answer to his, which pleased
my Pericles extremely, not perhaps for themselves, but
because I had followed his advice in writing them, and
had returned to him with the copy so speedily.

Alcibiades said he did not like them at all, and could

write better himself. We smiled at this, and his cousin said, " Do then, my boy !"

Would you believe it ? he not only wrote, but I fear (for he declares he did) actually sent these :

> O Satyr-son of Sophroniscus !
> Would Alcon cut me a hibiscus,
> I'd wield it as the goatherds do,
> And swing thee a sound stroke or two,
> Bewilder, if thou canst, us boys,
> Us, or the sophists, with thy toys —
> Thy *kalokagathons* . . beware !
> Keep to the good, and leave the fair.

Could he really be the composer? what think you? or did he get any of his wicked friends to help him? The verses are very bold, very scandalous, very shocking. I am vext and sorry; but what can be done? We must seem to know nothing about the matter.

The audacious little creature . . not very little, he is within four fingers of my height . . is half in love with me. He flames up at the mention of Socrates : can he be jealous?

Pericles tells me that the philosophers here are as susceptible of malice as of love. It may be so, for the plants which are sweet in some places are acrid in others.

He said to me, smiling, " I shall be represented in their schools as a sophist, because Aspasia and Alcibiades were unruly. O that boy! who knows but his mischievous verses will be a reason sufficient, in another year, why I am unable to command an army or harangue an assembly of the people?"

XX. XENIADES TO ASPASIA.

Aspasia! Aspasia! have you forgotten me? have you forgotten *us?* Our childhood was one, our earliest youth was undivided. Why should you not see me? Did you fear that you would have to reproach me for any fault I have committed? This would have pained you formerly ; ah, how lately !

Your absence . . not absence . . flight . . has broken my health, and left me fever and frenzy. Eumedes is certain I can only recover my health by composure. Foolish man! as if composure were more easy to recover than health. Was there ever such a madman as to say, " You will never have the use of your limbs again unless you walk and run!"

I am weary of advice, of remonstrance, of pity, of everything; above all, of life.

Was it anger (how dared I be angry with you?) that withheld me from imploring the sight of you? Was it pride? Alas! what pride is left me? I am preferred no longer; I am rejected, scorned, loathed. Was it always so? Well may I ask the question; for everything seems uncertain to me but my misery. At times I know not whether I am mad or dreaming. No, no, Aspasia! the past was a dream, the present is a reality. The mad and the dreaming do not shed tears as I do. And yet in these bitter tears are my happiest moments; and some angry demon knows it, and presses my temples that there shall fall but few.

You refused to admit me. I asked too little, and deserved the refusal. Come to me. This you will not refuse, unless you are bowed to slavery. Go, tell your despot this, with my curses and defiance.

I am calmer, but insist. Spare yourself, Aspasia, one tear, and not by an effort, but by a duty.

XXI. ASPASIA TO CLEONE.

Of all men living, what man do you imagine has come to Athens? Insensate! now you know. What other, so beloved, would ever have left Miletus! I wish I could be convinced that your coldness or indifference had urged him to this extravagance. I can only promise you we will not detain him. Athens is not a refuge for the perfidious or the flighty. But if he is unfortunate; what shall we do with him? Do? I will tell him to return. Expect him hourly.

XXII. ASPASIA TO XENIADES.

I am pained to my innermost heart that you are ill.

Pericles is not the person you imagine him. Behold his billet! And can not you think of me with equal generosity?

True, we saw much of each other in our childhood, and many childish things we did together. This is the reason why I went out of your way as much as I could afterward. There is another, too. I hoped you would love more the friend that I love most. How much happier would she make you than the flighty Aspasia! We resemble each other too much, Xeniades! we should never have been happy, so ill-mated. Nature hates these alliances: they are like those of brother and sister. I never loved any one but Pericles; none else attracts the admiration of the world. I stand, O Xeniades! not only above slavery, but above splendor, in that serene light which Homer describes as encompassing the Happy on Olympus. I will come to visit you within the hour; be calm, be contented! love me, but not too much, Xeniades!

XXIII. ASPASIA TO PERICLES.

Xeniades, whom I loved a little in my childhood, and (do not look serious now, my dearest Pericles!) a very little afterward, is sadly ill. He was always, I know not how, extravagant in his wishes, although not so extravagant as many others; and what do you imagine he wishes now? He wishes . . but he is very ill, so ill he cannot rise from his bed . . that I would go and visit him. I wonder whether it would be quite considerate: I am half inclined to go, if you approve of it.

Poor youth! he grieves me bitterly.

I shall not weep before him; I have wept so much here. Indeed, indeed, I wept, my Pericles, only because I had written too unkindly.

XXIV. PERICLES TO ASPASIA.

Do what your heart tells you: yes, Aspasia, do *all* it tells you. Remember how august it is: it contains the temple, not only of Love, but of Conscience; and a whisper is heard from the extremity of the one to the extremity of the other.

Bend in pensiveness, even in sorrow, on the flowery bank of youth, whereunder runs the stream that passes irreversibly! let the garland drop into it, let the hand be refreshed by it; but may the beautiful feet of Aspasia stand firm!

XXV. XENIADES TO ASPASIA.

You promised you would return. I thought you only broke hearts, not promises.

It is now broad daylight; I see it clearly, although the blinds are closed. A long sharp ray cuts off one corner of the room, and we shall hear the crash presently.

Come; but without that pale silent girl: I hate her. Place her on the other side of you, not on mine.

And this plane-tree gives no shade whatever. We will sit in some other place.

No, no; I will not have you call her to us. Let her play where she is .. the notes are low .. she plays sweetly.

XXVI. ASPASIA TO PERICLES.

See what incoherency! He did not write it; not one word. The slave who brought it, told me that he was desired by the guest to write his orders, whenever he found his mind composed enough to give any.

About four hours after my departure, he called him mildly, and said, " I am quite recovered."

He gave no orders, however, and spake nothing more for some time. At last he raised himself up, and rested on his elbow, and began (said the slave) like one inspired. The slave added, that finding he was indeed quite well again, both in body and mind, and capable of making as fine poetry as any man in Athens, he had written down every word with the greatest punctuality; and that, looking at him for more, he found he had fallen into as sound a slumber as a reaper's.

" Upon this I ran off with the verses," said he.

XXVII. CLEONE TO ASPASIA.

Comfort him. But you must love him, if you do. Well! comfort him. Forgive my inconsiderateness. You will not love him now. You would not receive him when your bosom was without an occupant. And yet you saw him daily. Others, all others, pine away before him. I wish I could solace my soul with poetry, as you have the power of doing. In all the volumes I turn over, I find none exactly suitable to my condition; part expresses my feelings, part flies off from them to something more light and vague. I do not believe the best writers of love-poetry ever loved. How could they write if they did? where could they recollect the thoughts, the words, the courage? Alas! alas! men can find all these, Aspasia, and leave us after they have found them. But in Xeniades there is no fault whatever: he never loved me; he never said he did; he fled only from my immodesty in loving him. Dissembler as I was, he detected it. Do pity him and help him; but pity me too, who am beyond your help.

XXVIII. PERICLES TO ASPASIA.

Tears, O Aspasia, do not dwell long upon the cheeks of youth. Rain drops easily from the bud, rests on the bosom of the maturer flower, and breaks down that one only which hath lived its day.

Weep, and perform the offices of friendship. The season of life, leading you by the hand, will not permit you to linger at the tomb of the departed; and Xeniades, when your first tear fell upon it, entered into the number of the blessed.

XXIX. ASPASIA TO CLEONE.

What shall I say to you, tender and sweet Cleone! The wanderer is in the haven of happiness; the restless has found rest.

Weep not; I have shed all your tears.. not all.. they burst from me again.

XXX. CLEONE TO ASPASIA

Oh! he was too beautiful to live! Is there anything that shoots through the world so swiftly as a sunbeam! Epialtes has told me everything. He sailed back without waiting at the islands; by your orders, he says.

What hopes could I, with any prudence, entertain? The chaplet you threw away would have cooled and adorned my temples; but how could he ever love another who had once loved you? I am casting my broken thoughts before my Aspasia; the little shells upon the shore, that the storm has scattered there, and that heedless feet have trampled on.

I have prayed to Venus; but I never prayed her to turn toward me the fondness that was yours. I fancied, I even hoped, you might accept it; and my prayer was, " Grant I may never love! Afar from me, O goddess! be the malignant warmth that dries up the dews of friendship."

XXXI. ASPASIA TO CLEONE.

Pericles has insisted on it that I should change the air, and has recommended to me an excursion to the borders of the state.

" If you pass them a little way," said he, " you will come to Tanagra, and that will inflame you with ambition."

The honor in which I hold the name of Corinna induced me to undertake a journey to her native place.
Never have I found a people so hospitable as the inhabitants.   Living at a distance from the sea, they are not
traders, nor adventurers, nor speculators, nor usurers,
but cultivate a range of pleasant hills, covered with
vines.   Hermes is the principal god they worship; yet I
doubt whether a single prayer was ever offered up to him
by a Tanagrian for success in thievery.

The beauty of Corinna is no less celebrated than her
poetry.   I remarked that the women speak of it with
great exultation, while the men applaud her genius; and
I asked my venerable host Agesilaus how he could
account for it.

"I can account for nothing that you ladies do," said
he, "although I have lived among you seventy-five years;
I only know that it was exactly the contrary while she
was living.   We youths were rebuked by you when we
talked about her beauty; and the rebuke was only softened by the candid confession, that she was *clever . . in
her way.*"

"Come back with me to Athens, O Agesilaus!" said
I, "and we will send Aristophanes to Tanagra."

XXXII. ASPASIA TO CLEONE.

I have been reading all the poetry of Corinna that I
could collect.   Certainly it is better than Hesiod's, or
even than Myrtis's, who taught her and Pindar, not the
rudiments of the art, for this is the only art in which the
rudiments are incommunicable, but what was good, what
was bad, in her verses; why it was so, and how she
might correct the worse and improve the better.

Hesiod, who is also a Bœotian, is admirable for the
purity of his life and soundness of his precepts, but there
is hardly a trace of poetry in his ploughed field.

I find in all his writings but one verse worth transcrib-
ing, and that only for the melody:

"In a soft meadow and on vernal flowers."

I do not wonder he was opposed to Homer. What an advantage to the enemies of greatness (that is, to mankind) to be able to match one so low against one so lofty!

The Greek army before Troy would have been curious to listen to a dispute between Agamemnon and Achilles, but would have been transported with ecstasy to have been present at one between the king of men and Thersites.

There are few who possess all the poetry of any voluminous author. I doubt whether there are ten families in Athens in which all the plays of Æschylus are preserved. Many keep what pleases them most; few consider that every page of a really great poet has something in it which distinguishes him from an inferior order; something which, if insubstantial as the aliment, serves at least as a solvent to the aliment, of strong and active minds.

I asked my Pericles what he thought of Hesiod.

"I think myself more sagacious," said he. "Hesiod found out that half was more than all; I have found out that one is."

XXXIII. ASPASIA TO CLEONE.

A slave brought to me, this morning, an enormous load of papers, as many as he could carry under both arms. They are treatises by the most celebrated philosophers. Some hours afterward, when the sun was declining, Pericles came in, and asked me if I had examined or looked over any portion of them. I told him I had opened those only which bore the superscription of famous names, but that, unless he would assist me, I was hopeless of reconciling one part with another in the same writers.

"The first thing requisite," said I, "is, that as many as are now at Athens should meet together, and agree upon a nomenclature of terms. From definitions we may go on to propositions; but we cannot make a step unless the foot rests somewhere."

He smiled at me. "Ah my Aspasia!" said he, "Philosophy does not bring her sons together; she portions them off early, gives them a scanty stock of worm-eaten furniture, a chair or two on which it is dangerous to sit down, and at least as many arms as utensils; then leaves them: they seldom meet afterward."

"But could not they be brought together by some friend of the mother?" said I, laughing.

"Aspasia!" answered he, "you have lived but few years in the world, and with only one philosopher . . yourself."

"I will not be contented with a compliment," said I, "and least of all from you. Explain to me the opinions of those about you."

He traced before me the divergencies of every sect, from our countryman Thales to those now living. Epimedea sat with her eyes wide open, listening attentively. When he went away, I asked her what she thought of his discourse. She half closed her eyes, not from weariness, but (as many do) on bringing out of obscurity into light a notable discovery; and, laying her forefinger on my arm, "You have turned his head," said she. "He will do no longer; he used to be plain and coherent; and now . . did ever mortal talk so widely? I could not understand one word in twenty, and what I could understand was sheer nonsense."

"Sweet Epimedea!" said I, "this is what I should fancy to be no such easy matter."

"Ah! you are growing like him already," said she; "I should not be surprised to find, some morning, a cupola at the top of this pretty head."

Pericles, I think I never told you, has a little elevation on the crown of his; I should rather say his head has a crown, others have none.

XXXIV. CLEONE TO ASPASIA.

Do, my dear Aspasia, continue to write to me about the poets; and if you think there is anything of Myrtis or Corinna, which is wanting to us at Miletus, copy it out. I do not always approve of the Trilogies. Nothing can be more tiresome, hardly anything more wicked, than a few of them. It may be well occasionally to give something of the historical form to the dramatic, as it is occasionally to give something of the dramatic to the historical; but never to turn into ridicule and buffoonery the virtuous, the unfortunate, or the brave. Whatever the Athenians may boast of their exquisite judgment, their delicate perceptions, this is a perversion of intellect in its highest place, unworthy of a Thracian. There are many bad tragedies both of Æschylus and Sophocles, but none without beauties, few without excellences: I tremble, then, at your doubt. In another century it may be impossible to find a collection of the whole, unless some learned and rich man, like Pericles, or some protecting king, like Hiero, should preserve them in his library.

XXXV. ASPASIA TO CLEONE.

Prudently have you considered how to preserve all valuable authors. The cedar doors of a royal library fly open to receive them; ay, there they will be safe . . and untouched.

Hiero is, however, no barbarian: he deserves a higher station than a throne; and he is raised to it. The protected have placed the protector where neither the malice of men nor the power of gods can reach him . . beyond Time . . above Fate.

XXXVI. CLEONE TO ASPASIA.

From the shortness of your last, I am quite certain that you are busy for me in looking out pieces of verse. If you cannot find any of Myrtis or Corinna, you may do what is better; you may compose a panegyric on all of our sex who have excelled in poetry. This will earn for you the same good office, when the world shall produce another Aspasia.

Having been in Bœotia, you must also know a great
deal more of Pindar than we do. Write about any of
them; they all interest me, and my mind has need of
exercise. It is still too fond of throwing itself down on
one place.

XXXVII. ASPASIA TO CLEONE.

And so, Cleone, you wish me to write a eulogy on
Myrtis and Corinna, and all the other poetesses that ever
lived; and this for the honor of our sex! Ah Cleone!
no studied eulogy does honor to any one. It is always
considered, and always ought to be, as a piece of plead-
ing, in which the pleader says everything the most in favor
of his client, in the most graceful and impressive manner
he can. There is a city of Greece, I hear, in which re-
ciprocal flattery is so necessary, that, whenever a member
of the assembly dies, his successor is bound to praise him
before he takes the seat.

I do not speak this from my own knowledge; indeed I
could hardly believe in such frivolity, until I asked Pericles if it were true; or rather, if there were any foundation at all for the report.

"Perfectly true," said he, "but the citizens of this city
are now become our allies; therefore do not curl your
lip, or I must uncurl it, being an archon."

Myrtis and Corinna have no need of me. To read and
recommend their works, to point out their beauties and
defects, is praise enough.

"How!" methinks you exclaim. "To point out defects! is that praising?"

Yes, Cleone; if with equal good faith and accuracy
you point out their beauties too. It is only thus a fair
estimate can be made; and it is only by such fair estimate that a writer can be exalted to his proper station.
If you toss up the scale too high, it descends again
rapidly below its equipoise; what it contains drops out,
and people catch at it, scatter it, and lose it.

We not only are inclined to indulge in rather more
than a temperate heat (of what we would persuade our-

;elves is wholesome severity) toward the living, but even
o peer sometimes into the tomb, with a wolfish appetite
or an unpleasant odor.

We must patronize, we must pull down; in fact we
nust be in mischief, men or women.

If we are capable of showing what is good in another,
ınd neglect to do it, we omit a duty; we omit to give
·ational pleasure, and to conciliate right good-will; nay
nore, we are abettors, if not aiders, in the vilest fraud,
he fraud of purloining from respect.   We are intrusted
vith letters of great interest; what a baseness not to
leliver them!

XXXVIII. ASPASIA TO CLEONE.

It is remarkable that Athens, so fertile in men of
ʒenius, should have produced no women of distinction,
vhile Bœotia, by no means celebrated for brightness of
ntellect in either sex, presented to the admiration of the
vorld her Myrtis and Corinna.   At the feet of Myrtis it
vas, that Pindar gathered into his throbbing breast the
;cattered seeds of poetry; and it was under the smile of
:he beautiful Corinna that he drew his inspiration and
vove his immortal crown.

He never quite overcame his grandiloquence.   The
ınimals we call *half-asses*, by a word of the sweetest
;ound, although not the most seducing import, he calls

"The daughters of the tempest-footed steeds!"

O Fortune! that the children of so illustrious a line
;hould carry sucking-pigs into the market-place, and
:abbage-stalks out of it!

XXXIX. CLEONE TO ASPASIA.

Will you always leave off, Aspasia, at the very moment
ʒou have raised our expectations to the highest?   A wit-
;icism, and a sudden spring from your seat, lest we should

3

see you smile at it, these are your ways; shame upon
you! Are you determined to continue all your life in
making every one wish something?

Pindar should not be treated like ordinary men.

XL. ASPASIA TO CLEONE.

I have not treated Pindar like an ordinary man; I conducted him into the library of Cleone, and left him there.
However, I would have my smile out, behind the door.
The verse I quoted, you may be sure, is much admired
by the learned, and no less by the brave and worthy men
whom he celebrates for charioteership, and other such
dexterities; but we of old Miletus have been always
taught that words should be subordinate to ideas, and we
never place the pedestal on the head of the statue.

Now do not tell anybody that I have spoken a single
word in dispraise of Pindar. Men are not too apt to
admire what is admirable in their superiors, but, on
the contrary, are apt to detract from them, and to seize on
anything which may tend to lower them. Pindar would
not have written so exquisitely if no fault had ever been
found with him. He would have wandered on among
such inquiries as those he began in:

"Shall I sing the wide-spreading and noble Ismenus?
or the beautiful and white-ankled Melie? or the glorious
Cadmus? or the mighty Hercules? or the blooming Bacchus?"

Now a poet ought to know what he is about before he
opens his lips; he ought not to ask, like a poor fellow in
the street, "Good people! what song will you have?"
This, however, was not the fault for which he was blamed
by Corinna. In our censures we are less apt to consider
the benefit we may confer than the ingenuity we can display.

She said, "Pindar! you have brought a sack of corn
to sow a perch of land; and, instead of sprinkling it
about, you have emptied the sack at the first step."

Enough: this reproof formed his character; it directed

s beat, it singled his aim, it concentrated his forces. It
as not by the precepts of Corinna, it was not by her
xample, it was by one witticism of a wise and lovely
oman, that he far excels all other poets in disdain of
iviality and choice of topics. He is sometimes very
dious to us in his long stories of families, but we may
2 sure he was not equally so to those who were con-
rned in the genealogy. We are amused at his clever-
ess in saving the shoulder of Pelops from the devouring
aw of a hungry god. No doubt he mends the matter ;
evertheless he tires us.

Many prefer his Dithyrambics to his Olympian, Isth-
ian, Pythian, and Nemean Odes. I do not ; nor is it
kely that he did himself. We may well suppose that he
xerted the most power on the composition, and the most
iought on the correction, of the poems he was to recite
efore kiugs and nations, in honor of the victors at those
olemn games. Here the choruses and bands of music
ere composed of the first singers and players in the
orld ; iu the others there were no performers but such
s happened to assemble on ordinary festivals, or at best
t a festival of Bacchus. In the Odes performed at the
ames, although there is not always perfect regularity of
orresponding verse, there is always enough of it to satisfy
ie most fastidious ear. In the Dithyrambics there is no
rder whatsoever, but verses and half verses of every
ind, cemented by vigorous and sounding prose.

I do not love dances upon stilts ; they may excite the
pplauses and acclamations of the vulgar, but we, Cleone,
xact the observance of established rules, and never
ut on slippers, however richly embroidered, unless they
air.

XLI. CLEONE TO ASPASIA.

We hear that between Athens and Syracuse there has
lways been much communication. Let me learn what
ou have been able to collect about the lives of Pindar
nd Æschylus in Sicily.

Is it not strange that the two most high-minded of poets

should have gone to reside in a foreign land, under the dominion of a king?

I am ashamed of my question already. Such men are under no dominion. It is not in their nature to offend against the laws, or to think about what they are, or who administers them; and they may receive a part of their sustenance from kings, as well as from cows and bees. We will reproach them for emigration, when we reproach a man for lying down in his neighbor's field because the grass is softer in it than in his own.

XLII. ASPASIA TO CLEONE.

Not an atom have I been able to collect in regard to the two poets, since they went to the court of Hiero; but I can give you as correct and as full information, as if I had been seated between them all the while.

Hiero was proud of his acquisition; the courtiers despised them, vexed them whenever they could, and entreated them to command their services and rely upon their devotion. What more? They esteemed each other; but poets are very soon too old for mutual love.

He who can add one syllable to this, shall have the hand of Cleone.

XLIII. CLEONE TO ASPASIA.

Torturing girl! And you, Aspasia, may justly say *ungrateful girl!* to me. You did not give me what I asked for, but you gave me what is better, a glimpse of you. This is the manner in which you used to trifle with me, making the heaviest things light, the thorniest tractable, and throwing your own beautiful brightness wherever it was most wanted.

But do not slip from me again. Æschylus, we know, is dead; we hear that Pindar is. Did they die abroad?

Ah poor Xeniades! how miserable to be buried by the stranger!

XLIV. ASPASIA TO CLEONE.

Æschylus, at the close of his seventieth year, died in Sicily. I know not whether Hiero received him with all the distinction he merited, or rewarded him with the same generosity as Pindar; nor indeed have I been able to learn, what would very much gratify me, that Pindar, who survived him four years and died lately, paid those honors to the greatest man of the most glorious age since earth rose out of chaos, which he usually paid with lavish hand to the prosperous and powerful. I hope he did; but the words wealth and gold occur too often in the poetry of Pindar.

Perhaps I may wrong him, for a hope is akin to a doubt; it may be that I am mistaken, since we have not all his poems even here in Athens. Several of these, too, particularly the Dithyrambics, are in danger of perishing. The Odes on the victors at the games will be preserved by the vanity of the families they celebrate; and, being thus safe enough for many years, their own merit will sustain them afterward. It is owing to a stout nurse that many have lived to an extreme old age.

Some of the Odes themselves are of little value in regard to poetry, but he exercises in all of them as much dexterity as the worthies he applauds had displayed in their exploits.

To compensate the disappointment you complained of, I will now transcribe for you an ode of Corinna to her native town, being quite sure it is not in your collection. Let me first inform you that the exterior of the best houses in Tanagra is painted with historical scenes, adventures of gods, allegories, and other things; and under the walls of the city flows the rivulet Thermodon. This is requisite to tell you of so small and so distant a place.

CORINNA TO TANAGRA.

From Athens.

Tanagra! think not I forget
    Thy beautifully storied streets;
Be sure my memory bathes yet
    In clear Thermodon, and yet greets
The blithe and liberal shepherd boy,
Whose sunny bosom swells with joy
When we accept his matted rushes
Upheav'd with sylvan fruit; away he bounds, and blushes.

A gift I promise; one I see
    Which thou with transport wilt receive,
The only proper gift for thee,
    Of which no mortal shall bereave
In later times thy mouldering walls,
Until the last old turret falls;
A crown, a crown from Athens won,
A crown no god can wear, beside Latona's son.

There may be cities who refuse
    To their own child the honors due,
And look ungently on the Muse;
    But ever shall those cities rue
The dry, unyielding, niggard breast,
Offering no nourishment, no rest,
To that young head which soon shall rise
Disdainfully, in might and glory, to the skies.

Sweetly where cavern'd Dirce flows
    Do white-armed maidens chant my lay,
Flapping the while with laurel rose
    The honey-gathering tribes away;
And sweetly, sweetly Attic tongues
Lisp your Corinna's early songs;
To her with feet more graceful come
The verses that have dwelt in kindred breasts at home.

O let thy children lean aslant
    Against the tender mother's knee,
And gaze into her face, and want
    To know what magic there can be
In words that urge some eyes to dance,
While others as in holy trance
Look up to heaven; be such my praise!
Why linger? I must haste, or lose the Delphic bays.

XLV. CLEONE TO ASPASIA.

Epimedea, it appears, has not corrupted very grossly
your purity and simplicity in dress.   Yet, remembering
your observation on armlets, I cannot but commend your
kindness and sufferance in wearing her emeralds.   Your
opinion was formerly, that we should be careful not to
subdivide our persons.   The arm is composed of three
parts ; no one of them is too long.   Now the armlet
intersects that portion of it which must be considered as
the most beautiful.   In my idea of the matter, the sandal
alone is susceptible of gems, after the zone has received
the richest.   The zone is necessary to our vesture, and
encompasses the person, in every quarter of the humanized world, in one invariable manner.   The hair, too, is
divided by nature in the middle of the head.   There is a
cousinship between the hair and the flowers ; and from
this relation the poets have called by the same name the
leaves and it.   They appear on the head as if they had
been seeking one another.   Our national dress, very
different from the dresses of barbarous nations, is not
the invention of the ignorant or the slave ; but the
sculptor, the painter, and the poet, have studied how best
to adorn the most beautiful object of their fancies and
contemplations.   The Indians, who believe that human
pains and sufferings are pleasing to the deity, make in-
cisions in their bodies, and insert into them imperishable
colors.   They also adorn the ears and noses and fore-
heads of their gods.   These were the ancestors of the
Egyptian ; we chose handsomer and better-tempered ones
for our worship, but retained the same decorations in our
sculpture, and to a degree which the sobriety of the
Egyptian had reduced and chastened.   Hence we retain
the only mark of barbarism which dishonors our national
dress, the use of ear-rings.   If our statues should all be
broken by some convulsion of the earth, would it be
believed by future ages that, in the country and age of
Sophocles, the women tore holes in their ears to let rings

into, as the more brutal of peasants do with the snouts of sows !

XLVI. ASPASIA TO CLEONE.

Cleone, I do not know whether I ought to write out for you anything of Mimnermus. What is amatory poetry without its tenderness? and what was ever less tender than his? Take, however, the verses, such as they are. Whether they make you smile or look grave, without any grace of their own they must bring one forward. Certainly they are his best, which cannot be said of every author out of whose rarer works I have added something to your collection.

> I wish not Thasos rich in mines,
> Nor Naxos girt around with vines,
> Nor Crete nor Samos, the abodes
> Of those who govern men and gods.
> Nor wider Lydia, where the sound
> Of tymbrels shakes the thymy ground,
> And with white feet and with hoofs cloven
> The dedal dance is spun and woven:
> Meanwhile each prying younger thing
> Is sent for water to the spring,
> Under where red Priapus rears
> His club amid the junipers.
> In this whole world enough for me
> Is any spot the gods decree;
> Albeit the pious and the wise
> Would tarry where, like mulberries,
> In the first hour of ripeness fall
> The tender creatures one and all.
> To take what falls with even mind
> Jove wills, and we must be resign'd.

XLVII. CLEONE TO ASPASIA.

There is less effrontery in those verses of Mimnermus than in most he has written. He is among the many poets who never make us laugh or weep; among the many whom we take into the hand like pretty insects, turn them over, look at them for a moment, and toss them into the grass again. The earth swarms with these; they live their season, and others similar come into life the next.

I have been reading works widely different from theirs; the odes of the lovely Lesbian. I think she has injured the phaleucian verse, by transposing one foot, and throwing it backward. How greatly more noble and more sonorous are those hendecasyllabics commencing the Scolion on Harmodius and Aristogiton, than the very best of hers, which, to my ear, labor and shuffle in their movement. Her genius was wonderful, was prodigious. I am neither blind to her beauties nor indifferent to her sufferings. We love forever those whom we have wept for when we were children; we love them more than even those who have wept for us. Now I have grieved for Sappho, and so have you, Aspasia! we shall not, therefore, be hard judges of her sentiments or her poetry.

Frequently have we listened to the most absurd and extravagant praises of the answer she gave Alcæus, when he told her he wished to say something, but shame prevented him. This answer of hers is a proof that she was deficient in delicacy and in tenderness. Could Sappho be ignorant how infantinely inarticulate is early love? Could she be ignorant that shame and fear seize it unrelentingly by the throat, while hard-hearted impudence stands at ease, prompt at opportunity, and profuse in declarations!

There is a gloom in deep love, as in deep water; there is a silence in it which suspends the foot, and the folded arms and the dejected head are the images it reflects. No voice shakes its surface; the Muses themselves approach it with a tardy and a timid step, and with a low and tremulous and melancholy song.

The best Ode of Sappho, the Ode to Anactoria,

"Happy as any god is he," etc.,

shows the intemperance and disorder of passion. The description of her malady may be quite correct, but I

confess my pleasure ends at the first strophe, where it begins with the generality of readers. I do not desire to
know the effects of the distemper on her body, and I
run out of the house into the open air, although the
symptoms have less in them of contagion than of un-
seemliness. Both Sophocles and Euripedes excite our
sympathies more powerfully and more poetically.

I will not interfere any farther with your reflections;
and indeed when I began, I intended to remark only the
injustice of Sappho's reproof to Alcæus in the first instance, and the justice of it in the second, when he renewed his suit to her after he had fled from battle. We
find it in the only epigram attributed to her:

> He who from battle runs away
> May pray and sing, and sing and pray;
> Nathless, Alcæus, howsoe'er
> Dulcet his song and warm his prayer
> And true his vows of love may be,
> He ne'er shall run away with me.

In my opinion no lover should be dismissed with contumely, or without the expression of commiseration, unless he has committed some bad action. O Aspasia! it
is hard to love and not to be loved again. I felt it early;
I still feel it. There is a barb beyond the reach of dit-
tany; but years, as they roll by us, benumb in some
degree our sense of suffering. Season comes after season, and covers as it were with soil and herbage, the flints
that have cut us so cruelly in our course.

XLVIII. ASPASIA TO CLEONE.

Alcæus, often admirable in his poetry, was a vain-
glorious and altogether worthless man. I must defend
Sappho. She probably knew his character at the beginning, and sported a witticism (not worth much) at his
expense. He made a pomp and parade of his generosity
and courage, with which in truth he was scantily supplied,

and all his love lay commodiously at the point of his pen, among the rest his first.

He was unfit for public life, he was unfit for private. Perverse, insolent, selfish, he hated tyranny because he could not be a tyrant. Sufficiently well-born, he was jealous and intolerant of those who were nothing less so, and he wished they were all poets that he might expose a weakness the more in them. For rarely has there been one, however virtuous, without some vanity and some iuvidiousness; despiser of the humble, detractor of the high, iconoclast of the near, and idolater of the distant.

Return we to Alcæus. Factitious in tenderness, factitious in heroism, addicted to falsehood, and unabashed at his fondness for it, he attacked and overcame every rival in that quarter. He picked up all the arrows that were shot against him, recocted all the venom of every point, and was almost an Archilochus in satire.

I do not agree with you in your censure of Sappho. There is softness by the side of power, discrimination by the side of passion. In this, however, I do agree with you, that her finest ode is not to be compared to many choruses in the tragedians. We know that Sappho felt acutely; yet Sappho is never pathetic. Euripides and Sophocles are not remarkable for their purity, the intensity, or the fidelity of their loves, yet they touch, they transfix, the heart. Her imagination, her whole soul, is absorbed in her own breast: *she* is the prey of the passions: *they* are the lords and masters.

Sappho has been dead so long, and we live so far from Lesbos, that we have the fewer means of ascertaining the truth or falsehood of stories told about her. Some relate that she was beautiful, some that she was deformed. Lust, it is said, is frequently the inhabitant of deformity; and coldness is experienced in the highest beauty. I believe the former case is more general than the latter ; but where there is great regularity of features I have often remarked a correspondent regularity in the affections and the conduct.)

XLIX. CLEONE TO ASPASIA.

Do you remember the lively Hegemon, whose curls you pressed down with your forefinger to see them spring up again? Do you remember his biting it for the liberty you had taken; and his kissing it to make it well; and his telling you that he was not quite sure whether some other kisses, here and there, might not be requisite to prevent the spreading of the venom? And do you remember how you turned pale? and how you laughed with me, as we went away, at his thinking you turned pale because you were afraid of it? The boy of fifteen, as he was then, hath lost all his liveliness, all his assurance, all his wit; and his radiant beauty has taken another character. His cousin Praxinoe, whom he was not aware of loving until she was betrothed to Callias, a merchant of Samos, was married a few months ago. There are no verses I read oftener than the loose dithyrambics of poor Hegemon. Do people love anywhere else as we love here at Miletus? But perhaps the fondness of Hegemon may abate after a time; for Hegemon is not a woman. How long and how assiduous are we in spinning that thread, the softest and finest in the web of life, which Destiny snaps asunder in one moment!

HEGEMON TO PRAXINOE.

Is there any season, O my soul,
When the sources of bitter tears dry up,
And the uprooted flowers take their places again
   Along the torrent-bed?

Could I wish it to live, it would be for that season,
To repose my limbs and press my temples there.
But should I not speedily start away
   In the hope to trace and follow thy steps!

Thou art gone, thou art gone, Praxinoe!
And hast taken far from me thy lovely youth,
Leaving me naught that was desirable in mine.
   Alas! alas! what hast thou left me?

The helplessness of childhood, the solitude of age,
The laughter of the happy, the pity of the scorner,
A colorless and broken shadow am I,
    Seen glancing in troubled waters.

My thoughts too are scattered; thou hast cast them off;
They beat against thee, they would cling to thee,
But they are viler than the loose dark weeds,
    Without a place to root or rest in.

I would throw them across my lyre; they drop from it;
My lyre will sound only two measures;
That Pity will never, never come,
    Or come to the sleep that awakeneth not unto her.

L. ASPASIA TO CLEONE.

Tell Hegemon that his verses have made a deeper impression than his bite, and that the Athenians, men and women, are pleased with them. (He has shown that he is a poet, by not attempting to show that he is overmuch of one.) Forbear to inform him that we Athenians disapprove of irregularity in versification ; we are little pleased to be rebounded from the end of a line to the beginning, as it often happens, and to be obliged to turn back and make inquiries in regard to what we have been about. There have latterly been many compositions in which it is often requisite to read twice over the verses which have already occupied more than a due portion of our time in reading once. The hop-skip-and-jump is by no means a pleasant or a graceful exercise, but it is quite intolerable when we invert it to a jump-skip-and-hop. I take some liberty in these strange novel compounds, but no greater than our friend Aristophanes has taken, and not only without reproof or censure, but with great commendation for it. However, I have done it for the first and last time, and before the only friend with whom they can be pardonable. Henceforward, I promise you, Cleone, I will always be Attic, or, what is gracefuller and better, Ionian. 'You shall forever hear my voice in my letters, and you shall know it to be mine, and mine only.) Already I have had imitators in the style of my conversations, but they have imitated others too, and this hath saved me. In mercy and pure beneficence to me, the gods have marred the resemblance. Nobody can recognize me in my metempsychosis. Those who had hoped and heard better of me, will never ask themselves, "Was Aspasia so wordy, so inelegant, affected, and perverse?" Inconsiderate friends have hurt me worse than enemies could do; they have hinted that the orations of Pericles have been retouched by my pen. Cleone! the gods themselves could not correct his language. Human ingenuity, with all the malice and impudence that usually accompany it, will never be able to remodel a single sentence, or to substitute a single word, in his speeches to the people. What wealth of wisdom has he not thrown away lest it encumber him in the Agora! how much more than ever was carried into it by the most popular of his opponents! Some of my expressions may have escaped from him in crowded places; some of his cling to me in retirement; we cannot love without imitating) and we are as proud in the loss of our originality as of our freedom. I am sorry that poor Hegemon has not had an opportunity of experiencing all this. Persuade his friends never to pity him, truly or feignedly, for (pity keeps the wound open;) persuade them rather to flatter him on his poetry, for never was there poet to whom the love of praise was not the first and most constant of passions. His friends will be the gainers by it: he will divide among them all the affection he fancies he has reserved for Praxinoe. With most men, nothing seems to have happened so long ago as an affair of love. Let nobody hint this to him at present. It is among the many truths that ought to be held back; it is among the many that excite a violent opposition at one time, and obtain at another (not much later) a very ductile acquiescence; he will receive it hereafter (take my word for him) with only one slight remonstrance . . *you are too hard upon us lovers;* then follows a shake of the head, not of abnegation, but of sanction, like Jupiter's.

Praxinoe, it seems, is married to a merchant, poor girl! I do not like these merchants. Let them have

vealth in the highest, but not beauty in the highest; cun-
ling and calculation can hardly merit both. At last they
uay aspire, if any civilized country could tolerate it, to
ıonors and distinctions. These, too, let them have, but
ıt Tyre and Carthage.

LI. CLEONE TO ASPASIA.

How many things in poetry, as in other matters, are
ikely to be lost because they are small! / Cleobuline of
Lindos wrote no long poem. Her lover was Cycnus of
Colophon. There is not a single verse of hers in all
hat city; proof enough that he took no particular care
of them. At Miletus she was quite unknown, not indeed
ıy name, but in her works, until the present month, when
ı copy of them was offered to me for sale. The first
hat caught my eyes was this:

> Where is the swan of breast so white
> It made my bubbling life run bright
>   On that one spot, and that alone,
> On which he rested; and I stood
> Gazing: now swells the turbid flood;
> Summer and he for other climes are flown!

I will not ask you at present to say anything in praise
of Cleobuline, but do be grateful to Myrtis and Corinna!

LII. ASPASIA TO CLEONE.

Grateful I am, and shall forever be, to Myrtis and
Corinna. But what odor of bud or incense can they wish
o be lavished on the empty sepulchre, what praises of
he thousand who praise in ignorance, or of the learned
who praise from tradition, when they remember that
hey subdued and regulated the proud unruly Pindar and
ıgitated with all their passion the calm, pure breast of
Cleone!

Send me the whole volume of Cleobuline; transcribe

uothing more. To compensate you as well as I can, and
indeed I think the compensation is not altogether an unfair one, here are two little pieces from Myrtis, auto-
graphs, from the library of Pericles.

> Artemia, while Arion sighs,
> Raising her white and taper finger,
> Pretends to loose, yet makes to linger,
> The ivy that o'ershades her eyes.
>
> "Wait, or you shall not have the kiss,"
> Says she; but he, on wing to pleasure,
> "Are there not other hours for leisure?
> For love is any hour like this?"
>
> Artemia! faintly thou respondest,
> As falsely deems that fiery youth;
> A god there is who knows the truth,
> A god who tells me which is fondest.

Here is another, in the same hand, a clear and elegant
one. Men may be negligent in their hand-writing, for
men may be in a hurry about the business of life; but I
never knew either a sensible woman or an estimable one
whose writing was disorderly.

Well, the verses are prettier than my reflection, and
equally true.

> *I will not love!*
>   .   .   . These sounds have often
>   Burst from a troubled breast;
> Rarely from one no sighs could soften,
>   Rarely from one at rest.

Myrtis and Corinna, like Anacreon and Sappho who
preceded them, were temperate in the luxuries of poetry.
They had enough to do with one feeling; they were occupied enough with one reflection. They culled but few
grapes from the bunch, and never dragged it across the
teeth, stripping off ripe and unripe.

LIII. CLEONE TO ASPASIA.

The verses of Myrtis, which you sent me last, are somewhat less pleasing to me than those others of hers which I

send you in return. A few loose ideas on the subject
(I know not whether worth writing) occur to me at this
moment. Formerly we were contented with schools of
philosophy; we now begin to talk about schools of
poetry. Is not that absurd? There is only one school,
the universe; only one school-mistress, Nature. Those
who are reported to be of such or such a school, are of
none; they have played the truant. Some are more
careful, some more negligent, some bring many dishes,
some fewer, some little seasoned, some highly. Ground,
however, there is for the fanciful appellation. The young
poets at Miletus are beginning to throw off their allegiance to the established and acknowledged laws of
Athens, and are weary of following in the train of the
graver who have been crowned. The various schools, as
they call them, have assumed distinct titles; but the
largest and most flourishing of all would be discontented,
I am afraid, with the properest I could inscribe it with,
the *queer*. We really have at present in our city more
good poets than we ever had; and the *queer* might be
among the best if they pleased. But whenever an obvious and natural thought presents itself, they either reject
it for coming without imagination, or they *phrygianize* it
with such biting and hot curling-irons, that it rolls itself
up impenetrably. They declare to us that pure and simple
imagination is the absolute perfection of poetry; and if
ever they admit a sentence or reflection, it must be one
which requires a whole day to unravel and wind it
smoothly on the distaff.

To me it appears that poetry ought neither to be all
body nor all soul. Beautiful features, limbs compact,
sweetness of voice, and easiness of transition, belong to
the deity who inspires and represents it. We may loiter
by the stream and allay our thirst as it runs, but we
should not be forbidden the larger draught from the
deeper well.

FROM MYRTIS.

Friends, whom she looked at blandly from her conch
And her white wrist above it, gem-bedewed,
Were arguing with Pentheusa; she had heard

4

Report of Creon's death, whom years before
She listened to, well-pleas'd; and sighs arose;
For sighs full often fondle with reproofs
And will be fondled by them.   When I came
After the rest to visit her, she said,
"Myrtis! how kind!   Who better knows than thou
The pangs of love? and my first love was he!"
Tell me (if ever, Eros! are reveal'd
Thy secrets to the earth) have they been true
To any love who speak about the first?
What! shall these holier lights, like twinkling stars
In the few hours assign'd them, change their place,
And, when comes ampler splendor, disappear?
Idler I am, and pardon, not reply,
Implore from thee, thus questioned; well I know
Thou strikest, like Olympian Jove, but once.

LIV. ASPASIA TO CLEONE.

Lysicles, a young Athenian, fond of travelling, has just
returned to us from a voyage in Thrace.   A love of observation, in other words curiosity, could have been his
only motive, for he never was addicted to commerce, nor
disciplined in philosophy; and indeed were he so, Thrace
is hardly the country he would have chosen.   I believe
he is the first that ever travelled with no other intention
than to see the cities and know the manners of barbarians.   He represents the soil as extremely fertile in its
nature, and equally well cultivated, and the inhabitants as
warlike, hospitable, and courteous.   All this is credible
enough, and perhaps as generally known as might be expected of regions so remote and perilous.   But Lysicles
will appear to you to have assumed a little more than the
fair privileges of a traveller, in relating that the people
have so imperfect a sense of religion as to bury the dead
in the temples of the gods, and the priests are so avaricious and shameless as to claim money for the permission
of this impiety.   He told us furthermore that he had seen
a magnificent temple, built on somewhat of a Grecian
model, in the interior of which there are many flat mar-
bles fastened with iron cramps against the walls, and serving for monuments.   Continuing his discourse, he assured

us that these monuments, although none are ancient, are of all forms and dimensions, as if the Thracians were resolved to waste and abolish the symmetry they had adopted ; and that they are inscribed in an obsolete language, so that the people whom they might animate and instruct, by recording brave and virtuous actions, pass them carelessly by, breaking off now and then a nose from a conqueror, and a wing from an agathodemon.

Thrace is governed by many princes. One of them, Teres, an Odrysan,* has gained great advantages in war. No doubt this is uninteresting to you, but it is necessary to the course of my narration. Will you believe it? yet Lysicles is both intelligent and trustworthy. . will you believe that, at the return of the Thracian prince to enjoy the fruits of his victory, he ordered an architect to build an arch for himself and his army to pass under, on their road into the city? As if a road, on such an occasion, ought not rather to be widened than narrowed? If you will not credit this of a barbarian, who is reported to be an intelligent and prudent man in other things, you will exclaim, I fear, against the exaggeration of Lysicles and my credulity, when I relate to you on his authority that, to the same conqueror, by his command, there has been erected a column sixty cubits high, supporting his effigy in marble !

Imagine the general of an army standing upon a column of sixty cubits to show himself! A crane might do it after a victory over a pigmy ; or it might aptly represent the virtues of a rope-dancer, exhibiting how little he was subject to dizziness.

I will write no more about it, for really I am beginning to think that some pretty Thracian has given poor Lysicles a love-potion, and that it has affected his brain.

---

* Teres not only governed the larger part of Thrace, but influenced many of the free and independent states in that country, and led into the field the Getes, the Agrianians, the Leæans, and the Pœonians. Sitalces, son of Teres, ravaged all Macedonia in the reign of Perdiccas.

LV. CLEONE TO ASPASIA.

Never will I believe that a people, however otherwise ignorant and barbarous, yet capable of turning a regular arch and of erecting a lofty column, can be so stupid and absurd as you have represented. What! bury dead bodies in the temples! cast them out of their own houses into the houses of the gods! Depend upon it, Aspasia, they were the bones of victims; and the strange uncouth inscriptions commemorate votive offerings, in the language of the priests, whatever it may be. So far is clear. Regarding the arch, Lysicles saw them removing it, and fancied they were building it. This mistake is really ludicrous. The column, you must have perceived at once, was erected, not to display the victor, but to expose the vanquished. A blunder very easy for an idle traveller to commit. Few of the Thracians, I conceive, even in the interior, are so utterly ignorant of Grecian arts, as to raise a statue at such a height above the ground that the vision shall not comprehend all the features easily, and the spectator see and contemplate the object of his admiration, as nearly and in the same position as he was used to do in the Agora.

The monument of the greatest man should be only a bust and a name. If the name alone is insufficient to illustrate the bust, let them both perish.

Enough about Thracians; enough about tombs and monuments. Two pretty Milesians, Agapentha and Peristera, who are in love with you for loving me, are quite resolved to kiss your hand. You must not detain them long with you: Miletus is not to send all her beauty to be kept at Athens; we have no such treaty.

LVI. ASPASIA TO CLEONE.

There is such a concourse of philosophers, all anxious to show Alcibiades the road to Virtue, that I am afraid they will completely block it up before him. Among the rest is my old friend Socrates, who seems resolved to transfer to him all the philosophy he designed for me, with very little of that which I presented to him in return.

And Alcibiades, who began with ridiculing him, now attends to him with as much fondness as Hyacinthus did to Apollo. The graver and uglier philosophers, however they differ on other points, agree in these: that beauty does not reside in the body, but in the mind; that philosophers are the only true heroes; and that heroes alone are entitled to the privilege of being implicitly obeyed by the beautiful.

Doubtless there may be very fine pearls in very uninviting shells; but our philosophers never wade knee-deep into the beds, attracted rather to what is bright externally.

LVII. CLEONE TO ASPASIA.

Alcibiades ought not to have captious or inquisitive men about him. I know not what the sophists are good for; I only know they are the very worst instructors. Logic, however unperverted, is not for boys; argumentation is among the most dangerous of early practices, and sends away both fancy and modesty. The young mind should be nourished with simple and grateful food, and not too copious. It should be little exercised until its nerves and muscles show themselves, and even then rather for air than anything else. Study is the bane of boyhood, the aliment of youth, the indulgence of manhood, and the restorative of age.

I am confident that persons like you and Pericles see little of these sharpers who play tricks upon words. It is amusing to observe how they do it, once or twice. As there are some flowers which you should smell but slightly to extract all that is pleasant in them, and which, if you do otherwise, emit what is unpleasant or noxious, so there are some men with whom a slight acquaintance is quite sufficient to draw out all that is agreeable; a more intimate one would be unsatisfactory and unsafe.

LVIII. ASPASIA TO CLEONE.

Pericles rarely says he likes anything ; but whenever he is pleased, he expresses it by his countenance, although when he is displeased he never shows it, even by the faintest sign.   It was long before I ventured to make the observation to him ; he replied :

" It would be ungrateful and ungentle not to return my thanks for any pleasure imparted to me, when a smile has the power of conveying them.   I never say that a thing pleases me while it is yet undone or absent, lest I should give somebody the trouble of performing or producing it.   As for what is displeasing, I really am insensible in general to matters of this nature ; and when I am not so, I experience more of satisfaction in subduing my feeling than I ever felt of displeasure at the occurrence which excited it.   Politeness is in itself a power, and takes away the weight and galling from every other we may exercise.   I foresee," he added, "that Alcibiades will be an elegant man, but I apprehend he will never be a polite one.   There is a difference, and a greater than we are apt to perceive or imagine.   Alcibiades would win without conciliating : he would seize and hold, but would not acquire.   The man who is determined to keep others fast and firm, must have one end of the bond about his own breast, sleeping and waking."

LIX. ASPASIA TO CLEONE.

Agapenthe and Peristera, the bearers of your letter, came hither in safety and health, late as the season is for navigation.   They complain of our cold climate in Athens, and shudder at the sight of snow upon the mountains in the horizon.

Hardly had they been seen with me, before the housewives and sages were indignant at their effrontery.   In fact, they gazed in wonder at the ugliness of our sex in

Attica, and at the gravity of philosophers, of whom
stories so ludicrous are related. I do not think I shall
be able to find them lovers here. Peristera hath lost a
little of her dove-like faculty (if ever she had much) at
the report which has been raised about her cousin and
herself. Dracontides was smitten at first sight by Agapenthe; she however was not at all by him, which is
usually the case when young men would warm us at
their fire before ours is kindled. For, honestly to confess
the truth, the best of us are more capricious than sensitive, and more sensitive than grateful. Dracontides is
not indeed a man to excite so delightful a feeling. He is
confident that Peristera must be the cause of Agapenthe's
disinclination to him ; for how is it possible that a young
girl of unperverted mind could be indifferent to Dracontides ? Unable to discover that any sorceress was employed against him, he turned his anger toward Peristera,
and declared in her presence that her malignity alone
could influence so abusively the generous mind of Agapenthe. At my request the playful girl consented to
receive him. Seated upon an amphora in the aviary,
she was stroking the neck of a noble peacock, while the
bird pecked at the berries on a branch of arbutus in her
bosom. Dracontides entered, conducted by Peristera,
who desired her cousin to declare at once whether it was
by any malignity of hers that he had hitherto failed to
conciliate her regard.

"O the ill-tempered frightful man !" cried Agapenthe ;
"does anybody that is not malicious ever talk of malignity?"

Dracontides went away, calling upon the gods for
justice.

The next morning a rumor ran through Athens, how
he had broken off his intended nuptials, on the discovery
that Aspasia had destined the two Ionians to the pleasures of Pericles. Moreover, he had discovered that one
of them, he would not say which, had certainly threads
of several colors in her thread-case, not to mention a
lock of hair, whether of a dead man, or no, might by
some be doubted ; and that the other was about to be

consigned to Pyrilampes, in exchange for a peacock and sundry smaller birds.

No question could be entertained of the fact, for the girls were actually in the house, and the birds in the aviary.

Agapenthe declares she waits only for the spring, and will then leave Athens for her dear Miletus, where she never heard such an expression as malignity.

"O what rude people the Athenians are!" said she.

LX. ASPASIA TO CLEONE.

Rather than open my letter again, I write another.

Agapenthe's heart is won by Mnasylos; I never suspected it.

On his return out of Thessaly (whither I fancy he went on purpose) he brought a cage of nightingales. There are few of them in Attica; and none being kept tame, none remain with us through the winter. Of the four brought by Mnasylos, one sings even in this season of the year. Agapenthe and Peristea were awakened in the morning by the song of a bird like a nightingale in the aviary. They went down together; and over the door they found these verses:

> Maiden or youth, who standest here,
> Think not, if haply we should fear
> A stranger's voice or stranger's face,
> (Such is the nature of our race)
> That we would gladly fly again
> To gloomy wood or windy plain.
> Certain we are we ne'er should find
> A care so provident, so kind,
> Altho' by flight we repossest
> The tenderest mother's warmest nest.
> O may you prove, as well as we,
> That even in Athens there may be
> A sweeter thing than liberty.

"This is surely the hand-writing of Mnasylos," said Agapenthe.

"How do you know his hand-writing?" cried Peristera.

A blush and a kiss, and one gentle push, were the answer.

Mnasylos, on hearing the sound of footsteps, had retreated behind a thicket of laurustine and pyracanthus, in which the aviary is situated, fearful of bringing the gardener into reproof for admitting him. However, his passion was uncontrollable; and Peristera declares, although Agapenthe denies it, that he caught a kiss upon each of his cheeks by the interruption. Certain it is, for they agree in it, that he threw his arms around them both as they were embracing, and implored them to conceal the fault of poor old Alcon, "who showed me," said he, "more pity than Agapenthe will ever show me."

"Why did you bring these birds hither?" said she, trying to frown.

"Because you asked," replied he, "the other day, whether we had any in Attica, and told me you had many at home."

She turned away abruptly, and, running up to my chamber, would have informed me why.

Superfluous confidence! Her tears wetted my cheek.

"Agapenthe!" said I, smiling, "are you sure you have cried for the last time, 'O what rude people the Athenians are!'"

LXI. ASPASIA TO PERICLES.

I apprehend, O Pericles, not only that I may become an object of jealousy and hatred to the Athenians, by the notice you have taken of me, but that you yourself, which affects me greatly more, may cease to retain the whole of their respect and veneration.

Whether to acquire a great authority over the people, some things are not necessary to be done on which Virtue and Wisdom are at variance, it becomes not me to argue or consider; but let me suggest the inquiry to you, whether he who is desirous of supremacy should devote the larger portion of his time to one person.

Three affections of the soul predominate : Love, Religion, and Power. The first two are often united ; the other stands widely apart from them, and neither is admitted nor seeks admittance to their society. I wonder then how you can love so truly and tenderly. Ought I not rather to say I *did* wonder ! Was Pisistratus affectionate? Do not be angry. It is certainly the first time a friend has ever ventured to discover a resemblance, although you are habituated to it from your opponents. In these you forgive it ; do you in me?

LXII. PERICLES TO ASPASIA.

Pisistratus was affectionate : the rest of his character you know as well as I do. You know that he was eloquent, that he was humane, that he was contemplative, that he was learned ; that he not only was profuse to men of genius, but cordial, and that it was only with such men he was familiar and intimate. You know that he was the greatest, the wisest, the most virtuons, excepting Solon and Lycurgus, that ever ruled any portion of the human race. Is it not happy and glorious for mortals, when, iustead of being led by the ears under the clumsy and violent hand of vulgar and clamorous adventurers, a Pisistratus leaves the volumes of Homer, and the conversation of Solon, for them !

We may be introduced to Power by Humanity, and at first may love her less for her own sake than for Humanity's, but by degrees we become so accustomed to her as to be quite uneasy without her.

Religion and Power, like the Cariatides in sculpture, never face one another ; they sometimes look the same way, but oftener stand back to back.

We will argue about them one at a time, and about the other in the triad too ; let me have the choice.

LXIII. ASPASIA TO PERICLES.

. We must talk over again the subject of your letter ; no, not talk, but write about it.

I think, Pericles, you who are so sincere with me, are never quite sincere with others. You have contracted this bad habitude from your custom of addressing the people. But among friends and philosophers, would it not be better to speak exactly as we think, whether ingeniously or not? Ingenious things, I am afraid, are never perfectly true ; however, I would not exclude them, the difference being wide between perfect truth and violated truth ; I would not even leave them in a minority ; I would hear and say as many as may be, letting them pass current for what they are worth. Anaxagoras rightly remarked that Love always makes us better, Religion sometimes, Power never.

LXIV. ASPASIA TO CLEONE.

Pericles was delighted with your letter on education. I wish he were as pious as you are ; occasionally he appears so. I attacked him on his simulation, but it produced a sudden and powerful effect on Alcibiades. You will collect the whole from a summary of our conversation.

"So true," said he, "is the remark of Anaxagoras, that it was worth my while to controvert it. Did you not observe the attention paid to it by young and old? I was unwilling that the graver part of the company should argue to-morrow with Alcibiades on the nature of love, as they are apt to do, and should persuade him that he would be the better for it.

"On this consideration I said, while you were occupied, 'O Anaxagoras ! if we of this household knew not how religious a man you are, your discourse would in some degree lead us to countenance the suspicion of your enemies. Religion is never too little for us ; it satisfies

all the desires of the soul. Love is but an atom of it,
consuming and consumed by the stubble on which it falls.
But when it rests upon the gods, it partakes of their nature, in its essence pure and eternal. Like the ocean,
Love embraces the earth ; and by love, as by the ocean,
whatever is sordid and unsound is borne away.'

" ' Love indeed works great marvels,' said Anaxagoras, ' but I doubt whether the ocean, in such removals,
may not peradventure be the more active of the two.'

" ' Acknowledge, at least,' said I, ' that the flame of
Love purifies the temple it burns in.'

" ' Only when first lighted,' said Anaxagoras. ' Generally the heat is either spent or stifling soon afterward ;
and the torch, when it is extinguished, leaves an odor
very different from myrrh and frankincense.'

" I think, Aspasia, you entered while he was speaking
these words."

He had turned the stream. Pericles then proceeded.

" Something of power," said he, " hath been consigned
to me by the favor and indulgence of the Athenians. I
do not dissemble that I was anxious to obtain it ; I do
not dissemble that my vows and supplications for the prosperity of the country were unremitted. It pleased the
gods to turn toward me the eyes of my fellow-citizens, but
had they not blessed me with religion they never would
have blessed me with power, better and more truly called
an influence on their hearts and their reason, a high and
secure place in the acropolis of their affections. Yes,
Anaxagoras ! yes, Meton ! I do say, had they not *blessed*
me with it ; for, in order to obtain it, I was obliged to
place a daily and a nightly watch over my thoughts and
actions. In proportion as authority was consigned to me,
I found it both expedient and easy to grow better, time
not being left me for sedentary occupations or frivolous
pursuits, and every desire being drawn on and absorbed
in that mighty and interminable, that rushing, renovating,
and purifying one, which comprehends our country. If
any young man would win to himself the hearts of the
wise and brave, and is ambitious of being the guide and
leader of them, let him be assured that his virtue will

give him power, and power will consolidate and maintain his virtue. Let him never, then, squander away the inestimable hours of youth in tangled and trifling disquisitions, with such as perhaps have an interest in perverting or unsettling his opinions. and who speculate into his sleeping thoughts and dandle his nascent passions. But let him start from them with alacrity, and walk forth with firmness ; let him early take an interest in the business and concerns of men ; and let him, as he goes along, look steadfastly at the images of those who have benefited his country, and make with himself a solemn compact to stand hereafter among them."

I had heard the greater part of this already, all but the commencement. At the conclusion Alcibiades left the room ; I feared he was conscious that something in it was too closely applicable to him. How I rejoiced when I saw him enter again, with a helmet like Pallas's on his head, a spear in his hand, crying, " To Sparta, boys ! to Sparta !"

Pericles whispered to me, but in a voice audible to those who sate further off, "Alcibiades, I trust, is destined to abolish the influence and subvert the power of that restless and troublesome rival."

LXV. ASPASIA TO PERICLES.

I disbelieve, O Pericles, that it is good for us, that it is good for men, women, or nations, to be without a rival.

Acquit me now of any desire that, in your generosity, you should resolve on presenting me with such a treasure, for I am without the ability of returning it. But have you never observed how many graces of person and demeanor we women are anxious to display, in order to humble a rival, which we were unconscious of possessing until opposite charms provoked them ?

Sparta can only be humbled by the prosperity and liberality of Athens. She was ever jealous and selfish ; Athens has been too often so. It is only by forbearance toward dependent states, and by kindness toward the

weaker, that her power can long preponderate. Strong
attachments are strong allies. This truth is so clear as
to be colorless, and I should fear that you would censure
me for writing what almost a child might have spoken,
were I ignorant that its importance hath made little impression on the breasts of statesmen.

I admire your wisdom in resolving to increase no farther
the domains of Attica; to surround her with the outworks
of islands, and more closely with small independent communities. It is only from such as these that Virtue can
come forward neither hurt nor heated; the crowd is too
dense for her in larger. But what is mostly our consideration, it is only such as these that are sensible of benefits. They cling to you afflictedly in your danger; the
greater look on with folded arms, nod knowingly, cry *sad
work!* when you are worsted, and turn their backs on you
when you are fallen.

LXVI. PERICLES TO ASPASIA.

There are things, Aspasia, beyond the art of Phidias. He may represent Love leaning upon his bow
and listening to Philosophy; but not for hours together:
he may represent Love, while he is giving her a kiss for
her lesson, tying her arms behind her; loosing them again
must be upon another marble.

LXVII. ASPASIA TO CLEONE.

The philosophers are less talkative in our conversations, now Alcibiades hath given up his mind to mathe-
matics and strategy, and seldom comes among them.

Pericles told me they will not pour out the rose-water
for their beards, unless into a Corinthian or golden vase.

"But take care," added he, "to offend no philosopher
of any sect whatever. Indeed to offend any person is the
next foolish thing to being offended. I never **do it**, unless when it is requisite **to discredit** somebody who might

otherwise have the influence to diminish my estimation.
Politeness is not always a sign of wisdom ; but the want
of it always leaves room for a suspicion of folly, if folly
and imprudence are the same. I have scarcely had time
to think of any blessings that entered my house with you,
beyond those which encompass myself ; yet it cannot but
be obvious that Alcibiades hath now an opportunity of
improving his manners, such as even the society of scho-
lastic men will never countervail. This is a high advantage on all occasions, particularly in embassies.
Well-bred men require it, and let it pass ; the ill-bred
catch at it greedily ; as fishes are attracted from the mud,
and netted, by the shine of flowers and shells."

LXVIII. ASPASIA TO CLEONE.

At last I have heard him speak in public.

Apollo may shake the rocks of Delphi, and may turn
the pious pale ; my Pericles rises with serenity ; his voice
hath at once left his lips and entered the heart of Athens.
The violent and desperate tremble in every hostile city ;
a thunderbolt seems to have split in the centre, and to have
scattered its sacred fire unto the whole circumference of
Greece.

The greatest of prodigies are the prodigies of a mortal ;
they are indeed the only ones : with the gods there are
none.

Alas ! alas ! the eloquence and the wisdom, the courage
and the constancy of my Pericles, must have their end ;
and the glorious shrine, wherein they stand preëminent,
must one day drop into the deformity of death !

O Aspasia ! of the tears thou art shedding, tears of
pride, tears of fondness, are there none (in those many)
for thyself ? Yes ; whatever was attributed to thee of
grace or beauty, so valuable for his sake whose partiality
assigned them to thee, must go first, and all that he loses
is a loss to thee ! Weep then on.

LXIX. PERICLES TO ASPASIA.

Do you love me? do you love me? Stay, reason upon it, sweet Aspasia! doubt, hesitate, question, drop it, take it up again, provide, raise obstacles, reply indirectly. Oracles are sacred, and there is a pride in being a diviner.

LXX. ASPASIA TO PERICLES.

I will do none of those things you tell me to do; but I will say something you forgot to say, about the insufficiency of Phidias.

He may represent a hero with unbent brows, a sage with the lyre of Poetry in his hand, Ambition with her face half-averted from the City, but he cannot represent, in the same sculpture, at the same distance, Aphrodite higher than Pallas. He would be derided if he did; and a great man can never do that for which a little man may deride him.

I shall love you even more than I do, if you will love yourself more than me. Did ever lover talk so? Pray tell me, for I have forgotten all they ever talked about. But, Pericles! Pericles! be careful to lose nothing of your glory, or you lose all that can be lost of me; my pride, my happiness, my content; everything but my poor weak love. Keep glory, then, for my sake!

LXXI. ASPASIA TO CLEONE.

I am not quite certain that you are correct in your decision, on the propriety of sculpturing the statues of our deities from one sole material. Those, however, of mortals and nymphs and genii should be marble, and marble only. But you will pardon a doubt, a long doubt, a doubt for the chin to rest upon in the palm of the hand, when Cleone thinks one thing and Phidias another. I debated with Pericles on the subject.

"In my opinion," said he, "no material for statuary
is so beautiful as marble ; and, far from allowing that two
or more materials should compose one statue, I would not
willingly see an interruption made in the figure of a god
or goddess, even by the folds of drapery. I would venture to take the cestus from Venus, distinguishing her
merely by her own peculiar beauty. But in the representations of the more awful Powers, who are to be venerated and worshipped as the patrons and protectors of
cities, we must take into account the notions of the people. In their estimate, gold and ivory give splendor and
dignity to the gods themselves, and our wealth displays
their power ! Beside . . but bring your ear closer . .
when they will not indulge us with their favor, we may
borrow their cloaks and ornaments, and restore them
when they have recovered their temper."

LXXII. ASPASIA TO CLEONE.

After I had written to you, we renewed our conversation on the same subject. I inquired of Pericles whether
he thought the appellation of *golden* was applied to Venus
for her precious gifts, or for some other reason. His
answer was :

"Small statues of Venus are more numerous than of
any other deity ; and the first that were gilt in Greece, I
believe, were hers. She is worshipped, you know, not
only as the goddess of beauty, but likewise as the goddess
of fortune. In the former capacity we are her rapturous
adorers for five years, perhaps ; in the latter, we perse-
vere for life. Many carry her image with them on their
journeys, and there is scarcely a house in any part of
Greece wherein it is not a principal ornament."

I remarked to him that Apollo, from the color of his
hair and the radiance of his countenance, would be more
appropriately represented in gold, and yet that the poets
were unmindful to call him the *golden.*

"They never found him so," said he ; "but Venus
often smiles upon them in one department. Little images

5

of her are often of solid gold, and are placed on the
breast or under the pillow.   Other deities are seldom of
such diminutive size or such precious materials.   It is
only of late that they have even borne the semblance of
them.   The Egyptians, the inventors of all durable colors, and, indeed, of everything else that is durable in the
arts, devised the means of investing other metals with
dissolved gold ; the Phœnicians, barbarous and indifferent to elegance and refinement, could only cover them
with lamular incrustations.   By improving the inventions
of Egypt, bronze, odious in its own proper color for the
human figure, and more odious for divinities, assumes a
splendor and majesty which almost compensate for marble itself."

" Metal," said I, " has the advantage in durability."

"Surely not," answered he ; " and it is more exposed
to invasion and avarice.   But either of them, under cover, may endure many thousand years, I apprehend, and
without corrosion.   The temples of Egypt, which have
remained two thousand, are fresh at this hour as when
they were first erected ; and all the violence of Cambyses
and his army, bent on effacing the images, has done little
more harm, if you look at them from a short distance,
than a single fly would do, in a summer day, on a statue
of Pentelican marble.   The Egyptians have labored more
to commemorate the weaknesses of man than the Grecians
to attest his energies.   This, however, must be conceded
to the Egyptians ; that they are the only people on earth
to whom destruction has not been the first love and principal occupation.   The works of their hands will outlive
the works of their intellect : here, at least, I glory in the
sure hope that we shall differ from them.   Judgment and
perception of the true and beautiful will never allow our
statuaries to represent the human countenance, as they
have done, in granite, and porphyry, and basalt.   Their
statues have resisted Time and War ; ours will vanquish
Envy and Malice.

"Sculpture has made great advances in my time ; Painting still greater ; for until the last forty years it was inelegant and rude.   Sculpture can go no farther ; Painting

can : she may add scenery and climate to her forms. She may give to Philoctetes, not only the wing of the sea-bird wherewith he cools the throbbing of his wound ; not only the bow and the quiver at his feet, but likewise the gloomy rocks, the Vulcanian vaults, and the distant fires of Lemnos, the fierce inhabitants subdued by pity, the remorseless betrayer, and the various emotions of his retiring friends.   Her reign is boundless, but the fairer and the richer part of her dominions lies within the Odyssea. Painting by degrees will perceive her advantages over Sculpture ; but if there are paces between Sculpture and Painting, there are parasangs between Painting and Poetry.   The difference is that of a lake confined by mountains, and a river running on through all the varieties of scenery, perpetual and unimpeded.   Sculpture and Painting are moments of life ; Poetry is life itself, and everything around it and above it.

" But let us turn back again to the position we set out from, and offer due reverence to the truest diviners of the gods.   Phidias, in ten days, is capable of producing what would outlive ten thousand years, if man were not resolved to be the subverter of man's glory.   The gods themselves will vanish away before their images."

O Cleone ! this is painful to hear.   I wish Pericles, and I, too, were somewhat more religious : it is so sweet and graceful.

LXXIII. CLEONE TO ASPASIA.

She, O Aspasia, who wishes to be more religious, hath much religion, although the volatility of her imagination and the velocity of her pursuits do not permit her to settle fixedly on the object of it.   How could I have ever loved you so, if I believed the gods would disapprove of my attachment, as they certainly would if you underrated their power and goodness !   They take especial care both to punish the unbeliever, and to strike with awe the witnesses of unbelief.   I accompanied my father, not long since, to the temple of Apollo ; and when we had performed the usual rites of our devotion, there came up to us a young man of somewhat pleasing aspect, with whose family ours was anciently on terms of intimacy. After my father had made the customary inquiries, he conversed with us about his travels. He had just left Ephesus, and said he had spent the morning in a comparison between Diana's temple and Apollo's. He told us that they are similar in design; but that the Ephesian goddess is an ugly lump of dark-colored stone; while our Apollo is of such transcendent beauty that, on first beholding him, he wondered any other god had a worshipper. My father was transported with joy at such a declaration.

"Give up the others," said he; "worship here, and rely on prosperity."

"Were I myself to select," answered he, "any deity in preference to the rest, it should not be an irascible, or vindictive, or unjust one."

"Surely not," cried my father . . "it should be Apollo; and *our* Apollo! What has Diana done for any man, or any woman! I speak submissively . . with all reverence . . I do not question."

The young man answered, "I will forbear to say a word about Diana, having been educated in great fear of her: but surely the treatment of **Marsyas** by Apollo was bordering on severity."

"Not a whit," cried my father, "if understood rightly."

"His assent to the request of Phaëton," continued the young man, "knowing (as he did) the consequences, seems a little deficient in that foresight which belongs peculiarly to the God of prophecy."

My father left me abruptly, ran to the font, and sprinkled first himself, then me, lastly the guest, with lustral water.

"We mortals," continued he gravely, "should not presume to argue on the gods after our own inferior nature and limited capacities. What appears to have been cruel might have been most kindly provident."

"The reasoning is conclusive," said the youth; "you have caught by the hand a benighted and wandering dreamer, and led him from the brink of a precipice. I see nothing left now on the road-side but the skin of Marsyas, and it would be folly to start or flinch at it."

My father had a slight suspicion of his sincerity, and did not invite him to the house He has attempted to come, more than once, evidently with an earnest desire to explore the truth.   Several days together he has been seen on the very spot where he made the confession to my father, in deep thought, and, as we hope, under the influence of the Deity.

I forgot to tell you that this young person is Thraseas, son of Phormio, the Coan.

LXXIV. ASPASIA TO CLEONE.

If ever there was a youth whose devotion was ardent, and whose face (I venture to say, although I never saw it) was prefigured for the offices of adoration, I suspect it must be Thraseas, son of Phormio, the Coan.

Happy the man who, when every thought else is dismissed, comes last and alone into the warm and secret foldings of a letter !

LXXV. ASPASIA TO CLEONE.

Alcibiades entered the library one day when I was writing out some verses.   He discovered what I was about by my hurry in attempting to conceal them.

" Alcibiades !" said I, " we do not like to be detected in anything so wicked as poetry.   Some day or other I shall, perhaps, have my revenge, and catch you committing the same sin with more pertinacity."

" Do you fancy," said he, " that I cannot write a verse or two, if I set my heart upon it?"

" No," replied I, " but I doubt whether your heart, in its lightness and volubility, would not roll off so slippery a plinth.   We remember your poetical talents, displayed in all their brightness, on poor Socrates."

" Do not laugh at Socrates," said he.   " The man is

by no means such a quibbler and impostor as some of his
disciples would represent him, making him drag along no
easy mule-load, by Hercules! no summer robe, no every-
day vesture, no nurse of an after-dinner nap, but a trail-
ing, troublesome, intricate piece of sophistry, interwoven
with flowers and sphynxes, stolen from an Egyptian temple, with dust enough in it to blind all the crocodiles as
far as to the cataracts, and to dry up the Nile at its highest
overflow.   He is rather fond of strangling an unwary in-
terloper with a string of questions, of which it is difficult
to see the length or the knots, until the two ends are about
the throat; but he lets him off easily when he has fairly
set his mark on him.   Anaxagoras tells me that there is
not a school in Athens where the scholars are so jealous
and malicious, while he himself is totally exempt from
those worst and most unphilosophical of passions; that
the parasitical weed grew up together with their very
root, and soon overtopped the plant, but that it only
hangs to his railing.   Now Anaxagoras envies nobody,
and only perplexes us by the admiration of his generosity, modesty, and wisdom.

"I did not come hither to disturb you, Aspasia! and
will retire when I have given you satisfaction, or *revenge;*
this, I think, is the word.   Not only have I written verses,
and, as you may well suppose, long after those upon the
son of Sophroniscos, but verses upon love."

"Are we none of us in the secret?" said I.

"You shall be," said he; "attend and pity."

I must have turned pale, I think, for I shuddered.   He
repeated these, and relieved me:

> I love to look on lovely eyes,
> And do not shun the sound of sighs,
>   If they are level with the ear;
> But if they rise just o'er my chin,
> O Venus! how I hate their din!
>   My own I am too weak to bear.

LXXVI. CLEONE TO ASPASIA.

D) you remember little Artemidora, the mild and bashful girl, whom you compared to a white blossom on the river, surrounded by innumerable slender reeds, and seen only at intervals as they waved about her, making way to the breeze, and quivering and bending?   Not having seen her for some time, and meeting Deiphobos, who is intimate with her family, I ventured to ask him whether he had been lately at the house.   He turned pale.   Imprudent and indelicate as I am, I accused him instantly, with much gayety, of love for her.   Accused!   O Aspasia, how glorious is it in one to feel more sensibly than all others the beauty that lies far beyond what they ever can discern!   From their earthly station they behold the Sun's bright disk: *he* enters the palace of the god.   Externally there is fire only; pure, inextinguishable æther fills the whole space within, and increases the beauty it displays.

"Cleone!" said he, "you are distressed at the apprehension of having pained me.   Believe me, you have not touched the part where pain lies.   Were it possible that a creature so perfect could love me, I would reprove her indiscretion; I would recall to her attention what surely her eyes might indicate at a glance, the disparity of our ages; and I would teach her, what is better taught by friendship than by experience, that youth alone is the fair price of youth.   However, since there is on either side nothing but pure amity, there is no necessity for any such discourse.   My soul could hardly be more troubled if there were.   Her health is declining while her beauty is scarcely yet at its meridian.   I will not delay you, O Cleone! nor will you delay me.   Rarely do I enter the temples; but I must enter here before I sleep.   Artemis and Aphroditè may perhaps hear me; but I entreat you, do you also, who are more pious than I am, pray and implore of their divine goodness, that my few years may be added to hers; the few to them any, the sorrowful (not then so) to the joyous."

He clasped my hand; I withdrew it, for it burnt me. Inconsiderate and indelicate before, call me now (what you must ever think me) barbarous and inhuman.

LXXVII. ASPASIA TO CLEONE.

The largest heart, O Cleone, is that which only one can
rest upon or impress; the purest is that which dares to
call itself impure; the kindest is that which shrinks
rather at its own inhumanity than at another's.　Cleone
barbarous! Cleone inhuman!　Silly girl! you are fit only
to be an instructress to the sillier Aspasia.　In some
things (in this for instance) I am wiser than you.　I
have truly a great mind to make you blush again, and so
make you accuse yourself a second time of indiscretion.
After a pause, I am resolved on it.　Now then, Artemidora is the very girl who preferred you to me both for
manners and beauty.　Many have done the same, no
doubt, but she alone to my face. (When we were sitting,
one evening in autumn, with our feet in the Mæander, her
nurse conducted her toward us.　We invited her to sit
down between us, which at first she was afraid of doing,
because the herbage had recovered from the drought of
summer and had become succulent as in spring, so that it
might stain her short white dress.　But when we showed
her how this danger might be quite avoided, she blushed,
and, after some hesitation, was seated. (Before long I
inquired of her who was her little friend, and whether
he was handsome, and whether he was sensible, and
whether he was courageous, and whether he was ardent.
She answered all these questions in the affirmative, excepting the last, which she really did not understand.　At
length came the twilight of thought and showed her
blushes.　I ceased to persecute her, and only asked her
which of us she liked the best and thought the most beautiful.　" I like Cleone the best," said she, "and think her
the most beautiful, because she took my hand and pitied
my confusion when such very strange questions were put
to me."　However, she kissed me when she saw I was
concerned at my impropriety; maybe a part of the kiss
was given as a compensation for the severity of her
sentence.

LXXVIII. ASPASIA TO CLEONE.

We are but pebbles in a gravel walk,
Some blacker and some whiter, pebbles still,
Fit only to be trodden on.

These words were introduced into a comedy lately written by Polus, a remarkably fat person, and who appears to have enjoyed life and liberty as much as any citizen in Athens. I happen to have rendered some services to Philonides the actor, to whom the speech is addressed. He brought me the piece before its representation, telling me that Polus and his friends had resolved to applaud the passage, and to turn their faces toward Pericles. I made him a little present, on condition that, in the representation, he should repeat the following verses in reply, instead of the poet's:

. . . . . . Fair Polus!
Can such fierce winds blow over such smooth seas?
I never saw a pebble in my life
So richly set as thou art: now, by Jove,
He who would tread upon thee can be none
Except the proudest of the elephants,
The tallest and the surest-footed beast
In all the stables of the kings of Ind.

The comedy was interrupted by roars of laughter; the friends of Polus slunk away, and he himself made many a violent effort to do the same; but Amphicydes, who stood next, threw his arms round his neck, crying:

"Behold another Codrus! devoting himself for his country. The infernal Powers require no black bull for sacrifice; they are quite satisfied. Eternal peace with Bœotia! eternal praise to her! what a present! where was he fatted?"

We had invited Polus to dine with us, and now condoled with him on his loss of appetite. The people of Athens were quite out of favor with him.

"I told them what they were fit for," cried he, "and

they proved it.   Amphicydes . . I do not say he has been
at Sparta . . I myself saw him, no long time ago, on the
road that leads to Megara . . that city rebelled soon after.
His wife died strangely ; she had not been married two
years, and had grown ugly and thin ; he might have used
her for a broom if she had hair enough . . perhaps he
did ; odd noises have been heard in the house.   I have no
suspicion or spite against any man living . . and, praise
to the gods ! I can live without being an informer."

We listened with deep interest, but could not understand the allusion, as he perceived by our looks.

" You will hear to-morrow," said he, " how unworthily
I have been treated.   Wit draws down Folly on us, and
she must have her fling.   It does not hit ; it does not hit."

Slaves brought in a ewer of water, with several nap-
kins.   They were not lost upon Polus, and he declared
that those two boys had more sagacity and intuition than
all the people in the theatre.

" In your house and your administration, O Pericles,
everything is timed well and done well, without our knowing how.   Dust will rise," said he, " dust will rise ; if
we would not raise it we must never stir.   They have
begun with those who would reform their manners ; they
will presently carry their violence against those who
maintain and execute the laws."

Supper was served.

" A quail, O best Polus !"*

" A quail, O wonderful ! may hurt me ; but being
recommended . . "

It disappeared.

" The breast of that capon . ."

" Capons, being melancholic, breed melancholy within."

" Coriander-seed might correct it, together with a few
of those white, plump pine-seeds."

" The very desideration !"

* O *best !* O *wonderful !* O *lady !* etc.
Ω βελτιστε: Ω θαυμασιε: Ω δεσποινα.

Conversation was never carried on without these terms, even
among philosophers, as we see in Plato, etc.

It was corrected.

"Tunny under oil, with marjoram and figs, pickled locusts and pistachioes . . Your stomach seems delicate."

"Alas! indeed it is declining. Tunny! tunny! I dare not, O festoon of the Graces! I dare not verily. Chian wine alone can appease its seditions."

They were appeased.

Some livers were offered him, whether of fish or fowl, I know not, for I can hardly bear to look at that dish. He waved them away, but turned suddenly round, and said, " Youth! I think I smell fennel."

"There is fennel, O mighty one!" replied the slave, "and not fennel only, but parsley and honey, pepper and rosemary, garlick from Salamis, and . . "

" Say no more, say no more; fennel is enough for moderate men and brave ones. It reminds me of the field of Marathon."

The field was won; nothing was left upon it.

Another slave came forward, announcing loudly and pompously, " Gosling from Brauron! Sauce . . prunes, mustard-seed, capers, fenu-greek, sesamum, and squills."

"Squills!" exclaimed Polus, " they soothe the chest. It is not every cook that is deep in the secrets of nature. Brauron! an ancient city; I have friends in Brauron; I will taste, were it only for remembrance of them."

He made several essays, several pauses.

" But when shall we come to the squills?" said he, turning to the slave; "the qualities of the others are negative."

The whole dish was, presently.

" Our pastry," said I, " O illustrious Polus! is the only thing I can venture to recommend at table; the other dishes are merely on sufferance, but really our pastry is good; I usually dine entirely upon it."

" Entirely!" cried he, in amaze.

"With a glass of water," added I, "and some grapes, fresh, or dry."

"To accompany you, O divine Aspasia! though in

good truth this sad pastry is but a sandy sort of road;
no great way can be made in it."

The diffident Polus was not a bad engineer, however,
and he soon had an opportunity of admiring the workmanship at the bottom of the salver.

Two dishes of roast meat were carried to him. I know
not what one was, nor could Polus easily make up his
mind upon it; experiment following experiment. Kid,
however, was an old acquaintance.

" Those who kill kids," said he, "deserve well of
their country, for they grow up mischievous: the gods,
aware of this, make them very eatable. They require
some management, some skill, some reflection: mint,
shalot, dandelion, vinegar: strong coercion upon them.
Chian wine, boy!"

"What does Pericles eat?"

"Do not mind Pericles! He has eaten of the quails,
and some roast fish, besprinkled with bay-leaves for sauce."

"Fish! ay, that makes him so vigilant. Cats . ."

Here he stopped, not however without a diversion in
his favor from me, observing that he usually dined on
vegetables, fish, and some bird: that his earlier meal
was his longest, confectionery, honey, and white bread,
composing it.

"And Chian or Lesbian?"

"He enjoys a little wine after dinner, preferring the
lighter and subacid."

"Wonderful man!" cried he; "and all from such
fare as that!"

When he rose from table he seemed by his countenance to be quiet again at heart; nevertheless he said in
my ear with a sigh, "Did I possess the power of Pericles, or the persuasion of Aspasia, by the Immortals! I
would enrich the galleys with a grand dotation. Every
soul of them should . . I, yes, every soul of them . .
monsters of ingratitude, hypocrites, traitors, they should
for Egypt, for Carthage, Mauritania, Numidia. He will
find out before long what dogs he has been skimming the
kettle for."

It required an effort to be perfectly composed, at a simile which I imagine has never been used in the Greek language since the days of Medea; but I cast down my eyes, and said consolatorily, "It is difficult to do justice to such men as Pericles and Polus."

He would now have let me into the secret, but others saved me.

Our farmers, in the number of their superstitions, entertain a firm belief that any soil is rendered more fertile by burying an ass's head in it. On this idea is founded the epigram I send you : it raised a laugh at dinner.

> Leave me thy head when thou art dead,
> Speusippus! Prudent farmers say
> An ass's skull makes plentiful
> The poorest soil; and ours is clay.

LXXIX. ASPASIA TO CLEONE.

Anaxagoras is the true, firm, constant friend of Pericles; the golden lamp that shines perpetually on the image I adore. Yet sometimes he speaks severely. On one of these occasions, Pericles took him by the hand, saying :

"O Anaxagoras! sincere and ardent lover of Truth! why do not you love her in such a manner as never to let her see you out of humor?"

"Because," said Anaxagoras, "you divide my affections with her, much to my shame."

Pericles was called away on business; I then said :

"O Anaxagoras! is not Pericles a truly great man?"

He answered, "If Pericles were a truly great man, he would not wish to appear different from what he is; he would know himself, and make others know him; he seems to guard against both. Much is wanting to constitute his greatness. He possesses, it is true, more comprehensiveness and concentration than any living; perhaps more than any since Solon; but he thinks that power over others is better than power over himself; as if a mob were worth a man, and an acclamation were worth a Pericles."

"But," said I, " he has absolute command over himself; and it is chiefly by exerting it that he has obtained an ascendancy over the minds of others."

" Has he rendered them wiser and more virtuous?" said he.

" You know best," replied I, "having lived much longer among them."

" Perhaps," said Anaxagoras, "I may wrong him; perhaps he has saved them from worse disasters."

" You think him, then, ambitious?" said I, with some sadness.

"Ambitious!" cried he; "how so! He might have been a philosopher, and he is content to be a ruler."

I was ill at ease.

"Come," said I, "Anaxagoras! come into the garden with me. It is rather too warm indeed out of doors, but we have many evergreens, high and shady, and those who, like you and me, never drink wine, have little to dread from the heat."

Whether the ilexes and bays and oleanders struck his imagination, and presented the simile, I cannot tell, but he thus continued in illustration of his discourse :

"There are no indeciduous plants, Aspasia! the greater part lose their leaves in winter, the rest in summer. It is thus with men. The generality yield and are stripped under the first chilly blasts that shake them. They who have weathered these, drop leaf after leaf in the sunshine. The virtues by which they arose to popularity, take another garb, another aspect, another form, and totally disappear. Be not uneasy; the heart of Pericles will never dry up, so many streams run into it."

He retired to his studies; I spoke but little that evening, and slept late.

LXXX. ASPASIA TO CLEONE.

How can I ever hope to show you, in all its brightness, the character of my friend? I will tell you how; by

following Love and Truth.   Like most others who have
no genius, I do not feel the want of it, at least not here.

A shallow water may reflect the sun as perfectly as a
deeper.

The words of Anaxagoras stuck to me like thistles.   I
resolved to speak in playfulness with the object of our
conversation.   First I began to hint at enemies.   He
smiled.

"The children in my orchard," said he, "are not yet
grown tall enough to reach the fruit ; they may throw at
it, but can bring none down."

"Do tell me, O Pericles!" said I, "now we are
inseparable forever, how many struggles with yourself
(to say nothing of others) you must have had, before
you attained the position you have taken."

"It is pleasanter," answered he, "to think of our
glory than of the means by which we acquired it."

"When we see the horses that have won at the
Olympian games, do we ask what oats they have eaten
to give them such velocity and strength?   Do those who
swim admirably, ever trouble their minds about the
bladders they swam upon in learning, or inquire what
beasts supplied them?   When the winds are filling our
sails, do we lower them and delay our voyage, in order
to philosophize on the particles of air composing them,
or to speculate what region produced them, or what
becomes of them afterward?"

LXXXI. CLEONE TO ASPASIA.

At last, Aspasia, you love indeed.   The perfections of
your beloved interest you less than the imperfections,
which you no sooner take up for reprehension, than
you admire, embrace, and defend.   Happy, happy, Aspasia! but are you wise and good and equable, and fond
of sincerity, as formerly?   Nay, do not answer me.
The gods forbid that I should force you to be ingenious,
and love you for it.   How much must you have lost before you are praised for that!

Archelaus, of all our philosophers the most quiet man, and the most patient investigator, will bring you this. He desires to be the hearer of Anaxagoras.

LXXXII. ASPASIA TO CLEONE.

I received our countryman with great pleasure. He was obliged to be *my* hearer for several hours: I hope his patience will never be so much tried by Anaxagoras. I placed them together at table; but Anaxagoras would not break through his custom; nothing of philosophy. Our repast would have been even less talkative than usual, had not Anaxagoras asked our guest whether the earlier Milesian authors, poets, or historians, had mentioned Homer.

"I find not a word about him in any one of them," replied he, "although we have the works of Cadmus and Phocylides, the former no admirable historian, the latter an indifferent poet, but not the less likely to mention him; and they are supposed to have lived within three centuries of his age. Permit my first question to you, in my search after truth, to be this: whether his age were not much earlier?"

"This is not the only question," said Anaxagoras, "on which you will hear from me the confession of my utter ignorance. I am interested in everything that relates to the operations of the human mind; and Pericles has in his possession every author whose works have been transcribed. The number will appear quite incredible to you: there cannot be fewer than two hundred. I find poetry to which is attributed an earlier date than to Homer's; but stupidity and barbarism are no convincing proofs. I find Cretan, Ionian, Laconian, and Bœotian, written certainly more than three centuries ago; the language is not copious, is not fluent, is not refined. Pericles says it is all of it inharmonious: of this I cannot judge; he can. Dropides and Mimnermus wrote no better verses than the servant-girls sing upon our staircases. Archilochus and Alcman, who lived a century earlier, composed much grander; but where there is at once ferocity and immodesty, either the age must have been barbarous or the poet must have been left behind it. Sappho was in reality the reviver of poetry, teaching it to humanize and delight; Simonides brought it to perfection. The muse of Lesbos, as she is called, and Alcæus, invented each a novel species of strophe. Aspasia prefers the poetry of Sappho and the metre of Alcæus, which, however, I think she informs us, is less adapted to her subjects than her own is."

"It appears to me," said I, "that every one who felt strong in poetry was ambitious of being an inventor in its measures. Archilochus, the last of any note, invented the iambic."

"True, O Aspasia!" said Pericles, "but not exactly in the sense usually received. He did not invent, as many suppose, the senarian iambic, which is coeval almost with the language itself, and many of which creep into the closest prose composition; but he was the first who subjoined a shorter to it, the barb to the dart, so fatal to Cleobule and Lycambes."

"His first," said I, "is like the trot of a mastiff, his second like the spring at the throat.

"Homer alone has enriched the language with sentences full of harmony. How long his verse was created, how long his gods had lived, before *him*, how long he himself before *us*, is yet uncertain, although Herodotus * is of opinion that he is nearer to us than Pericles and Anaxagoras admit. But these two philosophers place sun, moon, and stars beyond all reasonable limits, I know not how far off."

"We none of us know," said Pericles; "but Anaxagoras hopes that, in a future age, human knowledge will be more extensive and more correct; and Meton has encouraged us in our speculations. The heavenly bodies may keep their secrets two or three thousand years yet; but one or other will betray them to some wakeful favorite,

---

* The *Life of Homer*, appended to the works of Herodotus, is spurious.

6

some Endymion beyond Latmos, perhaps in regions un-
discovered, certainly in uncalculated times.   Men will
know more of them than they will ever know of Homer.
Our knowledge on this miracle of our species is unlikely
to increase."

LXXXIII. ASPASIA TO CLEONE.

Pericles, who is acknowledged to have a finer ear than
any of our poets or rhetoricians, is of opinion that the
versification in all the books, of both Iliad and Odyssea,
was modulated by the same master-key.   Sophocles, too,
certainly less jolted than you would suppose, by the deep
ruts, angular turns, and incessant jerks of the iambic,
tells me that he finds no other heroic verses at all resembling it in the rhythm, and that, to his apprehension, it is
not dissimilar in the two poems.

But I must continue, while I remember them perfectly,
the words of Pericles:

" The Ulysses of the *Iliad* and *Odyssea* is not the
same, but the Homer is.   Might not the poet have collected, in his earlier voyages, many wonderful tales about
the chieftain of Ithaca; about his wanderings and return;
about his wife and her suitors?   Might not afterward the
son or grandson have solicited his guest and friend to
place the sagacious, the courageous, the enduring man,
among the others whom he was celebrating in detached
poems, as leaders against Troy?   He describes with precision everything in Ithaca; it is evident he must have
been upon the spot.   Of all other countries, of Sicily, of
Italy, of Phrygia, he quite as evidently writes from tradition and representation.   Phrygia was subject to the
Assyrian kings at the time when he commences his siege.
The Greeks, according to him, had been ravaging the
country many years, and had swept away many cities.
What were the Assyrian kings doing?   Did the Grecians
lose no men by war, by climate, by disease, by time, in
the whole ten years?   Their horses must have been
strong and long-lived: an excellent breed! to keep their

teeth and mettle for five-and-twenty. I should have imagined that some of them must have got lamed, some few, perhaps, foundered; surely here and there a chariot can have had but one remaining, and he, in all probability, not in the very best condition. I cannot but think that Homer took from Sesostris the shield that he has given to Achilles. The Greeks never worked gold so skilfully as in this shield, until our own Phidias taught them; and even he possesses not the art of giving all the various colors to the metal, which are represented as designating the fruitage, and other things included in this stupendous work, and which the Egyptians in his time, and long earlier, understood. How happened it that the Trojans had Greek names, and the leader of the Greeks an Egyptian one? When I was at Byzantion, I had the curiosity to visit the imaginary scene of their battles. I saw many sepulchral monuments, of the most durable kind, conical elevations of earth, on which there were sheep and goats at pasture. There were ruins beyond, but neither of a great city nor of an ancient one. The only ancient walls I saw were on the European coast, those of Byzantion, which Aspasia claims as the structure of Miletus, and which the people of Megara tell us were founded by their forefathers less than two centuries ago. But neither Miletus nor Megara was built when these walls were entire. They belong to the unknown world, and are sometimes called Pelasgian, sometimes Cyclopean; appellations without meaning; signs that signify nothing; inscriptions that point out the road to places where there is neither place nor road. Walls of this massive structure surround the ruins of Phocœa, destroyed by Cyrus; they are also found in Tyrrhenia. Our acropolis was surmounted by such, until the administration of Themistocles, who removed the stones to serve as foundations to the works in the harbor; the occasion being urgent, and the magnitude of the blocks being admirably proper for that solid structure."

Cleone! are you tired? rest then.

LXXXIV. ASPASIA TO CLEONE.

Several times had Pericles been silent, expecting and inviting our guests to assist him in the investigation.

"I have no paradox to maintain, no partiality to defend," said he. "Some tell us that there were twenty Homers, some deny that there was ever one. It were idle and foolish to shake the contents of a vase in order to let them settle at last. We are perpetually laboring to destroy our delight, our composure, our devotion to superior power. Of all the animals upon earth we least know what is good for us. My opinion is, that what is best for us is our admiration of good. No man living venerates Homer more than I do. He was the only author I read when I was a boy, for our teachers are usually of opinion that wisdom and poetry are like fruit for children, unwholesome if too fresh. Simonides had indeed grown somewhat sound; Pindar was heating; Æschylus . . ay, but Æschylus was almost at the next door. Homer then nourished my fancy, animated my dreams, awoke me in the morning, marched with me, sailed with me, taught me morals, taught me language, taught me music and philosophy and war.

"Ah, were he present at this hour among us! that I might ask him how his deities entered Troy. In Phrygia there was but one goddess, the mother of all the gods, Cybele. Unlike our mortal mothers, she was displeased if you noticed her children; indeed, she disowned them. Her dignity, her gravity, her high antiquity, induced the natives of the islands, and afterward the other Greeks, to place their little gods under her protection, and to call her their mother. Jupiter had his Ida, but not the Phrygian; and Pallas was worshipped in her citadels, but not above the streams of Simois and Scamander. Our holy religion has not yet found its way far beyond us; like the myrtle and olive, it loves the sea air, and flourishes but upon few mountains in the interior. The Cabiri still hold Samothrace; and we may almost hear the cries of human victims in the north.

" If there were any true history of the times we are exploring, perhaps we might find in it that many excursions, combined and simultaneous, had utterly failed; and that the disasters of many chiefs engaged in them were partly concealed from the nations they governed by the sacred veil of poetry. Of those who are reputed to have sailed against Troy, none returned prosperous, none with the men he had led out; most were forbidden to land again upon their native shores, and some who attempted it were slain. Such is usually the fate of the unsuccessful. It is more probable that the second great naval expedition of the Greeks went out to avenge the disasters of the first, the Argonautic; and the result was nearly the same. Of the Argonauts few returned. Sparta lost her Castor and Pollux; Thessaly her Jason; and I am more disposed to believe that the head of Orpheus rolled down the Phasis than down the Hebrus.

"The poets gave successes which the gods denied. But these things concern us little; the poet is what we seek. Needless is it to remark that the *Iliad* is a work of much reflection and various knowledge; the *Odyssea* is the marvellous result of a vivid and wild imagination. Aspasia prefers it. Homer, in nearly the thirty years which I conceive to have intervened between the fanciful work and the graver, had totally lost his pleasantries. Polyphemus could amuse him no longer; Circe lighted up in vain her fires of cedar-wood; Calypso had lost her charms; her maidens were mute around her; the Lestrigons lay asleep; the Syrens sang

' Come hither, O passer by! come hither,
   O glory of the Achaians!'

and the smooth waves quivered with the sound, but the harp of the old man had no chord that vibrated.

In the *Odyssea* he invokes the Muse; in the *Iliad* he invokes her as a goddess he had invoked before. He begins the *Odyssea* as the tale of a family, to which he would listen as she rehearsed it; the *Iliad* as a song of warriors and divinities, worthy of the goddess herself to sing before the world.

" Demonstrate that metaphors are discoverable, drawn from things believed to have been uninvented in the Homeric age ; what does it prove ? Merely that Homer, who lived among the islands, and among those who had travelled into all the known regions of the world, had collected more knowledge than the shepherds and boar-hunters on the continent.

" Demonstrate that some books in the compilation retain slight traces of a language not exactly the same as the others. What then ? Might they not have been composed while he visited countries in which that dialect was indigenous ? or might they not have been found there at the first collection of the songs, having undergone some modification from the singers, adapted to the usages and phraseology of the people ?

" Who doubts that what was illegible or obscure in the time of Lycurgus was rendered clearer by the learned Spartan ? that some Cretan words, not the Dorian of Sparta, had crept in ; that others were substituted ; that Solon, Pisistratus, and Hipparchus, had also to correct a few of these corrections, and many things more ? They found a series of songs ; never was there a series of such length without an oversight or gap.

" Shall the *salpinx* be sounded in my ear ? Homer may have introduced it by way of allusion in one poem, not wanting it in the other. The Grecians of his time never used it in battle ; eastern nations did ; and, perhaps, had he known the Phrygians better, its blasts would have sounded on the plains of Troy. He would have discovered that trumpets had been used among them for many ages. We possess no knowledge of any nation who cultivated the science of music so early, or employed so great a variety of wind instruments, unless it be the Sidonian. Little did he know of Phrygia, and as little do we know of him. His beautiful creation lies displayed before us ; the creator is hidden in his own splendor. I can more easily believe that his hand constructed the whole, than that twenty men could be found, at nearly the same time, each of genius sufficient for the twentieth part ; because in many centuries there arose not a single one capable of such a production as that portion.

" Archilochus and Simonides are excellent only in their shorter poems; they could not have whistled so well throughout a long march. Difficulties are to be over-come on both sides. We have no grammarians worthy of the appellation ; none in any district of Greece has studied the origin and etymology of his language. We sing like the birds, equally ignorant whence our voice arises. What is worse, we are fonder of theories than of truth, and believe that we have not room enough to build up anything, until we subvert what we find before us. Be it so ; but let it be only what is obnoxious, what opposes our reason, what disturbs our tranquillity of mind ; not what shows us the extent of the one, the potency of the other, and, consoling us for being mortal, assures us that our structures may be as durable as those of the gods themselves. The name of Homer will be venerated as long as the holiest of theirs ; I dare not say longer ; I dare not say by wiser men. I hope I am guilty of no impiety ; I should aggravate it by lowering Homer, the loftiest of their works."

LXXXV. CLEONE TO ASPASIA.

We are losing, day by day, one friend or other. Arte-midora of Ephesus was betrothed to Elpenor, and their nuptials, it was believed, were at hand. How gladly would Artemidora have survived Elpenor. I pitied her almost as much as if she had. I must ever love true lovers on the eve of separation. These indeed were little known to me until a short time before. We became friends when our fates had made us relatives. On these occasions there are always many verses, but not always so true in feeling and in fact as those which I shall now transcribe for you :

> " Artemidora! Gods invisible,
>   While thou art lying faint along the couch,
>   Have tied the sandal to thy veined feet,

And stand beside thee, ready to convey
Thy weary steps where other rivers flow.
Refreshing shades will waft thy weariness
Away, and voices like thine own come nigh,
Soliciting, nor vainly, thy embrace."
Artemidora sigh'd, and would have press'd
The hand now pressing hers, but was too weak.
Fate's shears were over her dark hair unseen
While thus Elpenor spake : he look'd into
Eyes that had given light and life erewhile
To those above them, those now dim with tears
And watchfulness. Again he spake of joy
Eternal. At that word, that sad word, *joy*,
Faithful and fond her bosom heav'd once more,
Her head fell back : one sob, one loud deep sob
Swell'd through the darken'd chamber ; 'twas not hers :
With her that old boat incorruptible,
Unwearied, undiverted in its course,
Had plashed the water up the farther strand.

LXXXVI. ASPASIA TO CLEONE.

Aristophanes often dines with us ; nevertheless he is
secretly an enemy of Pericles, and, fearing to offend him
personally, is satirical on most of our friends.   Meton,
whose character you know already, great in astronomy,
great in geometry, great in architecture, was consulted
by Pericles on beautifying the streets of the city, which
are close and crooked.   No sooner had Aristophanes
heard this, than he began to compose a comedy, entitled
The Birds.   He has here represented our quiet contemplative Meton, with a rule and compass in his hands,
uttering the most ludicrous absurdities.   Meton is a
plain, unassuming, inoffensive man, and never speaks
inconsiderately.   The character is clumsily drawn ; but
that fault was easily corrected, by representing poor
Meton under the chastisement of the cudgel.   There is
so much wit in this, I doubt whether any audience can
resist it.   There is magic in every stroke, and what was
amiss is mended and made whole again ere the hammer
falls.   How easy a way of setting all things to rights,
with only one dissentient voice !

In the same comedy is ridiculed the project of Pericles, on a conformity of weights and measures in Attica and her dependencies.   More wit! another beating!

When Aristophanes made us the next visit, Pericles, after greeting him with much good-nature, and after various conversations with him, seemed suddenly to recollect something, and, with more familiarity than usual, took him gently by the elbow, led him a little aside, and said with a smile, and in a low voice:

" My dear friend Aristophanes! I find you are by no means willing to receive the same measure as you give ; but remember, the people have ordered the adjustment, the surest preservative against fraud, particularly that by which the poorer are mostly the sufferers.   Take care they do not impeach you, knowing as you do how inefficient is my protection.   It is chiefly on such an occasion I should be sorry to be in a minority."

Aristophanes blushed, and looked alarmed.   Pericles took him by the hand, whispering in his ear, " Do not let us enter into a conspiracy against Equity, by attacking the uniformity of weights and measures ; nor against Comedy, by giving the magistrates a pretext to forbid its representation."

Aristophanes turned toward Pentarces, who stood near him, and said :

" I can write a comedy as well as most ; Pericles can act one better than any."

Aristophanes, in my opinion, might have easily been the first lyric poet now living, except Sophocles and Euripides ; he chose rather to be the bitterest satirist. How many, adorned with all the rarities of intellect, have stumbled on the entrance into life, and have made a wrong choice on the very thing which was to determine their course forever!   This is among the reasons, and perhaps is the principal one, why the wise and the happy are two distinct classes of men.

LXXXVII. ASPASIA TO CLEONE.

I had retired before Aristophanes went home.   On my

return, it was evident that some one present had in-
veighed against the poet's effrontery, for I was in time to
catch these words of Pericles:

" Why should I be angry with the writers of comedy?
Is it because they tell me of the faults I find in myself?
Surely not; for he who finds them in himself may be
quite certain that others have found them in him long
before, and have shown much forbearance in the delay.

" Is it because I am told of those I have not discovered
in me? Foolish indeed were this. I am to be angry, it
seems, because a man forewarns me that I have enemies
in my chamber, who will stab me when they find me
asleep, and because he helps me to catch them and dis-
arm them.

" But it is such an indignity to be ridiculed! I in-
curred a greater when I threw myself into the way of
ridicule: a greater still should I suffer if I tried whether
it could be remedied by resentment.

" Ridicule often parries resentment, but resentment
never yet parried ridicule."

LXXXVIII. ASPASIA TO HERODOTUS.

Herodotus! if there is any one who admires your
writings more than another, it is I. No residence in
Attica will ever make me prefer the dialect to ours; no
writer will charm my ear as you have done; and yet you
cannot bring me to believe that the sun is driven out of
his course by storms; nor any of the consequences you
deduce from it, occasioning the overflow of the Nile.
The opinion you consider as unfounded, namely, that it
arises from the melting of the snows, and from the pe-
riodical rains on the mountains of Ethiopia, is, however,
that of Pericles and Anaxagoras, who attribute it also to
Thales, in their estimation the soundest and shrewdest
of philosophers. They appear to have very strange notions about the sun, about his magnitude, his position,
and distance; and I doubt whether you could persuade
them that the three stoutest winds are able to move him

one furlong. I am a great doubter, you see; but they, I do assure you, are greater. Pericles is of opinion that natural philosophy has made but little progress; and yet that many more discoveries have burst open before the strenuous inquirer than have been manifested to the world; that some have been suppressed by a fear of the public, and some by a contempt for it.

"In the intellectual," said he, "as in the physical, men grasp you firmly and tenaciously by the hand, creeping close at your side, step for step, while you lead them into darkness; but when you conduct them into sudden light, they start and quit you."

O Herodotus! may your life and departure be happy! But how can it be expected! No other deities have ever received such honors as you have conferred upon the Muses; and alas, how inefficient are they to reward or protect their votaries!

LXXXIX. CLEONE TO ASPASIA.

The tragedy of Phrynicus, on the devastation of our city by the Persians, will outlast all the cities now flourishing on earth.* Heavy was the mulct to which the poet was condemned by the Athenians for the tears he drew from them in the theatre.

Is it not remarkable that we have never found any Milesian poem on the same subject? Surely there must have been several. Within how short a period have they perished! Lately, in searching the houses of such inhabitants as were suspected of partiality to the interests of Lacedæmon, these verses were discovered. They bear the signature of *Aletheia, daughter of Charidemus and Astyage.*

We have often heard her story. Often have we sat upon the mound of ruins under which she lies buried;

---

* This tragedy, which produced a more powerful effect than any other on record, has failed, however, to fulfil the prophecy of Cleone: the Ode of Aletheia, on which she places so small a value, has outlived it.

often have we plucked from it the white cyclamen, sweetest of all sweet odors, and played with its stiff reverted little horns, pouring forth a parsimonious fragrance, won only when we applied to them tenderly and closely.

Whether poor Aletheia gave for life more than life's value, it were worse than curiosity to inquire. She loved her deliverer; and, at the instigation of many less gentle, she was slain for loving him. When the city was again in possession of the citizens, she was stoned to death for favoring the invader; and her mother rushed forward and shared it. These are things you know; her poem, her only one extant, you do not. You will find in it little of poetry, but much of what is better and rarer, true affection.

ALETHEIA TO PHRAORTES.

Phraortes! where art thou?
The flames were panting after us, their darts
Had pierced to many hearts
Before the gods, who heard nor prayer nor vow;

Temples had sunk to earth, and other smoke
O'er riven altars broke
Than curled from myrrh and nard,
When like a god among
Arm'd hosts and unarm'd throng
Thee I discern'd, implored, and caught one brief regard.

Thou passest: from thy side
Sudden two bowmen ride
And hurry me away.
Thou and all hope were gone ..
They loos'd me .. and alone
In a closed tent 'mid gory arms I lay.

How did my tears then burn
When, dreading thy return,
Behold thee reappear!
Nor helm nor sword nor spear ..

In violet gold-hemm'd vest
Thou camest forth; too soon!
Fallen at thy feet, claspt to thy breast,
I struggle, sob, and swoon.

"O send me to my mother! bid her come,
    And take my last farewell!
One blow! . . enough for both . . one tomb . .
    'Tis there *our* happy dwell."

    Thou orderest: call'd and gone
At once they are who breathe for thy command.
Thou stoodest nigh me, soothing every moan,
    And pressing in both thine my hand.

    Then, and then only, when it tore
      My hair to hide my face;
    And gently did thy own bend o'er
The abject head war-doomed to dire disgrace.

    Ionian was thy tongue,
And when thou badest me to raise
That head, nor fear in aught thy gaze,
    I dared look up . . but dared not long.

    "Wait, maiden, wait! if none are here
Bearing a charm to charm a tear,
There may (who knows?) be found at last
Some solace for the sorrow past."

    My mother, ere the sounds had ceas'd,
      Burst in, and drew me down:
Her joy o'erpowered us both, her breast
    Covered lost friends and ruin'd town.

    Sweet thought! but yielding now
To many harsher! By what blow
Art thou dissevered from me? War,
    That hath career'd too far,
Closeth his pinions. "Come, Phraortes, come
    To thy fond friends at home!"

Thus beckons Love. Away then, wishes wild!
    O may thy mother be as blest
    As one whose eyes will sink to rest
    Blessing thee for her rescued child!

    Ungenerous still my heart must be:
    Throughout the young and festive train
    Which thou revisitest again
May none be happier (this I fear) than she!

XC. ASPASIA TO CLEONE.

Perhaps I like the Ode of Aletheia more than you do, because you sent it me; and you perhaps would have liked it more than I, had I sent it you. There are writings which must lie long upon the straw before they mellow to the taste; and there are summer fruits which cannot abide the keeping.

My heart assures me that Aletheia, had she lived, might have excelled in poetry; and the loss of a lover is a help to it. We must defer our attempts to ascertain her station in the world of poetry; for we never see the just dimensions of what is close before our eyes. Faults are best discovered near, and beauties at some distance.

Aletheia, who found favor with Cleone, is surely not unworthy to take her seat in the library of Pericles.

I will look for a cyclamen to place within the scroll; I must find it, and gather it, and place it there myself. Sweet, hapless Aletheia!

XCI. ASPASIA TO CLEONE.

Nothing is pleasanter to me than exploring in a library. What a delight in being a discoverer! Among a loose accumulation of poetry, the greater part excessively bad, the verses I am about to transcribe are perhaps the least so.

> Life passes not as some men say,
> If you will only urge his stay,
>   And treat him kindly all the while.
> He flies the dizzy strife of towns,
> Cowers before thunder-bearing frowns,
> But freshens up again at song and smile.

> Ardalia! we will place him here,
> And promise that nor sigh nor tear
>   Shall ever trouble his repose.
> What precious seal will you impress
> To ratify his happiness?
> That rose thro' which you breathe? Come, bring that rose.

XCII. ASPASIA TO CLEONE.

Knowing how desirous I have always been to learn the history of Athens for these last fifty years, and chiefly that part of it in which my Pericles has partaken so largely ; and to reward my forbearance in abstaining from every close and importunate inquiry, he placed a scrap of paper in my hands this morning.

" Read that," said he.

It was no easy matter ; few sentences would have been legible without my interpreter ; indeed there were not many unerased.

" This speech," replied he, " occupied me one whole night, and somewhat of the next morning ; I had so very much *not* to say."

Aware that the party of Cimon would interest the people in his behalf, so that a leader from among his relatives or friends might be proposed and brought forward, Pericles was resolved to anticipate these exertions. See his few words :

" We have lost, O Athenians ! not a town, nor a battle ; these you would soon regain ; but we have lost a great man, a true lover of his country, Cimon, son of Miltiades.

" I well remember the grief you manifested at the necessity of removing him for a time, from among the insidious men who would have worked upon his generous temper, ductile as gold. Never could I have believed I had sufficient interest with some I see before me, firm almost unto hardness, whose patriotism and probity had been the most alarmed ; but they listened to me with patience, and revoked the sentence of banishment. Cimon returned from Sparta, took the command of your armies, vanquished the Persians, and imposed on them such conditious as will humble their pride forever.

" Our fathers were ungenerous to his ; we will, as becomes us, pay their debts, and remove the dust from their memory. Miltiades was always great, and only once unsuccessful ; Cimon was greater, and never unfortunate but in the temporary privation of your affections. History offers us no example of so consummate a commander.

"I propose that a statue be erected to Cimon, son of Miltiades, vanquisher of the Persians."

XCIII. ASPASIA TO CLEONE.

There are secrets which not even love should try to penetrate. I am afraid of knowing who caused the banishment of Cimon; certainly he was impeached by Pericles, who nevertheless praised him highly whenever his name was mentioned. He has allowed me to transcribe his speech after the sentence of the judges, and with it his letter of recall.

TO THE ATHENIANS,

On the Banishment of Cimon.

In your wisdom, O Athenians, you have decreed that Cimon, son of Miltiades, be exiled from our city.

Whatever may have been the errors or the crimes of Cimon, much of them should, in justice to yourselves, and in humanity to the prosecuted, be ascribed to the perversity of that faction, which never ceases or relaxes in its attempts to thwart your determinations, and to deprive you of authority at home, of respect in the sight of Greece.

But I adjure you to remember the services both of Cimon and of Miltiades; and to afford the banished man no reason or plea to call in question your liberality. Permit the rents of his many farms in Attica to be carried to him in Sparta; and let it never be said that a citizen of Athens was obliged to the most illiberal and penurious of people for a sustenance. Not indeed that there is any danger of Sparta entertaining him too honorably. She may pay for services; but rather for those which are to be performed than for those which have been ; and to the man, rather who may do her harm, than to him who can do it no longer.

Let us hope that at some future day Cimon may be aware of his mistake, and regard with more veneration the image of his father than the throne of his father's enemy.

XCIV. PERICLES TO CIMON.

There are few cities, O Cimon, that have men for their inhabitants. Whatever is out of Greece, and not Grecian, is nearer the animal world than the intellectual; some even in Greece are but midway. Leave them behind you; return to your country and conquer her assailants. Wholesome is the wisdom that we have gathered from misfortune, and sweet the repose that dwells upon renown.

XCV. ASPASIA TO CLEONE.

Generally we are little apt to exaggerate merit. In our maladies of the mind the cold fit usually is longer and more intense than the hot, and our dreams are rarely of water in the desert. We must have been among the departed before we experience this sensation. In our road through life, we may happen to meet with a man casting a stone reverentially to enlarge the cairn of another, which stone he had carried in his bosom to sling against that very other's head. Seriously, my Cleone, I am inclined to think that even in these dark days (as they are called) of literature we may occasionally catch a glimpse of poetry. We should be laughed at if we ventured to compare the living with the dead, who always are preferable, but there are choruses in Sophocles and Euripides as pathetical as those tender words of Sappho in her invocation to Hesperos : "Thou bringest the wine, thou bringest the kid, thou bringest the maiden to her mother." Certainly these words are very unsophistical, and they who have seen others weep at them, weep also.

7

But pardon me, if looking attentively, you find no letter in the sentence obliterated by a tear of mine. Sometimes I fancy that the facility and pliancy of our language is the reason why many of the most applauded verses are written with more intenseness of feeling and less expenditure of thought. What is graceful must be easy; but many things are very easy which are not very graceful. There is a great deal even of Attic poetry in which a slight covering of wax is drawn over a bundle of the commonest tow and tatters; we must not bring it too near the lamp . . But it is something to abstain from an indulgence in grossness, prolixity, and exaggeration, which are never the signs of fertility, but frequently the reverse. This abstinence is truly Attic, but Attic not exclusively: for Pindar has given manifold examples of it, and is heavy and tedious then only when he wipes away the foam off his bit with old stories and dry genealogies.

SPEECH OF PERICLES,

On the Defection of Eubœa and Megara.

Eubœa has rejected our authority and alliance, Megara our friendship. Under what pretext? That we have employed in the decoration of our city the sums of money they stipulated to contribute annually; a subsidy to resist the Persians. What! must we continue a war of extermination with Persia, when she no longer has the power to molest us? when peace has been sworn and proclaimed? Do we violate the compact with our confederates? No; men of Athens! our fleets are in harbor, every ship in good condition; our arsenals are well stored; and we are as prompt and as able now to repel aggression as we ever were.

Are our dues then to be withholden from us, because we have anticipated our engagements? because our navy and our army are in readiness before they are wanted? because, while our ungrateful allies were plotting our ruin, we were watching over their interests and provid-

ing for their security? States, like private men, are
subject to the distemper of ingratitude, erasing from their
memory the impression of past benefits; but it appears
to be peculiar to the Megarians to recompense them with
hatred and animosity. Not only have we protected them
from aggression, by building for them the very walls
from which they now defy us; but, when Mardonius
sent against them, at Mount Cithæron, the whole force
of the Median cavalry, under the command of Magestios,
and when they called aloud to every near battalion of
the Grecian army, and when Pausanias in vain repeated
the exhortation, three hundred Athenians, led by Olym-
piodoros, son of Lampon, threw themselves forward from
Erythrai, and, after losing many brave comrades, rescued
from imminent death the fathers of those degenerate men
who are now in the vanguard of conspirators against us.
Ingratitude may be left to the chastisement of the gods,
but the sword must consolidate broken treaties. No
state can be respected if fragment after fragment may be
detached from it with impunity; if traitors are permitted
to delude and discompose the contented, and to seduce the
ignorant from their allegiauce; if loyalty is proclaimed
a weakness, sedition a duty, conspiracy wisdom, and rebellion heroism. It is a crime, then, for us to embellish our
city! it is a reproach to enlarge and fortify our harbors!
In vain have we represented to the clamorous and refractory, that their annual contributions are partly due to us
for past exertions, and partly the price of our protection,
at this time and in future; and not against Persia only,
but against pirates. Our enemies have persuaded them
that rebellion and war are better things; our enemies,
who were lately theirs, and who, by this perfidious insti-
gatiou, are about to become so more cruelly than ever.
Are Athenians avaricious? are Athenians oppressive?
Even the slaves in our city have easier access to the com-
forts and delights of life than the citizens of almost any
other. Until of late the Megarians were proud of our
consanguinity, and refused to be called the descendants
of Apollo, in hopes to be acknowledged as the children of
Pandiou. Although in later times they became the allies

of Sparta, they cannot but remember that we have always
been their friends, often their deliverers; and it is only
for their dishonesty and perfidy that we now are resolved
at last to prohibit them from the advantages of our ports
Sparta and Corinth have instigated them; Corinth,
whose pride and injustice have driven Corcyra, with her
fleets, to seek deliverance in the Piræus.   What have we
to fear from so strange a union as that of Corinth and
Sparta?   Are any two nations so unlike? so little formed
for mutual succor or for mutual esteem?   Hitherto we
have shared both our wealth and our dangers with Eubœa.
At the conclusion of a successful war, at the signature
of a most honorable and advantageous peace, we are derided and reproached.   What is it they discover to despise
in us?   I will tell you what it is.   It is the timid step of
blind men; this they saw in us while they were tamper-
ing with Sparta.   Not ashamed of their seduction, they
now walk hand in hand, with open front, and call others
to join in their infamy.   They have renounced our amity,
they have spurned our expostulations, they have torn our
treaties, and they have defied our arms.   At the peril of
being called a bad citizen, I lament your blindness, O
Megara and Eubœa!

XCVI. ASPASIA TO CLEONE.

I find, among the few records in my hands, that Pericles went in person, and conquered the faithless Megara
and the refractory Eubœa.   Before he sailed to attack the
island, he warned the Athenians against an inconsiderate
parsimony, which usually terminates in fruitless expenditure.   He told them plainly that Eubœa was capable of
a protracted and obstinate resistance; and he admonished
them that, whatever reverses the arms of Athens might
experience, they should continue the war, and consider
the dominion of the island a thing necessary to their existence as a nation; that whoever should devise or counsel the separation of Eubœa from Athens, be declared
guilty of treason, and punished with death.

" If Thebes, in a future war," said he, " should take possession of this productive country, and shut up, as she easily might, the passage of the Euripus, she would gain an ascendancy over us, from which we never could recover. Losses, defeats, inadequate supplies, may tempt her ; she would always have Sparta for an ally on such an occasion. Indeed, it is wonderful that the Bœotians, as brave a race of men as any in Greece, and stronger in body, should not have been her masters. Perhaps it is the fertility of her own territory that kept her content with her possessions, and indisposed the cultivators of so rich a soil from enterprise and hazard. Eubœa is no less fertile than Bœotia, from which she is separated by the distance of a stone's throw. Give me fifty galleys, and five thousand men, and Eubœa shall fall ere Sparta can come to her assistance."

XCVII. ASPASIA TO CLEONE.

Perpetual as have been the wars of Attica, she is over-peopled. A colony hoisted sail for the Chersonese ; another to repeople the ruined walls of Sybaris. Happy the families whose fathers give them lands to cultivate, instead of keeping them in idleness at home ; such are the founders of colonies. The language of this city is spoken in Italy, in Sicily, in Asia, in Africa, and even on the coast of Gaul, among the yelpings and yells of Kimbers and Sicambers.

Surely the more beneficent of the gods must look down with delight on these fruit-trees planted in the forest. May the healthfullest dews of heaven descend on them !

We are now busied in the Propylæa ; they, although unfinished, are truly magnificent. Which will remain the longest, the traces of the walls or of the colonies? Of the future we know nothing, of the past little, of the present less ; the mirror is too close to our eyes, and our own breath dims it.

XCVIII. CLEONE TO ASPASIA.

I have only time to send you a few perfumes and a few verses. These I transcribe out of a little volume of Erinna; the perfumes came to me from Syria.

Blessed be the man whose beneficent providence gave the flowers another life! We seem to retain their love when their beauty has departed.

ERINNA TO LEUCONÖE.

If comfort is unwelcome, can I think
    Reproof aught less will be?
The cup I bring to cool thee, wilt thou drink,
    Fever'd Leuconöe?

Rather with Grief than Friendship wouldst thou dwell,
    Because Love smiles no more!
Bent down by culling bitter herbs, to swell
    A cauldron that boils o'er.

XCIX. ASPASIA TO CLEONE.

Thanks for the verses! I hope Leuconöe was as grateful as I am, and as sensible to their power of soothing.

Thanks, too, for the perfumes! Pericles is ashamed of acknowledging he is fond of them; but I am resolved to betray one secret of his: I have caught him several times *trying* them, as he called it.

How many things are there that people pretend to dislike, without any reason, as far as we know, for the dislike or the pretence!

I love sweet odors. Surely my Cleone herself must have breathed her very soul into these! Let me smell them again: let me inhale them into the sanctuary of my breast, lighted up by her love for their reception.

But, ah Cleone! what an importunate and exacting creature is Aspasia! Have you no willows fresh peeled? none lying upon the bank for baskets, white, rounded, and delicate, as your fingers! How fragrant they were formerly! I have seen none lately. Do you remember the cross old Hermesionax? how he ran to beat us for breaking his twigs? and how, after looking in our faces, he seated himself down again, finished his basket, disbursed from a goat-skin a corroded clod of rancid cheese, put it in, pushed it to us, forced it under my arm, told us to carry it home *with the gods!* and lifted up both hands and blest us?

I do not wish *that* one exactly; cheese is the cruellest of deaths to me; and Pericles abhors it.

I am running over trifling occurrences which you must have forgotten. You are upon the spot, and have no occasion to recall to memory how the munificent old basketmaker looked after us, not seeing his dog at our heels; how we coaxed the lean, shaggy, suspicious animal; how many devices we contrived to throw down, or let slip, so that the good man might not observe it, the pestilence you insisted on carrying; how many names we called the dog by, ere we found the true one, *Cyrus;* how, when we had drawn him behind the lentisk, we rewarded him for his assiduities, holding each an ear nevertheless, that he might not carry back the gift to his master; and how we laughed at our fears, when a single jerk of the head served at once to engulf the treasure and to disengage him.

I shall always love the smell of the peeled willow. Have you none for me? Is there no young poplar, then, with a tear in his eye on bursting into bud? I am not speaking by metaphor and Asiatically. I want the poplars, the willows, the water-lilies, and the soft green herbage. How we enjoyed it on the Mæander! what liberties we took with it! robbing it of the flowers it had educated, of those it was rearing, of those that came confidently out to meet us, and of those that hid themselves. None escaped us. For these remembrances, green is the color I love best. It brings me to the *Fortunate Island* and my Cleone; it brings me back to Childhood, the proud little nurse of Youth, brighter of eye and lighter of heart than Youth herself.

These are not regrets, Cleone; they are respirations, necessary to existence. You may call them half-wishes if you will. We are poor indeed when we have no half-wishes left us. The heart and the imagination close the shutters the instant they are gone.

Do not chide me then for coming to you after the blossoms and buds and herbage: do not keep to yourself all the grass on the Mæander. We used to share it; we will now. I love it wherever I can get a glimpse of it. It is the home of the eyes, ever ready to receive them, and spreading its cool couch for their repose.

C. CLEONE TO ASPASIA.

Demophile, poor honest faithful creature! has yielded to her infirmities. I have spent almost as many hours with her in these last autumnal months, as I did in the earliest of my existence. She could not carry me in her arms again, but she was happy when mine were about her neck, and said they made her stronger. Do you remember how often she dropt my hand to take yours, because you never cried? saying:

"People never weep nor work, themselves, who can make others weep and work for them. That little one will have weeper and worker too about her presently. Look at her, Cleone! Cannot you look like that? Have not you two lips and two eyes? Aspasia has not three. Try now! Mind how I do it!"

Good, simple heart!

When she was near her end, she said to me:

"Do you ever go and read those names and bits of verses on the stones yonder? You and Aspasia used formerly. Some of them tell us to be sad and sorry for folks who died a hundred years ago; others to imitate men and women we never should have had a chance of seeing, had they been living yet. All we can learn from them is this: that our city never had any bad people in it, but has been filled with weeping and wailing from its foundation upward."

These things puzzled Demophile; she was somewhat vext that she could not well comprehend them, but praised the gods that our house was safe, when many others must have been rent asunder: such a power of lamentation!

"My name," said she, "I believe, is a difficult and troublesome one to pinfold in a tombstone: nobody has ever tried how it would sound in verse; but if you and Aspasia think me worth remembering, I am sure you could do more with it than others could; and you would lead your litle ones. when the gods have given you any, to come and see it, and tell them many things of old Demophile."

I assured her that, if I outlived her, I would prove, in the manner she wished, that my memory and love outlived her likewise.

She died two days afterward.

Nothing is difficult, not even an epitaph, if we prefer the thoughts that come without calling. and receive the first as the best and truest. I would not close my eyes to sleep until I had performed my promise.

> Demophile rests here: we will not say
> That she was aged. lest ye turn away;
> Nor that she long had suffered: early woes
> Alone can touch you; go. and pity those!

CI. ASPASIA TO CLEONE.

Ah poor Demophile! she remembered me then!   How sorry I am I cannot tell her I remember her!

Cleone! there are little things that leave no little regrets. I might have said kind words, and perhaps have done kind actions. to many who now are beyond the reach of them. One look on the unfortunate might have given a day's happiness; one sigh over the pillow of sickness might have insured a night's repose; one whisper might have driven from their victim the furies of despair.

We think too much upon *what* the gods have given us, and too little *why*.

We both are young; and yet we have seen several who loved us pass away; and we never can live over again as we lived before. A portion of our lives is consumed by the torch we follow at their funerals. We enter into another state of existence, resembling, indeed, and partaking of the former, but another! it contains the substance of the same sorrows, the shadow of the same joys. Alas! how true are the words of the old poet:

> We lose a life in every friend we lose,
> And every death is painful but the last.

I often think of my beautiful nurse, Myrtale, now married very happily in Clazomenai. My first verses were upon her. These are the verses I thought so good, that I wrote a long dissertation on the trochaic metre, to prove it the most magnificent of metres; and I mentioned in it all the poets that ever wrote, from epigrammatic to epic, praising some and censuring others, a judge without appeal upon all.

How you laughed at me! Do you remember the lines? I wonder they are not worse than they are.

> Myrtale! may heaven reward thee
> For thy tenderness and care!
> Dressing me in all thy virtues,
> Docile, duteous, gentle, fair.
>
> One alone thou never heededst,
> I can boast that one alone;
> Grateful beats the heart thy nurseling,
> Myrtale! 'tis all thy own.

CII. PERICLES TO ASPASIA.

Receive old Lycoris, and treat her affably. She has much influence in her tribe. The elderly of your sex possess no small authority in our city, and I suspect that in others, too, they have their sway. She made me tremble once. Philotas asked her how she liked my speech, I forget upon what occasion; she answered:

" His words are current words, and ring well ; but unless he gives us more of them for the trouble of our attendance, he shall not be archon, I promise him."

Now I know not how long I could protract a speech, nor how long I could keep my head under water ; these are accomplishments I have never studied. Lycoris and I are still friends, however. In my favor she has waived her promise, and lets me be an archon.*

CIII. ASPASIA TO CLEONE.

It is difficult and unsafe to pick up a pearl dropped by Alcman. Usually it is moist with the salt of its habitation ; and something not quite cleanly may be found adhering to it. Here, however, is one which even my chaste Cleone may look down on with complacency.

> " So pure my love is, I could light
>   The torch on Aglac's wedding-night,
>   Nor bend its flame with sighs,
>   See, from beneath, her chamber-door
>   Unclose, and bridemaids trip before,
>   With undejected eyes."
>
> Cupid stood near and heard this said,
> And full of malice shook his head,
> Then cried, " I'll trust him when he swears
> He cannot mount the first three stairs ;
> Even then I'll take one look below
> And see with my own eyes 'tis so."

And even Mimnermus, who bears but an indifferent character with the chaste, is irreproachable in those verses, which he appears to have written in the decline of life.

CIV. PERICLES TO ASPASIA.

Send me a note whenever you are idle and thinking of me, dear Aspasia ! Send it always by some old slave,

---

* Plutarch says he never was archon ; he means, perhaps, *first* archon.

ill-dressed.   The people will think it a petition, or something as good, and they will be sure to observe the pleasure it throws into my countenance.   Two winds at once
will blow into my sails, each helping me onward.

If I am tired, your letter will refresh me ; if occupied,
it will give me activity.   Beside, what a deal of time we
lose in business !

CV. ASPASIA TO PERICLES.

Would to heaven, O Pericles ! you had no business at
all, but the conversation of your friends.   You must
always be the greatest man in the city, whoever may be
the most popular.   I wish we could spend the whole day
together ; must it never be?   Are you not already in
possession of all you ever contended for?

It is time, methinks, that you should leave off speaking
in public, for you begin to be negligent and incorrect.   I
am to write you a note whenever I am idle and thinking
of you !

Pericles ! Pericles ! how far is it from idleness to think
of you !   We come to rest before we come to idleness.

CVI. PERICLES TO ASPASIA.

In our republic it is no easy thing to obtain an act of
divorce from power.   It usually is delivered to us by the
messager of Death, or presented in due form by our
judges where the oyster keeps open house.

Now, oysters are quite out of season in the summer
of life ; and life, just about this time, I do assure you, is
often worth keeping.   I thought so even before I knew
you, when I thought but little about the matter.   It is a
casket not precious in itself, but valuable in proportion to
what Fortune, or Industry, or Virtue, has placed within
it.

CVII. ASPASIA TO CLEONE.

When Pericles is too grave and silent, I usually take up my harp and sing to it ; for music is often acceptable to the ear when it would avoid or repose from discourse. He tells me that it not only excites the imagination, but invigorates eloquence and refreshes memory ; that playing on my harp to him is like besprinkling a tessellated pavement with odoriferous water, which brings out the images, cools the apartment, and gratifies the senses by its fragrance.

"That instrument," said he, "is the rod of Hermes, it calls up the spirits from below, or conducts them back again to Elysium. With what ecstasy do I throb and quiver under those refreshing showers of sound!"

> Come sprinkle me soft music o'er the breast,
>   Bring me the varied colors into light
> That now obscurely on its tablet rest,
>   Show me its flowers and figures fresh and bright.
>
> Waked at thy voice and touch, again the chords
>   Restore what restless years had moved away,
> Restore the glowing cheeks, the tender words,
>   Youth's short-lived spring and Pleasure's summer-day.

I believe he composed these verses while I was playing, although he disowns them, asking me whether I am willing to imagine that my execution is become so powerless.

You remember my old song; it was this I had been playing :

> The reeds were green the other day,
> Among the reeds we loved to play,
>   We loved to play while they were green.
> The reeds are hard and yellow now,
> No more their tufted heads they bow
>   To beckon us behind the scene.
>
> "What is it like?" my mother said,
> And laid her hand upon my head;
>   "Mother! I cannot tell indeed.
> I've thought of all hard things I know,
> I've thought of all the yellow too,
>   It only can be like the reed."

CVIII. ASPASIA TO CLEONE.

Panenos is our best painter; he was educated by Phei-
lias, who excels all the painters in correctness of design.
Panenos has travelled into Egypt, in which country, he
tells us, the colors are as fresh upon the walls of the
temples as when they were painted, two thousand years
ago.   Pericles wishes to have a representation of me in
the beginning of every Olympiad.   Alas! what an imprudence!   The most youthful lover never committed
one greater.

I will not send a stranger to you, Cleone!   I will send
the fugitive of Miletus when Epimedea was giving her
the lecture in the bath.   Be quiet now; say nothing;
even the bath itself is quite imaginary.

Panenos plays upon the harp.   I praised him for the
simplicity and melody of the tune, and for his execution.
He was but little pleased.

"Lady," said he to me, "a painter can be two things:
he can be painter and statuary, which is much the easier;
make him a third, and you reduce him to nothing."

"Yet Pericles," said I, "plays rather well."

"*Rather well*, I can believe," said he, "because I know
that his master was Damon, who was very skilful and
very diligent.   Damon, like every clever composer I
have met with, or indeed ever heard of, was a child in
levity and dissipation.   His life was half feast, half
concert."

"But, Panenos," said I, "surely we may be fond of
music, and yet stand a little on this side of idiocy."

"Aspasia!" he replied, "he who loves not music is a
beast of one species; he who overloves it is a beast of
another, whose brain is smaller than a nightingale's, and
his heart than a lizard's.   Record me one memorable
saying, one witticism, one just remark, of any great
musician, and I consent to undergo the punishment of
Marsyas.   Some among them are innocent and worthy
men; not many, nor the first.   Dissipation, and, what is
strange, selfishness, and disregard to punctuality in en-

gagements, are common and nearly general in the more distinguished of them.

" O Music! how it grieves me, that imprudence, intemperance, gluttony, should open their channels into thy sacred stream ! "

Panenos said this : let us never believe a word of it. He himself plays admirably, although no composer.

CIX. CLEONE TO ASPASIA.

O Aspasia! have you heard (you surely must) that the people of Samos have declared war against us? It is hardly sixty years since our beautiful city was captured and destroyed by the Persians. In vain hath she risen from her ashes with fresh splendor ! Another Phrynicus will have, perhaps, to write another tragedy upon us.

Is it an offence to be flourishing and happy?

The unfortunate meet and embrace ; the fortunate meet and tear each other to pieces. What wonder that the righteous gods allow to prosperity so brief a space !

CX. ASPASIA TO CLEONE.

Be composed and tranquil : read the speech of Pericles to the Athenians.

SPEECH OF PERICLES.

The Milesians, it appears, have sent embassadors to you, O men of Athens! not entreating the coöperation of your arms, but the interposition of your wisdom and integrity. They have not spoken, nor indeed can they deem it necessary to speak, of dangers recently undergone together with you, of ancient, faithful, indissoluble alliances, or the glory of descending from the same forefathers. On this plea Miletus might have claimed as a right what she solicits as a favor.

Samos, O Athenians, has dared to declare war against

the people of Miletus. She envies us our commerce, and, unable to find a plea for assailing us, strikes our friend in our sight, and looks impudently in our faces to see whether we will resent it.

No, Athenians, we will not resent it, until we have sent embassadors, to ask her why she has taken up arms against the peaceful and unoffending? It were well were it permitted us to abstain. Yes, I feel I am hazarding your favor by recommending delay and procrastination; but I do not apprehend that we are losing much time. We have weapons, we have ships, we have the same soldiers who quelled braver enemies. The vanquished seem again to be filling up the ranks we have thinned. They murmur, they threaten, they conspire, they prepare (and preparation denounces it) hostility. Let them come forth against us. Wealth rises up to our succor in that harbor; Glory stands firm, and bids them defiance on those walls.

Wait, wait! twenty days only. Ten. Not ten?

Little becomes it me, O Athenians! to oppose your wishes or to abate your ardor.

Depart, then, heralds! and carry with you war.

CXI. ASPASIA TO CLEONE.

I have asked Pericles to let me see all his speeches. He declared to me that he has kept no copies, but promised that he would attempt to recover some of them from his friends. I was disappointed and grieved, and told him I was angry with him. He answered thus, taking me by the hand:

"So, you really are angry that I have been negligent in the preservation of my speeches, after all my labor in modelling and correcting them. You are anxious that I should be praised as a writer, by writers who direct the public in these matters. Aspasia! I know their value. Understand me correctly and comprehensively. I mean partly the intrinsic worth of their commendations, and partly (as we pay in the price of our utensils) the fashion.

I have been accused of squandering away both the public money and my own ; nobody shall ever accuse me of
paying three obols for the most grandly embossed and
most sonorous panegyric. I would excite the pleasure (it
were too much to say the admiration) of judicious and
thoughtful men ; but I would neither soothe nor irritate
these busybodies. I have neither honey nor lime for ants.
We know that good writers are often gratified by the
commendation of bad ones ; and that even when the
learned and intelligent have brought the materials to
crown their merits, they have looked toward the door at
some petulant, smirking page, for the thread that was to
bind the chaplet. Little do I wish to hear what I am,
much less what I am not. Enough for me to feel the
consciousness and effect of health and strength ; surely
it is better than to be told by those who salute me, that
I am looking very well.

"You may reply that the question turns not upon com-
pliments, but upon censure.

"Really I know not what my censurers may write,
never having had the advantage of reading their lucubrations ; all I know is this : if I am not *their* Pericles, I
am at least the Pericles of Aspasia and the Athenians."

CXII. ASPASIA TO CLEONE.

We were conversing on oratory and orators, when Anaxagoras said, looking at Pericles, and smiling :

" They are described by Hesiod in two verses, which
he applies to himself and the poets :

> ' Lies very like the truth we tell,
> And, when we wish it, truth as well.' "

Meton relaxed from his usual seriousness, but had no
suspicion of the application, saying :

" Cleverly applied, indeed ! "

Pericles enjoyed equally the simplicity of Meton and
the slyness of Anaxagoras, and said :

" Meton ! our friend Anaxagoras is so modest a man,

8

that the least we can do for him is to acknowledge his
claims as heir-general to Hesiod : see them registered."

I have never observed the temper of Pericles either
above or below the enjoyment of a joke ; he invites and
retaliates, but never begins, lest he should appear to take
a liberty.

There are proud men of so much delicacy that it almost conceals their pride, and perfectly excuses it.

Meton never talks, but answers questions with great
politeness, although with less clearness and precision
than you would expect. I remarked to him, one evening, that mathematicians had great advantages over
others in disputation, from the habitude they had acquired of exactness in solving their problems.

" We mathematicians," answered he, " lay claim to this
precision. I need not mention to you, Aspasia, that of
all the people who assemble at your house, I am the only
one that ever wants a thought or word. We are exact
in our own proper workmanship. Give us time, and we
can discover what is false in logic ; but I never was acquainted with a mathematician who was ready at correcting in himself a flaw of ratiocination, or who produced
the fitting thing in any moderate time. Composition is
quite beyond our sphere. I am not envious of others ;
but I often regret in myself that, while they are deliver-
ing their opinions freely and easily, I am arranging mine ;
and that, in common with all the mathematicians of my
acquaintance, I am no prompt debater, no acute logician
no clear expositor, but begin in hesitation and finish in
confusion."

I assure you, Cleone, I have been obliged to give order
and regularity to these few words of the wise contemplative Meton, and to remove from among them many that
were superfluous and repeated. When he had paused, I
told him I sometimes wished he would exercise his powerful mind in conversation.

" I have hardly time," said he, " for study, much less
for disputation. Rarely have I known a disputant who,
however dexterous, did not either drive by Truth or over
her, or who stopped to salute her, unless he had some-

thing fine or novel to display. He would stumble over my cubes and spheres, and I should leave my leg in his noose."

" And yet Anaxagoras and you agree well together," said I.

" Anaxagoras," replied he, " usually asks me short questions, and helps me himself to explain them. He comes to me when I am alone, and would find no pleasure in showing to others my perplexity. Seldom do I let him go again, until he has given me some help or some incitement in my studies. He suggests many things."

" Silence, good Meton !" cried Anaxagoras, " or I may begin to talk of a luminary whose light has not yet reached the earth."

The three men smiled : they have some meaning uncommunicated to me. Perhaps it is a remark of Pericles, in encouragement of Anaxagoras, that, while others pass before us like a half-obol tow-link across a dark alley, and dazzle and disappear, his loftier light has not yet come down to the intellects of his fellow-citizens ; or perhaps it may really have a reference to some discovery in astronomy.

Pericles goes in person to command the expedition against Samos. He promises me it will soon be ready to sail, and tells me to expect him back again within a few months. Artemon is preparing machines of great magnitude for the attack of the city. He teaches me that the Samians are brave and wealthy, and that no city is capable of such a resistance. Certainly never were such preparations. I hope, at least, that the report of them will detain your enemies at home, and at all events that, before they land, you will leave Miletus and come to me. The war is very popular at Athens ; I dare say it is equally so at Samos, equally so at Miletus. Nothing pleases men like renewing their ancient alliance with the brutes, and breaking off the more recent one with their fellow-creatures.

> War, is it, O grave heads ! that ye
> With stern and stately pomp decree ?
> Inviting all the gods from far
> To join you in the game of war !

Have ye then lived so many years
To find no purer joy than tears?
And seek ye now the highest good
In strife, in anguish, and in blood?
Your wisdom may be more than ours,
But you have spent your golden hours,
And have, methinks, but little right
To make the happier fret and fight.
Ah! when will come the calmer day
When these dark clouds shall pass away?
When (should two cities disagree)
The young, the beauteous, and the free,
Rushing with all their force, shall meet
And struggle with embraces sweet,
Till they who may have suffer'd most
Give in, and own the battle lost.

Philosophy does not always play fair with us. She often eludes us when she has invited us, and leaves us when she has led us the farthest way from home. Perhaps it is because we have jumped up from our seats at the first lesson she would give us, and the easiest, and the best. There are few words in the precept —

Give pleasure : receive it :
Avoid giving pain : avoid receiving.

For the duller scholar, who may find it difficult to learn the whole, she cuts each line in the middle, and tells him kindly that it will serve the purpose, if he will but keep it in his memory.

CXIII. CLEONE TO ASPASIA.

Will you never be serious even upon the most serious occasions? There are so many Grecian states, on both continents and in the islands, that surely some could always be found both willing and proper to arbitrate on any dissension. If litigations are decided by arbiters when two men contend (as they often are), surely it would be an easier matter with cities and communities; for they are not liable to the irritation arising from violent words, nor to the hatred that springs up afresh between two men who strive for property, every time they come within sight. I believe the Greeks are the happiest people upon earth, or that ever are likely to exist upon it; and chiefly from their separation into small communities, independent governments, and laws made by the people for the people! But unless they come to the determination that no war whatever shall be undertaken until the causes of quarrel are examined, and the conditions of accommodation are proposed by others, from whom impartiality is most reasonably to be expected, they will exist without enjoying the greatest advantage that the gods have offered them. Religious men, I foresee, will be sorry to displease the God of battles. Let him have all the kingdoms of the world to himself, but I wish he would resign to the quieter deities our little Greece.

Preparations are going on here for resistance to the Samians, and we hear that Athenian ships are cruising off their island.

In case of necessity, everything is ready for my departure to the sources of the Mæander. I will prove to you that I am not hurried nor frightened; I have leisure to write out what, perhaps, may be the last verses written in Miletus, unless we are relieved.

LITTLE AGLAE,

To her Father, on her Statue being called like her.

> Father! the little girl we see
> Is not, I fancy, so like me;
> You never hold her on your knee.
>
> When she came home the other day
> You kiss'd her; but I cannot say
> She kiss'd you first and ran away.

CXIV. ASPASIA TO CLEONE.

Herodotus, on returning from his victory at the Olympian games, was the guest of Pericles. You saw him

afterward; and he might have told you that Pericles
was urgent with him to remain at Atheus. True, as a
stranger, he would have been without influence here in
political affairs. It is evident that he desires no such
thing, but prefers, as literary men should always do,
tranquillity and retirement. These he may enjoy in perfection where he is, and write the truth intrepidly. Pericles has more than once heard from him. Life passes in
no part of the world so easily and placidly as among
the Grecian colonies in Italy. They rarely quarrel;
they have room enough, men enough, wealth enough,
and not too much. One petty tyrant has sprung up
among them lately, and has imprisoned, exiled, and
murdered, the best citizens.

Pericles was asked his advice what should be done
with him. He answered:

"I never interfere in the affairs of others. It appears
to me that, where you have nothing but a weasel to
hunt, you should not bring many dogs into the field, nor
great ones; but in fact the rat-catcher is the best
counsellor on these occasions: he neither makes waste
nor noise."

The tyrant, we hear, is sickening, and many epitaphs
are already composed for him; the shortest is —

> The pigmy despot Mutinas lies here;
> He was not godless; no; his god was Fear.

Herodotus tells us, that throughout the lower Italy
poverty is unknown; every town well governed, every
field well ploughed, every meadow well irrigated, every
vineyard pruned scientifically. The people choose their
higher magistrates from the most intelligent, provided
they are not needy. The only offices that are salaried
are the lower, which all the citizens have an equal chance
of attaining; some by lot, some by suffrage. This is
the secret why the governments are peaceful and durable. No rich man can become the richer for them;
every poor man may, but honestly and carefully.

CXV. CLEONE TO ASPASIA.

Corinna was honored in her native place as greatly as
abroad. This is the privilege of our sex. Pindar and
Æschylus left their country, not because the lower orders
were indifferent or unjust to them, but because those who
were born their equals could not endure to see them rise
their superiors.

What a war against the gods is this!

It seems as if it were decreed by a public edict, that
no one shall receive from them any gift above a certain
value; and that, if they do receive it, they shall be permitted to return the gods no thanks for it in their native
city.

So then! republics must produce genius, and kings reward it!

So then! Hiero and Archelaus must be elevated to the
rank of Cimon and Pericles! O shame! O ignominy!

What afflicts me deeply is the intelligence we receive
that Herodotus has left Ionia. He was crowned at the
Olympian games; he was invited to a public festival in
every city he visited throughout the whole extent of
Greece; even his own was pleased with him: yet he too
has departed; not to Archelaus or to Hiero, but to the
retirement and tranquillity of Italy.

I do believe, Aspasia, that studious men, who look so
quiet, are the most restless men in existence.

ORATION OF PERICLES TO THE SOLDIERS ROUND SAMOS.

Little time is now left us, O Athenians, between the
consideration and the accomplishment of our duties.
The justice of the cause, when it was first submitted to
your decision in the Agora, was acknowledged with
acclamations: the success of it you have insured by your
irresistible energy. The port of Samos is in our possession, and we have occupied all the eminences round her
walls. Patience is now as requisite to us as to the

enemy; for, although every city which can be surrounded
can be captured, yet in some, where courage and numbers have been insufficient to drive off the besieger, Nature and Art may have thrown up obstacles to impede
his progress.   Such is Samos; the strongest fortress in
Europe, excepting only Byzantion.   But Byzantion fell
before our fathers; and unless she become less deaf to
the reclamations of honor, less indifferent to the sancti-
tude of treaties, unless she prefer her fellow-soldiers to
her common enemy, freedom to aristocracy, friends to
strangers, Greeks to Asiatics, she shall abase her Thracian fierceness before *us*.   However, we will neither
spurn the suppliant nor punish the repentant; our arms
we will turn forever, as we turn them now, against the
malicious rival, the alienated relative, the apostate confederate, and the proud oppressor.   Where a sense of
dignity is faint and feeble, and where reason hath lain
unexercised and inert, many nations have occasionally
been happy, and even flourishing, under kings: but oligarchy hath ever been a curse to all, from its commencement to its close.   To remove it eternally from the
vicinity of Miletus, and from the well-disposed of that
very city by which hostilities are denounced against her,
is at once our interest and our duty.   For oligarchs in
every part of the world are necessarily our enemies,
since we have always shown our fixed determination to
aid and support with all our strength the defenders of
civility and freedom.   It is not in our power (for against
our institutions and consciences we Athenians can do
nothing), it is not in our power, I repeat it, to sit idly
by, while those who were our fellow-combatants against
the Persian, and who suffered from his aggression even
more than we did, are assailed by degenerate Ionians,
whose usurpation rests on Persia.   We have enemies
wherever there is injustice done to Greeks; and we will
abolish that injustice, and we will quell those enemies.
Wherever there are equal laws we have friends; and
those friends we will succor, and those laws we will
maintain.   On which side do the considerate and religious look forward to the countenance of the gods? Often

have they deferred, indeed, their righteous judgments, but never have they deserted the long-suffering and the brave. Upon the ground where we were standing when you last heard my appeal to you, were not Xerxes and his myriads encamped? What drove them from it? The wisdom, force, and fortitude breathed into your hearts by the immortal gods. Preserve them with equal constancy ; and your return, I promise you, shall not have been more glorious from Salamis than from Samos.

CXVI. ASPASIA TO CLEONE.

I must always send you poetry when I find it, whether in a greater quantity or a smaller : not indeed all I happen to find ; for certainly the most part even of careful collections is mere trash. If there is a word too much in sense or sentiment, it is no poem ; just as, if there is a syllable in a verse too much, it is no metre. I speak only of these shorter ; not of those which are long enough to stretch ourselves on and sleep in. But there are poetical cooks so skilful in dividing the tendons of their cub-fed animals, that they contrive to fill a capacious dish with a few couples of the most meagre and tottering. From Athens you shall have nothing that is not Attic. I wish I could always give you the names of the authors.

> Look at that fountain! Gods around
> Sit and enjoy its liquid sound.
> Come, come : why should not we draw near?
> Let them look on : they cannot hear.
> But if they envy what we do,
> Say, have not gods been happy too?

The following were composed on a picture in which Cupid is represented tearing a rose-bud :

> Ah Cupid! Cupid! let alone
> That bud above the rest :
> The Graces wear it in their zone,
> Thy mother on her breast.

Does it not grieve thee to destroy
So beautiful a flower?
If thou must do it, cruel boy,
Far distant be the hour!
If the sweet bloom (so tinged with fire
From thy own torch) must die,
Let it, O generous Love! expire
Beneath a lover's sigh.

The next is *A Faun to Eriopis*, a wood nymph, who had permitted a kiss, and was sorry for it.

Tell me, Eriopis, why
Lies in shade that languid eye?
Hast thou caught the hunter's shout
Far from Dian, and without
Any sister nymph to say
Whither leads the downward way?
Trust me: never be afraid
Of thy Faun, my little maid!
He will never call thee *Dear*,
Press thy finger, pinch thy ear,
To admire it overspread
Swiftly with pellucid red,
Nor shall broad and slender feet
Under fruit-laid table meet.
Doth not he already know
All thy wandering, all thy woe?
Come! to weep is now in vain,
I will lead thee back again.
Slight and harmless was the slip
That but soil'd the sadden'd lip.
Now the place is shown to me
Peace and safety shall there be.

CXVII. CLEONE TO ASPASIA.

Samos has fallen. Pericles will have given you this information long before my letter can reach you, and perhaps the joy of the light-hearted Athenians will be over ere then. So soon dies away the satisfaction of great exploits, even of such as have swept a generation from before us, have changed the fortunes of a thousand more, and indeed have shaken the last link in the remotest. We hear, but perhaps the estimate is exaggerated, that the walls of Miletus, of Ephesus, of Priene, are in comparison to Samos as the fences of a farm-yard are to them. Certain it is that the vanquished fleet was more formidable than the united navies of Corinth and of Carthage, which are rated as next in force to the Athenian.

By this conquest we are delivered from imminent danger; yet, I am ashamed to say it, our citizens are ungrateful already. It is by the exertions of the Athenians that they are not slaves; and they reason as basely as if they were. They pretend to say that it was jealousy of Samos, and the sudden and vast increase of her maritime power, but by no means any affection for Miletus, which induced them to take up arms! Athens had just reason for hostility; why should she urge, in preference, unjust ones? Alas! if equity is supported by violence, little can be the wonder if power be preceded by falsehood. Such a reflection may be womanish; but are not all peculiarly so which are quiet, compassionate, and consistent? The manly mind, in its continual course of impediments and cataracts, receives and gives few true images; our stagnant life in this respect has greatly the advantage.

Xanthus, the friend (you remember) of poor Xeniades, fought as a volunteer in the Athenian army, and was intrusted with the despatches to our government.

"Xanthus!" said the general, "your countrymen will hereafter read your name, although it is not written here; for we conquerors of Samos are no little jealous one of another. Go and congratulate the Milesians: they will understand us both."

I asked him many questions. He replied with much simplicity, "I was always too much in it to know any thing about it. The principal thing I remember is, that Pericles (I was told) smiled at me for a moment in the heat of battle, and went on to another detachment."

CXVIII. ASPASIA TO CLEONE.

The wind, I understand, has delayed my last letter in harbor, and continues adverse. Every day we receive some fresh vessel from Samos, and some new intelligence. True is it, we discover, that the prevailing party had been supported at once by the Peloponnesians and the Persians. The chastisement of the delinquents is represented as much too mild. "They would have made us slaves, let us make them so." Such, with scourges and tortures, were the denunciations of the people and the soldiery; and more vehemently in Samos than in Miletus. The leaders of the oligarchy (now supprest forever) were two men of low extraction, Lysimachus and Elpenor. We daily hear some story, well known in Samos only, of these incendiaries. Lysimachus was enriched by the collocation of his wife with an old dotard, worn out by gluttony and disordered in intellect. By his last testament, made when he had lost his senses, he bequeathed her fifty talents. The heirs refused to pay them; and Lysimachus would have pleaded her cause before the people, had they not driven him away with shouts and stones. Nevertheless, he was thought a worthy champion of the faction, and the rather as his hatred of his fellow-citizens and former companions must be sincere and inextinguishable. Elpenor is far advanced in age. His elder son was wounded by accident, and died within the walls. Avarice and parsimony had always been his characteristics, under the veil, however, of morality and religion. The speech he made at the funeral is thus reported:

"It hath been, O men of Samos! the decree of the immortal gods, whose names be ever blessed! ..

"Hold hard there! Cannot you see that there are no more sparks in the pyre? .. the wine smells sadly .. throw no more on them .. take it home to the cellar ..

"To remove from my aged eyes, from my frail embraces, the delight of my life, the staff of my declining years, all spent in the service of my beloved country. It

is true I have another son, rising out of his adolescence . .
here beside me. . .

"O my child! Molismogis! Molismogis! on such a
melancholy occasion dost thou, alas! tie indissolubly and
wastefully that beautiful piece of packthread? Thy poor,
bereaved mother may want it; and it will fail her in the
hour of need."

Two torches were borne before the funeral. One of
them presently gave signs rather prematurely emblem-
atical of our mortal state, and could be restored to its
functions by no exertion of the bearer, first waving it
gently toward his companion, then shaking it with all
his might, horizontally, vertically, diagonally, then holding it down despondingly to the earth. Elpenor beckoned
to him, and asked him, in his ear, how much he had paid
for it.

"Half a drachma."

"Fraud!" cried Elpenor; "fraud, even at the tomb!
before the dead, and before the gods of the dead! From
whom did you make the purchase?"

"From Gylippides, son of Agoracles."

"Tell Gylippides, son of Agoracles," calmly said Elpenor, "that in my love of equity, in my duty to the
state, in my piety to the gods, in my pure desire to preserve the tranquillity of his conscience, I cite him before
the tribunal unless he refund an obol." Then aloud, "It
was not in this manner, O Athenians! that our forefathers
revereuced the dead."

He gave way under his grief, and was carried back
with little commiseration. Elpenor is among the richest
men in Greece, unless the conquerors have curtailed his
treasures. It is but reasonable that everything such men
possess should compensate the people for years of rapine,
disunion, and turbulence; for the evil laws they enacted,
and for the better they misadministered and perverted.

CXIX. CLEONE TO ASPASIA.

Worse verses, it may be, than any of those which you
lately sent to me, affect me more. There is no giddiness

in looking down the precipices of youth ; it is the rapidity
and heat of its course that brings the giddiness. When
we are near its termination, a chilly thrill comes over us
whether we look before or behind. Yet there is something like enchantment in the very sound of the word
youth, and the calmest heart, at every season of life, beats
in double time to it. Never expect a compensation for
what you send me, whether prose or poetry ; but expect
a pleasure, because it has given me one. Now here are
the worse verses for the better, the Milesian for the
Attic :

> We mind not how the sun in the mid-sky
> Is hastening on ; but when the golden orb
> Strikes the extreme of earth, and when the gulfs
> Of air and ocean open to receive him,
> Dampness and gloom invade us ; then we think,
> Ah ! thus it is with Youth. Too fast his feet
> Run on for sight ; hour follows hour ; fair maid
> Succeeds fair maid ; bright eyes bestar his couch ;
> The cheerful horn awakens him ; the feast,
> The revel, the entangling dance, allure,
> And voices mellower than the Muse's own
> Heave up his buoyant bosom on their wave.
> A little while, and then . . Ah Youth ! dear Youth !
> Listen not to my words . . but stay with me !
> When thou art gone, Life may go too ; the sigh
> That follows is for thee, and not for Life.

CXX. ASPASIA TO CLEONE.

Enough, enough is it for me to see my Pericles safe at
home again. Not a word has he spoken, not a question
have I asked him, about the odious war of Samos. He
made in Samos, I hear, a most impressive oration, to celebrate the obsequies of these brave soldiers who fell. In
Athens, where all is exultation, he has rendered the slain
the most glorious and triumphant, and the fatherless the
proudest, of the living. But at last how little worth is
the praise of eloquence ! Elpenor and Lysimachus lead
councils and nations ! Great gods ! surely ye must pity
us when we worship you ; we, who obey, and appear to

reverence, the vilest of our species! I recover my step;
I will not again slip iuto this offal. Come, and away to
Xanthus. Ay, ay, Cleone! Simplicity, bravery, well-
merited and well-borne distinction! Take him, take him:
we must not all be cruel . . to ourselves.

CXXI. CLEONE TO ASPASIA.

Aspasia! you mistake. Grant me the presence of
friendship and the memory of love! It is only in this
condition that a woman can be secure from fears and
other weaknesses. I may admire Xanthus; and there is
pleasure in admiration. .If I thought I could love him,
I should begin to distrust and despise myself. I would
not desecrate my heart, even were it in ruins; but I am
happy, very happy; not indeed altogether as I was in
early youth; perhaps it was youth itself that occasioned
it. Let me think so! Indulge me in the silence and solitude of this one fancy. If there was anything else, how
sacred should it ever be to me! Ah yes, there was! and
sacred it is, and shall be.

Laodamia saw with gladness, not with passion, a god,
conductor of her sole beloved. The shade of Xeniades
follows the steps of Xanthus.

CXXII. CLEONE TO ASPASIA.

Parties of pleasure are setting sail, every day, almost,
for Samos. We begin to be very brave; we women, I
mean. I suspect that no few of us take an unworthy delight in the humiliation and misery of the fair Samians.
Not having seen, nor intending to see them myself, I can
only tell you what I have heard of their calamities.

Loud outcries were raised by the popular orators
against such of them as were suspected of favoring the
Persian faction, and it was demanded of the judges that
they should be deported and exposed for slaves. This
menace, you may well imagine, caused great anxiety and

alarm, even among those who appeared to be quite resigned to such a destiny while the gallant young Athenians were around the walls. But, to be sold! and the
gods alone know to whom! old morose men, perhaps, and
jealous women! Some suspect it was at the instigation
of Pericles that a much severer chastisement has befallen
them. They have been condemned to wear the habiliments of Persians. Surely no refinement of cruelty can
surpass the decree, by which a Greek woman is divested
of that beautiful dress which alone can be called an ornament to the female form. This decree has been carried
into execution ; and you would pity even the betrayers of
their country. Whether in ignorance of what the Persian habit is, or from spite and malice, the Samian ladies
are obliged to wear sleeves of sufficient amplitude to conceal a traitor in each ; and chains intersecting the forehead with their links and ornaments ; and hair not divided
along the whole summit of the head, but turned back
about the centre, to make them resemble the heads of
some poisonous snakes. Furthermore, the dresses are
stripped ignominiously off the shoulders, as for some
barely conceivable punishment, and fastened round the
arms in such a manner that, when they attempt to reach
anything, or even to move, they are constrained to shrug
and writhe, like the uncleanliest persons. Beside, they
are quite at the mercy of any wicked idler in the street,
who, by one slight touch, or by treading on the hem,
might expose them far more undisguisedly to the gazes of
the multitude. This barbarian garb has already had such
an effect, that two have cast themselves into the sea ; and
others have entreated that they may, as was first threatened, rather be sold for slaves.

CXXIII. CLEONE TO ASPASIA.

Odious as undoubtedly was the conduct of the Samian
oligarchy and priesthood, and liable as are all excesses to
a still farther exaggeration in the statement of them, you
will hardly believe the effrontery of the successful dema-

gogues. Not contented with undeniable proofs, in regard to the enormous and mismanaged wealth torn away from the priests of Bacchus, they have invented the most improbable falsehood that the malevolence of faction ever cast against the insolence of power. They pretend that certain men, some of ancient family, more of recent, had conspired to transmit the reins of government to their elder sons. Possession for life is not long enough! They are not only to pass laws, but (whenever it so pleases) to impede them! They decree that the first-born male is to be the wisest and best of the family, and shall legislate for all Samos! Democracy has just to go one step farther, and to persuade the people (ready at such times to believe anything) that the oligarchy had resolved to render their power hereditary, not only for one generation, but for seven. The nation, so long abused in its understanding, would listen to and believe the report, ignorant that arbitrary power has never been carried to such extravagance even in Persia itself, although it is reported that in India the lower orders of people were hereditarily subject to the domination of a privileged class. But this may be false; and indeed it must be, if what is likewise told us concerning them be true, which is, that they have letters among them.

CXXIV. ASPASIA TO CLEONE.

You have given me in your two last a great deal of curious information, about the discoveries that the demagogues made, or pretended to have made, in Samos. It is credible enough that the oligarchs were desirous of transmitting their authority to their children; but that they believed so implicitly in the infatuation of the citizens, or the immutability of human events, as to expect a continuation of power in the same families for seven generations, is too gross and absurd, even to mislead an insurgent and infuriated populace. He indeed must be composed of mud from the Nile, who can endure with patience this rancorous fabrication. In Egypt, we are

9

told by Herodotus in his *Erato*, that " the son of a herald is of course a herald ; and, if any man hath a louder
voice than he, it goes for nothing."

Hereditary heralds are the proper officers of hereditary
lawgivers ; and both are well worthy of dignity where
the deities are cats.

Strange oversight ! that no provision should ever have
been devised, to insure in these tutelar and truly household gods an equal security for lineal succession !

CXXV. ASPASIA TO CLEONE.

Abuses of many kinds, and of great enormity, have
been detected by the Samians in their overthrown government.   What exasperates the people most, and indeed
the most justly, is the discovery that the ruling families
have grossly abused the temples, to the high displeasure
of the gods.   Sacrilege has been carried to such a
pitch, that some among them have appointed a relative
or dependent to the service of more than one sanctuary.
You remember that anciently all the worship of this
island was confined to Juno.   She displeased the people,
I know not upon what occasion, and they suffered the
greater part of her fanes to fall in ruins, and transferred
the richest of the remainder to the priests of Bacchus.
Several of those who had bent the knee before Juno,
took up the thyrsus with the same devotion.   The people
did indeed hope that the poor and needy, and particularly
such as had lost their limbs in war, or their parents or
their children by shipwreck, would be succored out of
the wealth arising from the domains of the priesthood ;
and the rather as these domains were bequeathed by religious men, whose whole soul rested upon Juno, and whose
bequest was now utterly frustrated, by taking them from
the sister of Jupiter and giving them exclusively to his
son.   Beside, it was recollected by the elderly, that out
of these vast possessions aid was afforded to the state
when the state required it ; and that, wherever there
stood one of these temples, hunger and sickness, sorrow

and despair, were comforted and assuaged. The people, it appears, derived no advantages from the change, and only grew more dissatisfied and violent; for, if those who had officiated in the temples of Juno were a little more licentious than became the ministers of a goddess, they did not run into the streets, and through the country places, drunk and armed; nor did they seize upon the grapes because they belonged to Bacchus; nor upon the corn because it is unwholesome to drink wine without bread; nor upon the cattle because man cannot live on bread alone. These arguments you may suspect of insufficiency; what then will you think when you hear another reason of theirs, which is, that the nation has no right to take from them what belongs to the goddess? The people cry, "How then can it belong to you?" Pushed upon this side, they argue that they should not be deprived of their salaries, because they are from land. "What!" reply the citizens, " are not gold and silver the products of land also?" But long possession . . " We will remedy that too, as well as we can." The soldiers and sailors have the most reason to complain, when they see twelve priests in the enjoyment of more salary than seven thousand of the bravest combatants. The military are disbanded and deprived of pay at the instant when their services are no longer necessary; yet no part, it appears, of a superfluous and idle priesthood is to be reduced or regulated; on the contrary, it is rapacious and irreligious to take away three temples from a venerable occupant of four. Was ever soldier so impudent as to complain that rations were not allowed him in four detachments of his army? The downfall of the whole faction will be of little benefit to Samos, while these insults and iniquities press upon the people. Unless those who are now intrusted with power resolve to abolish the gross abuses of the priesthood, the wealth of which is greater and worse applied in Samos than it is even in those countries where the priests are sovrans, and venerated as deities, little imports it by whom they are governed, or what gods they venerate. It is better to be ruled by the kings of Lacedæmon, and wiser to salute in worship the sun of Persia. Never surely will the island be pacified, until what was taken from Juno shall also be taken from Bacchus, and until the richest priest be reduced in his emoluments far below the level of a polemarch.

CXXVI. ASPASIA TO CLEONE.

Those of your letters, my Cleone, which relate to the affairs of Samos, and especially to the priests of Juno and Bacchus, have led me into many reflections. The people of Athens are the most religious of any upon earth; but I doubt whether they are the most just, the most generous, the most kindly. There is not a friend, whatever benefit they may have received from him, whom they would not abandon or denounce, on a suspicion of irreverence to Pallas; and those in general are the most fanatical and furious whom, as goddess of wisdom, she has least favored. Your neighbors the Samians are more judicious in their worship of Juno. They know that, as long as Jupiter hath a morsel of ambrosia, she will share it, although he may now and then indulge in a draught of nectar to which her lips have no access. The Samians have discovered that wealth is not a requisite of worship, and that a temple needs not a thousand parasangs of land for its enclosure. If we believed that gods could be jealous, we might fear that there would be much ill blood between Juno and Bacchus. It is more probable that they will look on calmly, and let their priests fight it out. The Persians in these matters are not quite so silly as we are. Herodotus tells us that, instead of altars and temples, the verdure of the earth is chosen for their sacrifice; and music and garlands, prayers and thanksgivings, are thought as decent and acceptable as comminations and blood. It does not appear that they are less moral or less religious than those who have twenty gods, and twenty temples for each. The wiser men in Athens tell us that the vulgar have their prejudices. Where indeed is the person who never has repeated this observation? Yet believe me, Cleone, it is

utterly untrue.   The vulgar have not *their* prejudices :
they have the prejudices of those who ought to remove
them if they had any.   Interested men give them, not their
religion, but clubs and daggers for enforcing it ; taking
from them, in return, their time, their labor, their benev-
olence, their understanding, and their wealth.   And are
such persons to be invested with the authority of lawgivers and the splendor of satraps?   The Samians have
decided that question.   Priests of Bacchus, let them dif-
fuse the liberality and joyousness, and curtail a little
from the swaggering stateliness of him whom the poet
calls, in his dithyrambic,

> " The tiger-borne and mortal-mothered god."

CXXVII. ASPASIA TO CLEONE.

Hephæstion, whom I never have mentioned to you,
and whom indeed I hardly know by name, is going to
Italy, and has written this poem on the eve of his departure.   It is said that his verses are deficient in tenderness
and amenity.   Certain it is that he by no means indulges
in the display of them, whatever they may be.   When
Pericles had read the following, I asked him what he
thought of the author.   "I think," replied Pericles, "that
he will never attempt to deprive me of my popularity."

I am afraid he is an ill-tempered man : yet I hear he
has suffered on many occasions, and particularly in regard to his fortune, very great injustice, with equally
great unconcern.   He is never seen in the Agora, nor in
the theatre, nor in the temples, nor in any assemblage of
the people, nor in any society of the learned ; nor has he
taken the trouble to enter into a confederacy or strike a
bargain, as warier men do, with any praiser ; no, not
even for the loan of a pair of palms in the Keramicos.

I have now said all I believe you will think it requisite
for me to say, on a citizen so obscure, and so indifferent
a poet.   Yet even he, poor man ! imagines that his ef-
fusions must endure.   This is the most poetical thought

I can find in him ; but perhaps he may have written what
is better than my specimen.

THE IAMBICS OF HEPHÆSTION.

Speak not too ill of me, Athenian friends !
Nor ye, Athenian sages, speak too ill !
From others of all tribes am I secure.
I leave your confines : none whom you caress,
Finding me hungry and athirst, shall dip
Into Cephisus the gray bowl to quench
My thirst, or break the horny bread, and scoop
Stiffly around the scanty vase, wherewith
To gather the hard honey at the sides,
And give it me for having heard me sing.
Sages and friends ! a better cause remains
For wishing no black sail upon my mast.
'Tis, friends and sages ! lest, when other men
Say words a little gentler, ye repent,
Yet be forbidden by stern pride to share
The golden cup of kindness, pushing back
Your seats, and gasping for a draught of scorn.
Alas ! shall this too, never lack'd before,
Be, when you most would crave it, out of reach !
Thus on the plank, now Neptune is invoked,
I warn you of your peril : I *must* live,
And ye, O friends ! howe'er unwilling, *may*.

CXXVIII. CLEONE TO ASPASIA.

Aspasia ! I have many things to say in reply to your
last letter.

Believe me, I can take little interest in any ill-tempered
man.   Hephæstion is this, you tell me, and there is nothing in his *Iambics* to make me doubt it.   Neither do they
contain, you justly remark, anything so characteristic of
a poet as the confidence he expresses that he shall live.
All poets, good and bad, are possessed by this confidence ;
because the minds of them all, however feeble, however
incapacious, are carried to the uttermost pitch of enthusiasm.   In this dream, they fancy they stand upon the
same eminence, or nearly so, and look unto the same distance.   But no poet or other writer, supposing him in his
senses, could ever think seriously that his works will be

eternal; for whatever had a beginning must also have an end; and in this predicament are languages. Like the fowls of the air, they are driven from the plains and take refuge in the mountains, until at last they disappear, leaving some few traces, some sounds imperfectly caught up. Highly poetical works, or those in which eloquence is invested with the richest attributes of poetry, are the only ones that can prolong the existence of a dialect. Egypt and Phœnicia and Chaldæa, beyond doubt, contain many treatises on the arts and sciences, although unpublished, and preserved only by the priesthood, or by the descendants of the authors and discoverers. These are certainly to pass away before inventions and improvements more important. But if there is anything of genius in their hymns, fables, or histories, it will remain among them, even when their languages shall have undergone many variations; and afterward, when they are spoken no longer, it will be incorporated with others, and finally be claimed as original and indigenous, by nations the most remote and dissimilar. Many streams, whose fountains are now utterly dried up, have flowed from afar to be lost in the ocean of Homer. Our early companions, the animals of good old Æsop, have spoken successively in every learned tongue. And now a few words on that gentlest and most fatherly of masters. Before we teach his fables to children, we should study them attentively ourselves. They were written for the wisest and the most powerful, whose wisdom they might increase, and whose power they might direct. There are many men, of influence and authority, apt enough to take kindly a somewhat sharp bite from a dog or monkey, and to be indignant at the slightest touch on the shoulder from a fellow-creature. It is improbable that a fable will do many of them much good, but it may do a little to one in twenty, and the amount is by no means unimportant in that number of generations. The only use of Æsop to children, after the delight he gives them, is the promotion of familiarity and friendship with animals, in proportion as they appear to deserve it: and a great use indeed it is. If I were not afraid that one or other of these vigilant creatures might snap at me, I would now begin to quarrel a little with you. And yet I think I should have on my side some of the more sagacious, were I to reprehend you for letting an ill-tempered man render you supercilious and unjust. How do you know, pray, that Hephæstion may not live? and quite as long as he fancies he shall; a century, or two, or three. Even in the *Iambics* there is a compression and energy of thought, which the best poets sometimes want; and there is in them as much poetry as was necessary on the occasion. The poet has given us, at one stroke, the true impression of a feature in his character; which few have done, and few can do, excepting those features only which are nearly alike in the whole fraternity.

Doubtless we are pleased to take our daily walk by streams that reflect the verdure and the flowers; but the waters of a gloomy cavern may be as pellucid and pure, and more congenial to our graver thoughts and bolder imaginations.

For any high or any wide operation, a poet must be endued, not with passion indeed, but with power and mastery over it; with imagination, with reflection, with observation, and with discernment. There are, however, some things in poetry which admit few of these qualities. Comedy, for instance, would evaporate under too fervid a fancy; and the sounds of the Ode would be dulled and deadened by being too closely overarched with the fruitage of reflection. Homer in himself is subject to none of the passions; but he sends them all forth on his errands, with as much precision and velocity as Apollo his golden arrows. The hostile gods, the very Fates themselves, must have wept with Priam in the tent before Achilles: Homer stands unmoved.

Aspasia! there is every reason why a good-natured person should make us good-natured, but none whatever why an ill-natured one should make us ill-natured: neither of them ought to make us unjust. You do not know Hephæstion, and you speak ill of him on the report of others, who perhaps know him as little as you do. You would shudder if I ventured to show you the position y·

have taken. Ill-tempered you cannot be ; you would not be unfair : what if, in the opinion of your friends, you should be a more shocking thing than either ! what, in the name of the immortal gods ! if I should have found you, on this one occasion, a somnambulist on the verge of vulgarity ! Take courage : nobody has seen it but myself. If there are bad people in the world, and maybe there are plenty, we ought never to let it be thought that we are near enough to be aware of it. Again to Hephæstion. It is better to be austere than ambitious ; better to live out of society than to court the worst. How many of the powerful, even within the confines of their own household, will be remembered less affectionately and lastingly than tame sparrows and talking daws ! and, among the number of those who are destined to be known hereafter, of how many will the memory be laden with contempt or with execration ! To the wealthy, proud, and arrogant, the gods have allotted no longer an existence, than to the uteusils in their kitchens or the vermin in their sewers ; while, to those whom such perishables would depress and villify, the same eternal beings have decreed and ratified their own calm consciousness of plastic power, of immovable superiority, with a portion (immeasurably great) of their wisdom, their authority, and their duration.

CXXIX. CLEONE TO ASPASIA.

We have kept your birthday, Aspasia ! On these occasions I am reluctant to write anything. Politeness, I think, and humanity, should always check the precipitancy of congratulation. Nobody is felicitated on losing. Even the loss of a bracelet or tiara is deemed no subject for merriment and alertness in our friends and followers. Surely then the marked and registered loss of an irreparable year, the loss of a limb of life, ought to excite far other sensations. So long is it, O Aspasia ! since we have read any poetry together, I am quite uncertain whether you know the Ode to Asteröessa.

Asterŏessa! many bring
The vows of verse and blooms of spring
   To crown thy natal day.
Lo, *my* vow too amid the rest!
" Ne'er mayst thou sigh from that white breast,"
   O take them all away !

For there are cares and there are wrongs,
And withering eyes and venom'd tongues;
   They now are far behind;
But come they must : and every year
Some flowers decay, some thorns appear,
   Whereof these gifts remind.

Cease, raven, cease! nor scare the dove
With croak around and swoop above;
   Be peace, be joy, within!
Of all that hail this happy tide
My verse alone be cast aside!
   Lyre, cymbal, dance, begin!

Although there must be some myriads of odes written
on the same occasion, yet, among the number on which I
can lay my hand, none conveys my own sentiment so
completely.

Sweetest Aspasia, live on ! live on ! but rather, live
back the past !

CXXX. ASPASIA TO CLEONE.

The Hecatompedon, which many of the citizens begin
to call the *Parthenon*, is now completed, and waits but
for the goddess. A small temple, raised by Cimon in
honor of Theseus, is the model. This until lately was
the only beautiful edifice in the Athenian dominions.
Pericles is resolved that Athens shall not only be the
mistress, but the admiration of the world, and that her
architecture shall, if possible, keep pace with her military
and intellectual renown. Our countrymen, who have
hitherto been better architects than the people of Attica,
think it indecorous and degrading, that Ionians, as the
Athenians are, should follow the fashion of the Dorians,
so inferior a race of mortals. Many grand designs were
offered by Ictinos to the approbation and choice of the

public.   Those which he calls Ionian, are the gracefuller.
Crateros, a young architect, perhaps to ridicule the finery
and extravagance of the Corinthians, exposed to view a
gorgeous design of slender columns and top-heavy capitals, such as, if ever carried into execution, would be incapable of resisting the humidity of the sea-breezes, or
even the action of the open air, uninfluenced by them.
These, however, would not be misplaced as indoor ornaments, particularly in bronze or ivory ; and indeed small
pillars of such a character would be suitable enough to
highly-ornamented apartments.   I have conversed on the
subject with Ictinos, who remarked to me that what we
call the Doric column is in fact Egyptian, modified to the
position and the worship ; and that our noblest specimens
are but reduced and petty imitations of those ancient and
indestructible supporters, to the temples of Thebes, of
Memphis and of Tentyra.   He smiled at the ridicule cast
on the Corinthians by the name designating those florid
capitals, but agreed with me that, on a smaller scale, in
gold or silver, they would serve admirably for the recep-
tacles of wax-lights on solemn festivals.   He praised the
designs of our Ionian architects, and acknowledged that
their pillars alone deserve the appellation of Grecian, but
added that, in places liable to earthquakes, inundations,
or accumulations of sand, the solider column was in its
proper situation.   The architraves of the Parthenon are
chiselled by the scholars of Pheidias, who sometimes gave
a portion of the design.   It is reported that two of the
figures bear the marks of the master's own hand ; he
leaves it to the conjecture of future ages which they are.
Some of the young architects, Ionian and Athenian, who
were standing with me, disputed not only on the relative
merits of their architecture, but of their dialect.   One of
them, Psamiades of Ephesus, ill enduring the taunt of
Brachys the Athenian, that the Ionian, from its open
vowels, resembles a pretty pulpy hand which could not
close itself, made an attack on the letter T usurping the
place of S, and against the augments.

    " Is it not enough," said he, "that you lisp, but you
must also stammer ? "

Let us have patience if any speak against us, O Cleone! when a censure is cast on the architecture of Ictinos and on the dialect of Athens.

CXXXI. CLEONE TO ASPASIA.

When the weather is serene and bright, I think of the young Aspasia; of her liveliness, her playfulness, her invitations to sit down on the grass; and her challenges to run, to leap, to dance, and if nobody was near, to gambol. The weather at this season is neither bright nor serene, and I think the more of my Aspasia, because I want her more. Fie upon me! And yet on the whole —

> Happy to me has been the day,
> The shortest of the year,
> Though some, alas! are far away
> Who made the longest yet more brief appear.

I never was formed for poetry; I hate whatever I have written, five minutes afterward. A weakly kid likes the warm milk, and likes the drawing of it from its sources; but place the same before her, cold, in a pail, and she smells at it and turns away.

Among the *Tales* lately come out here, many contain occasional poetry. In the preface to one, the scene of which lies mostly in Athens, the author says:

"My reader will do well to draw his pen across the verses; they are not good for him. The olive, especially the Attic, is pleasing to few the first time it is tasted."

This hath raised an outcry against him; so that of the whole fraternity he is the most unpopular.

"The gods confound him with his Atticisms!" exclaim the sober-minded. "Is not the man contented to be a true and hearty Carian? Have we not roses and violets, lilies and amaranths, crocuses and sowthistles? Have we not pretty girls and loving ones; have we not desperate girls and cruel ones, as abundantly as elsewhere? Do not folks grieve and die to his heart's content? We possess the staple: and by Castor and Pollux! we can bleach it

and comb it and twist it, as cleverly as the sharpest of
your light-fingered locust-eaters."

You will soon see his works, among others more voluminous.   In the meanwhile, I cannot end my letter in a
pleasanter way than with a copy of these verses, which
are nearer to the shortest than to the best:

> Perilla! to thy fates resign'd,
>   Think not what years are gone:
> While Atalanta look't behind
>   The golden fruit roll'd on.
>
> Albeit a mother may have lost
>   The plaything at her breast,
> Albeit the one she cherish't most,
>   It but endears the rest.
>
> Youth, my Perilla, clings on Hope,
>   And looks into the skies
> For brighter day; she fears to cope
>   With grief, she shrinks at sighs.
>
> Why should the memory of the past
>   Make you and me complain?
> Come, as we could not hold it fast,
>   We'll play it o'er again.

CXXXII. ASPASIA TO CLEONE.

There are odes in Alcæus which the pen would stop
at, trip at, or leap over.   Several in our collection are
wanting in yours; this among them:

> Wormwood and rue be on his tongue,
>   And ashes on his head,
> Who chills the feast and checks the song
>   With emblems of the dead!
>
> By young and jovial, wise and brave,
>   Such mummers are derided.
> His sacred rites shall Bacchus have,
>   Unspared and undivided.
>
> Couch't by my friends, I fear no mask
>   Impending from above,
> I only fear the later flask
>   That holds me from my love.

Show these to any priest of Bacchus, especially to any
at Samos, and he will shake his head at you, telling you
that Bacchus will never do without his masks and mysteries, which it is holier to fear than the *later flask*. On
this subject, he would prove to you, all fears are empty
ones.

CXXXIII. ASPASIA TO CLEONE.

In ancient nations there are grand repositories of wisdom, although it may happen that little of it is doled
out to the exigencies of the people.   There is more in the
fables of Æsop than in the schools of our Athenian
philosophers ; there is more in the laws and usages of
Persia, than in the greater part of those communities
which are loud in denouncing them for barbarism.   And
yet there are some that shock me. We are told by Herodotus, who tells us whatever we know with certainty a
step beyond our thresholds, that a boy in Persia is kept
in the apartments of the women, and prohibited from
seeing his father, until the fifth year.   The reason is,
he informs us, that if he dies before this age, his loss
may give the parent no uneasiness.   And such a custom
he thinks commendable. Herodotus has no child, Cleone !
If he had, far other would be his feelings and his judgment.   Before that age how many seeds are sown, which
future years, and distant ones, mature successively ! How
much fondness, how much generosity, what hosts of other
virtues, courage, constancy, patriotism, spring into the
father's heart from the cradle of his child !   And does
never the fear come over him, that what is most precious
to him upon earth is left in careless or perfidious, in unsafe or unworthy hands?   Does it never occur to him
that he loses a son in every one of these five years?
What is there so affecting to the brave and virtuous man
as that which perpetually wants his help and cannot cal.
for it !   What is so different as the speaking and the
mute !   And hardly less so are inarticulate sounds, and
sounds which he receives half-formed, and which he delights to modulate, and which he lays with infinite care

and patience, not only on the tender attentive ear, but on the half-open lips, and on the eyes, and on the cheeks; as if they all were listeners. In every child there are many children; but coming forth year after year, each somewhat like and somewhat varying. When they are grown much older, the leaves (as it were) lose their pellucid green, the branches their graceful pliancy.

Is there any man so rich in happiness that he can afford to throw aside these first five years? is there any man who can hope for another five so exuberant in unsating joy?

O my sweet infant! I would teach thee to kneel before the gods, were it only to thank 'em for being Athenian and not Persian.

CXXXIV. ASPASIA TO CLEONE.

Our good Auaxagoras said to me this morning, "You do well, Aspasia, to read history in preference to philosophy, not only on the recommendation, but according to the practice of Pericles. A good historian will also be a good philosopher, but will take especial care that he be never caught in the attitude of disquisition or declamation. The golden vein must run through his field, but we must not see rising out of it the shaft and the machinery. We should moderate or repress our curiosity and fastidiousness. Perhaps at no time will there be written, by the most accurate and faithful historian, so much of truth as untruth. But actions enow will come out with sufficient prominence before the great tribunal of mankind, to exercise their judgment and regulate their proceedings. If statesmen looked attentively at everything past, they would find infallible guides in all emergencies. But leaders are apt to shudder at the idea of being led, and little know what different things are experiment and experience. The sagacity of a Pericles himself is neither rule nor authority to those impetuous men, who would rather have rich masters than frugal friends.

"The young folks from the school of your suitor Socrates, who begin to talk already of travelling in Egypt when the plague is over, are likely to return with a distemper as incurable, breaking bulk with demons and dreams. They carry stem and stern too high out of the water, and are more attentive to the bustling and bellying of the streamers, than to the soundness of the mast, the compactness of the deck, or the capacity and cleanliness of the hold."

CXXXV. ASPASIA TO CLEONE.

Anaxagoras told me yesterday that he had been conversing with some literary men, philosophers and poets, who agreed in one thing only, which is, that we are growing worse day after day, both in morality and intellect. Hints were thrown out that philosophy had mistaken her road, and that it was wonderful how she could be at once so dull and so mischievous. The philosophers themselves made this complaint : the poets were as severe on poetry, and were amazed that we were reduced so low as to be the hearers of Sophocles and Euripides, and three or four more, who, however, were quite good enough for such admirers.

"It is strange," said Anaxagoras, "that we are unwilling to receive the higher pleasures, when they come to us and solicit us, and when we are sure they will do us great and lasting good ; and that we gape and pant after the lower, when we are equally sure they will do us great and lasting evil. I am incapable," continued he, "of enjoying so much pleasure from the works of imagination as these poets are, who would rather hate Euripides and Sophocles than be delighted by them, yet who follow the shade of Orpheus with as ardent an intensity of love as Orpheus followed the shade of Eurydice. Ignorant as I am of poetry, I dared not hazard the opinion that our two contemporaries were really deserving of more commendation on the score of verse, inferior as they might in originality be to Marsyas and Tha-

myris and the Centaur Chiron; and to the philosophers
I could only say, My dear friends! let us keep our temper firmly and our tenets laxly; and let any man correct
both who will take the trouble. I come to you, Aspasia,
to console me for the derision I bring home with me."

I kissed his brow, which was never serener, and
assured him that he possessed more comfort than any
mortal could bestow upon him, and that he was the
only one living who never wanted any.

"I am not insensible," said he, "that every year, at
my time of life, we lose some pleasure; some twig that
once blossomed, cankers."

I never was fond of looking forward; I have invariably checked both hopes and wishes. It is but fair
then that I should be allowed to turn away my eyes from
the prospect of age: even if I could believe that it
would come to me as placidly as it has come to Anaxagoras, I would rather lie down to sleep before the knees
tremble as they bend. With Anaxagoras I never con-
verse in this manner; for old men more willingly talk of
age than hear others talk of it; and neither fool nor
philosopher likes to think of the time when he shall talk
no longer. I told my dear old man that, having given a
piece of moral to the philosophers, he must not be so unjust as to refuse a like present to the poets. About an
hour before I began my letter, he came into the library,
and, to my great surprise, brought me these verses,
telling me that, if they were satirical, the satire fell
entirely upon himself.

> Pleasures! away; they please no more.
> Friends! are they what they were before?
> Loves! they are very idle things,
> The best about them are their wings.
> The dance! 'tis what the bear can do;
> Music! I hate your music too.
>
> Whene'er these witnesses that Time
> Hath snatcht the chaplet from our prime,
> Are call'd by Nature, as we go
> With eye more wary, step more slow,
> And will be heard and noted down,
> However we may fret or frown,

10

Shall we desire to leave the scene
Where all our former joys have been?
No, 'twere ungrateful and unwise!
But when die down our charities
For human weal and human woes,
Then is the time our eyes should close.

CXXXVI. ASPASIA TO CLEONE.

We hear that another state has been rising up gradually to power, in the centre of Italy. It was originally
formed of a band of pirates from some distant country,
who took possession of two eminences, fortified long before, and overlooking a wide extent of country. Under
these eminences, themselves but of little elevation, are
five hillocks, on which they enclosed the cattle by night.
It is reported that here were the remains of an ancient and
extensive city, which served the robbers for hiding-places;
and temples were not wanting in which to deprecate the
vengeance of the gods for the violences and murders they
committed daily. The situation is unhealthy, which
perhaps is the reason why the city was abandoned, and
is likewise a sufficient one why it was rebuilt by the
present occupants. They might perpetrate what depre-
dations they pleased, confident that no force could long
besiege them in a climate so pestilential. Relying on
this advantage, they seized from time to time as many
women as were requisite for any fresh accession of vagabonds, rogues, and murderers.

The Sabines bore the loss tolerably well, until the
Romans (so they call themselves) went beyond all
bounds, and even took their cattle from the yoke. The
Sabines had endured all that it became them to endure;
but the lowing of their oxen from the seven hills reached
their hearts and inflamed them with revenge. They are
a pastoral, and therefore a patient people, able to undergo the exertions, and endure the privations, of war,
but, never having been thieves, the Romans over-matched
them in vigilance, activity, and enterprise; and have
several times since made incursions into their country

and forced them to disadvantageous conditions. Emboldened by success, they ventured to insult and exasperate the nearest of the Tyrrhenian princes.

The Tyrrhenians are a very proud and very ancient nation, and, like all nations that are proud and ancient, excel chiefly in enjoying themselves. Demaratos the Corinthian dwelt among them several years; and from the Corinthians they learned to improve their pottery, which, however, it does not appear that they ever have carried to the same perfection as the Corinthian, the best of it being indifferently copied, both in the form and in the figures on it.

Herodotus has written to Pericles all he could collect relating to them; and Pericles says the account is interesting. For my part I could hardly listen to it, although written by Herodotus and read by Pericles. I have quite forgotten the order of events. I thing they are such as neither you nor any one else, excepting those who live near them, will ever care about. But the Tyrrhenians really are an extraordinary people. They have no poets, no historians, no orators, no statuaries, no painters; they say they once had them; so much the more disgraceful. The Romans went out against them and dispersed them, although they blew many trumpets bravely, and brought (pretty nearly into action) many stout soothsayers. The enemy, it appears, has treated them with clemency; they may still feed soothsayers, blow horns, and have wives in common.

I hope it is near your bedtime; if it is, you will thank me for my letter.

CXXXVII. ASPASIA TO CLEONE.

Who would have imagined that the grave, sedate Pericles could take such delight in mischief! "After reading my dissertation on the Tyrrhenians and Romans, he gave it again into my hands, saying:

"Pray amuse your friend Cleone with your first attempt at history."

I sent it off, quite unsuspicious. In the evening he
looked at me with a smile of no short continuance, and
said, at last:

"Aspasia! I perceive you are emulous of our Halicar-
nassian; but pray do not publish that historical Essay
either in his name or your own. He does not treat the
Romans quite so lightly as you do, and shows rather more
justice to the Tyrrhenians. You forgot to mention some
important facts recorded by him, and some doubts as
weighty. We shall come to them presently.

"Having heard of the Romans, but nothing distinctly,
I wished to receive a clearer and a fuller account of them,
and wrote to Herodotus by the first ship that sailed for
Tarentum. The city where he is residing lies near it,
and I gave orders that my letter should be taken thither,
and delivered into his hands. Above a year is elapsed,
during which time Herodotus tells me he has made all the
inquiries which the pursuit of his studies would allow;
that he is continuing to correct the errors, elucidate the
doubtful points, and correct the style and arrangement of
his history; and that, when he has completed it to his
mind, he shall have time and curiosity to consider with
some attention this remarkable tribe of barbarians.

"At present he has not been able to answer my questions; for never was writer so sedulous in the pursuit and
examination of facts. What he sees, he describes clearly;
what he hears, he relates faithfully; and he bestows the
same care on the composition as he had bestowed on the
investigation.

"The Romans, I imagined, had been subdued by
Numa, a Sabine; for it can hardly be credited that so
ferocious a community sent a friendly invitation to be
governed and commanded by the prince of a people they
had grossly and repeatedly insulted. What services had
he rendered them? or by what means had they become
acquainted with his aptitude for government? They had
ever been rude and quarrelsome; he was distinguished
for civility and gentleness. They had violated all that
is most sacred in public and private life; virgins were
seized by treachery, detained by force, and compelled to

wipe the blood of their fathers off the sword of their rav-
ishers. A fratricide king had recently been murdered by
a magistracy of traitors. What man in his senses would
change any condition of life to become the ruler of such
a nation? None but he who had conquered and could
control them; none but one who had swords enough for
every head among them. Absolute power alone can tame
them, and fit them for anything better; and this power
must reside in the hands of a brave and sagacious man,
who will not permit it to be shared, or touched, or questioned. Under such a man such a people may become
formidable, virtuous, and great. It is too true that, to be
martial, a nation must taste of blood in its cradle. Philosophers may dispute it; but time past has written it
down, and time to come will confirm it. Of these matters the sophists can know nothing; he who understands
them best will be the least inclined to discourse on them.

    "Another thing I doubted, and wished to know.
Numa is called a Sabine. The Sabines are illiterate
still; in the time of Numa they were ruder; they had no
commerce, no communication with countries beyond Italy;
and yet there are writers who tell us that he introduced
laws, on the whole not dissimilar to ours, and corrected
the calendar. Is it credible? Is it possible? I am disposed to believe that both these services were rendered by
the son of Demaratos, and that the calendar might have
been made better, were it not requisite on such an occasion, more than almost any other, to consult the superstition of the populace.

    "I myself am afraid of touching the calendar here in
Athens, many as have been my conferences with Metou
on the subject. Done it shall be; but it must be either
just before a victory or just after.

    "If the Sabine had sent an embassy, or even an indi-
vidual, to Athens, in order to collect our laws, the ar-
chives of the city would retain a record of so wonderful
an event. He certainly could not have picked them up
in the pastures or woodlands of his own country. But the
Corinthians know them well, and have copied most of
them. All nations are fond of pushing the date of their

civilization as high up as possible, and care not how re-
motely they place the benefits they have received.   And
probably some of the Romans, aware that Numa was
their conquerer, helped to abolish the humiliating suspicion, by investing him successively with the robes of a
priest, of a legislator, and of an astronomer.

"His two nearest successors were warriors and conquerors.   The third was the son of that Demaratos of
whom we have spoken, and who, exiled from Corinth, settled among the Tyrrhenians, and afterward, being rich
and eloquent, won over to his interest the discontented
and venal of the Romans ; at all times the great majority.
We hear that he constructed of hewn stone a long, a spacious, and a lofty channel, to convey the filth of the town
into the river ; we hear, at the same time, that the town
itself was fabricated of hurdles and mud, upon ruins of
massy workmanship ; that the best houses were roofed
with rushes, and that the vases of the temples were
earthen.   Now, kings in general, and mostly those whose
authority is recent and insecure, think rather of amusing
the people by spectacles, or pampering their appetites by
feasts and donatives, or dazzling their imagination by pomp
and splendor.   Theatres, not common sewers, suited best
the Romans.   Their first great exploit was performed in
a theatre, at the cost of the Sabines.   Moreover they
were religious, and stole every god and goddess they
could lay their hands on.   Surely so considerate a person
as the son of Demaratos would have adapted his magnificence to the genius of the people, who never cared about
filth, but were always most zealous in their devotions.
This we might imagine would occur to him as more and
more requisite on the capture of every town or village ;
for, when the Romans had killed the inhabitants, they
transferred the gods very diligently into their city, that
they might not miss their worshippers.   Now the gods
must have wanted room by degrees, and might not have
liked their quarters.   Five hundred temples could have
been erected at less expense than the building of this stupendous duct.   Did the son of Demaratos build it then?

"The people are still ignorant, still barbarous, still

cruel, still iutractable ; but they are acute in the perception of their interests, and have established at last a form
of government more resembling the Carthaginian than
ours. As their power does not arise from commerce,
like the power of Carthage, but strikes its roots into the
solid earth, its only sure foundation, it is much less subject to the gusts of fortune, and will recover from a shock
more speedily. Neither is there any great nation in contact with them. When they were much weaker, the
Tyrrhenians conquered them, under the command of
their prince Porsena ; but thought they could leave them
nowhere less inconveniently than iu the place they themselves had abandoned. The Sabines, too, conquered them
a second time, and imposed a king over them, but were
so unsuspicious and inconsiderate as not to destroy the
city, and parcel out the inhabitants for Greece, Sicily, and
Africa.

" Living as they did on their farms, with no hold upon
the Romans but a king, who, residing in the city with
few of his own countrymen about him, was rather a host-
age than a ruler, his authority was soon subverted. The
Sabines at this time are partly won by conquest, and
partly domiciliated by consanguinity. The Tyrrhenians
are spent and effete. The government of the Romans,
from royal, is now become aristocratical ; and the people,
deprived of their lawful share in the lands they conquered
from so many enemies, swear hatred to kings, and sigh
for their return. One flagrant crime consumed the regal
authority ; a thousand smouldering ones eat deep into the
consular. The military system stands apart, admirable
in its formation ; and, unless that, too, falls, the Roman
camps will move forward year after year, until the mountains and the seas of Italy shall not contain them. They
are heirs to the wealth of worn-out nations, and, when
they have seized upon their inheritance, they will fight
with braver. The Romans will be to Italy what the
Macedonians at some future day will be to Greece.

" The old must give way to the young, nations like
men, and men like leaves."

CXXXVIII. ASPASIA TO CLEONE.

Buildings of high antiquity have usually been carried by the imagination much higher still. But, by what we hear of the Tyrrhenians, we may believe that in their country there are remains of earlier times than in ours. Everything about them shows a pampered, and dissolute, and decaying people.

You will hardly think a sewer a subject for curiosity and investigation; yet nothing in Europe is so vast and so well-constructed as the sewer at Rome, excepting only the harbor walls and propylæa, built recently here at Athens, under the administration of Pericles. I have asked him some further questions on the wonderful work still extant in the city occupied by the Romans. I will now give you his answer:

" Do not imagine that, unable as I am to ascertain the time when the great sewer of Rome was constructed, I am desirous of establishing one opinion in prejudice of another, or forward in denying that a rich Corinthian might have devised so vast an undertaking. But in Corinth herself we find nothing of equal magnitude, nothing at all resembling its architecture; the Tyrrhenians, who are stated to have been employed in building it, have ceased for many ages to be capable of anything similar; all their great fabrics may be dated more than a thousand years before the age of Tarquin. I feel no interest in the support of an hypothesis. Take it, or reject it; I would rather that you rejected it, if you would replace it with another and a better. Many things pass across the mind, which are neither to be detained in it with the intention of insisting on them as truths, nor are to be dismissed from it as idle and intrusive. Whatever gives exercise to our thoughts, gives them not only activity and strength, but likewise range. We are not obliged to continue on the training-ground; nor, on the other hand, is it expedient to obstruct it or plough it up. The hunter, in quest of one species of game, often finds another, and always finds what is better, freshness, and earnestness, and ani-

mation.   Were I occupied in literature, I should little
fear stumbling in my ascent toward its untrodden and
abstruser scenery : being a politician, I know that a single false step is a fall, and a fall is a ruin.   We may
begin wrong, and continue so with impunity ; but we
must not deviate from wrong to right."

He said this with one of his grave smiles ; and then
to me :

" A slender shrub, the ornament of your private walk,
may with moderate effort be drawn straight again from
any obliquity ; but such an attempt, were it practicable,
would crack every fibre in the twisted tree that over-
shades the forest."

CXXXIX. CLEONE TO ASPASIA.

Who told you, Aspasia, that instead of poetry, of history, of philosophy, our writers at Miletus are beginning
to compose a species of tales founded on love or madness, and ending in miserable death or wealthy marriage ;
and that at the conclusion of the work a strict account is
rendered of all estrays, of all that had once come into it
and had disappeared?   Very true, the people at large run
after the detail of adventures, and are as anxious to see
the termination as they are to reach the bottom of an amphora ; but I beseech you never to imagine that we are
reduced in our literature to such a state of destitution, as
to be without the enjoyment of those treasures which our
ancestors left behind them.   No, Aspasia, we are not yet
so famished that a few morsels of more nutritious food
would overpower us.   I assure you, we do not desire to
see a death or a marriage set upon the table every day.   We
are grateful for all the exercises and all the excursions of
intellect, and our thanks are peculiarly due to those by
whose genius our pleasure in them is increased or varied.
If we have among us any one capable of devising an
imaginary tale, wherein all that is interesting in poetry is
united with all that is instructive in history, such an

author will not supersede the poets and historians, but
will walk between them, and be cordially hailed by both.

CXL. ASPASIA TO CLEONE.

When we are dull we run to music. I am sure you
must be dull enough after so much of history and of politics. My Pericles can discover portents in Macedonia
and Italy: Anaximander could see mountains in the
moon; I desire to cast my eyes no farther than to
Miletus.

Take your harp.

ODE TO MILETUS.

Maiden there was whom Jove
Illuded into love,
  Happy and pure was she;
Glorious from her the shore became,
And Helle lifted up her name
To shine eternal o'er the river-sea.

And many tears are shed
Upon thy bridal-bed.
Star of the swimmer in the lonely night!
  Who with unbraided hair
  Wipedst a breast so fair,
Bounding with toil, more bounding with delight.

But they whose prow hath past thy straits
And, ranged before Byzantion's gates,
Bring to the god of sea the victim due,
  Even from the altar raise their eyes,
  And drop the chalice with surprise,
And at such grandeur have forgotten you.

At last there swells the hymn of praise,
And who inspires those sacred lays?
  "The founder of the walls ye see."
What human power could elevate
Those walls, that citadel, that gate?
  "Miletus, O my sons! was he."

Hail, then, Miletus! hail beloved town,
  Parent of me and mine!
But let not power alone be thy renown,
  Nor chiefs of ancient line,

Nor visits of the gods, unless
   They leave their thoughts below,
And teach us that we most should bless
   Those to whom most we owe.

Restless is Wealth; the nerves of Power
   Sink, as a lute's in rain:
The gods lend only for an hour
   And then call back again

All else than Wisdom; she alone,
   In Truth's or Virtue's form,
Descending from the starry throne
   Thro' radiance and thro' storm,

Remains as long as godlike men
   Afford her audience meet,
Nor Time nor War tread down again
   The traces of her feet.

Always hast thou, Miletus, been the friend,
   Protector, guardian, father, of the wise;
Therefore shall thy dominion never end
   Till Fame, despoil'd of voice and pinion, dies.

With favoring shouts and flowers thrown fast behind,
   Arctinos ran his race,
No wanderer he, alone and blind . .
   And Melesander was untorn by Thrace.

There have been, but not here,
Rich men who swept aside the royal feast
   On child's or bondman's breast,
Bidding the wise and aged disappear.

Revere the aged and the wise,
Aspasia! but thy sandal is not worn
   To trample on these things of scorn;
By his own sting the fire-bound scorpion dies.

CXLI. ASPASIA TO CLEONE.

To-day there came to visit us a writer who is not yet
an author: his name is Thucydides. We understand
that he has been these several years engaged in preparation for a history. Pericles invited him to meet Herod-

otus, when that wonderful man had returned to our
country, and about to sail from Athens. Until then, it
was believed by the intimate friends of Thucydides that
he would devote his life to poetry, and such is his vigor
both of thought and of expression, that he would have been
the rival of Pindar. Even now he is fonder of talking
on poetry than any other subject, and blushed when history was mentioned. By degrees, however, he warmed,
and listened with deep interest to the discourse of Pericles
on the duties of a historian.

" May our first Athenian historian not be the greatest ! " said he, " as the first of our dramatists has been,
in the opinion of many. Æschylus was the creator of
Tragedy, nor did she ever shine with such splendor, ever
move with such stateliness and magnificence, as at her
first apparition on the horizon. The verses of Sophocles
are more elaborate, the language purer, the sentences
fuller and more harmonious ; but in loftiness of soul, and
in the awfulness with which he invests his characters,
Æschylus remains unrivalled and unapproached.

" We are growing too loquacious, both on the stage
and off. We make disquisitions which render us only
more and more dim-sighted, and excursions that only
consume our stores. If some among us who have acquired celebrity by their compositions, calm, candid, contemplative men, were to undertake the history of Athens
from the invasion of Xerxes, I should expect a fair and
full criticism on the orations of Antiphon, and experience no disappointment at their forgetting the battle of
Salamis. History, when she has lost her Muse, will lose
her dignity, her occupation, her character, her name.
She will wander about the Agora ; she will start, she
will stop, she will look wild, she will look stupid, she will
take languidly to her bosom doubts, queries, essays, dis-
sertations, some of which ought to go before her, some
to follow, and all to stand apart. The field of History
should not merely be well tilled, but well peopled. None
is delightful to me, or interesting, in which I find not as
many illustrious names as have a right to enter it. We
might as well in a drama place the actors behind the

scenes, and listen to the dialogue there, as in a history push valiant men back, and protrude ourselves with husky disputations. Show me rather how great projects were executed, great advantages gained, and great calamities averted. Show me the generals and the statesmen who stood foremost, that I may bend to them in reverence; tell me their names, that I may repeat them to my children. Teach me whence laws were introduced, upon what foundation laid, by what custody guarded, in what inner keep preserved. Let the books of the treasury lie closed as religiously as the Sibyl's; leave weights and measures in the market-place, Commerce in the harbor, the Arts in the light they love, Philosophy in the shade: place History on her rightful throne, and, at the sides of her, Eloquence and War.

"Aspasia! try your influence over Thucydides : perhaps he would not refuse you the pleasure of hearing a few sentences of the work he has begun. I may be a plagiary if I am a listener, and yet I would request permission to be present."

Thucydides was pleased at this deference, and has promised to return soon.

CXLII. ASPASIA TO CLEONE.

Polynices, a fishmonger, has been introduced upon the stage. He had grown rich by his honesty and good nature; and latterly, in this hot season, had distributed among the poorer families the fish he could not sell in the daytime at a reasonable price. Others of the same trade cried out against his unfairness, and he was insulted and beaten in the market-place. So favorable an incident could not escape the sagacious scent of our comic writers. He was represented on the stage as aiming at supreme power, riding upon a dolphin through a stormy sea, with a lyre in one hand, a dog-fish in the other, and singing—

> I, whom you see so high on
> A dolphin's back, am not Arion,
> But (should the favoring breezes blow me faster)
> Cecropians! by the gods! . . your master!

The people were indignant at this, and demanded with loud cries the closing of the theatre, and the abolition of comedies forever.

What the abuse of the wisest and most powerful men in the community could not effect, the abuse of a fish-monger has brought about.

The writers and actors of comedy came in a body to Pericles, telling him they had seen the madness of the people, and had heard with wonder and consternation that it was supported by some of the archons.

He answered, that he was sorry to see Comedy with a countenance so altered as to make him tremble for her approaching dissolution; her descent into the regions of Tragedy. He wondered how the archons should deem it expedient to correct those, whose office and employment it had hitherto been to correct *them;* and regretted his inability to interpose between two conflicting authorities; he must leave it entirely to the people, who would soon grow calmer, and renew their gratitude to their protectors and patrons.

In the midst of these regrets the theatre for comedy was closed. The poets and actors, as they departed, made various observations.

"Dogs sweat and despots laugh inwardly," said Hegesias. "Did you note his malice? the Sisyphus!"

"We have nothing left for it," said Hipponax, "but to fall on our knees among the scales, fins, and bladders at the fish-stall."

"Better," said Aristophanes, "make up to Religion, and look whether the haughty chieftain has no vulnerable place in his heel for an arrow from that quarter."

"He has broken your bow," said Pherecydes; "take heed that the people do not snatch at the string; they have shown that they can pull hard, and may pull where we would not have them."

CXLIII. ASPASIA TO CLEONE.

Thucydides has just left us. He has been reading to me a portion of history. At every pause I nodded to

Pericles, who, it seems to me, avoided to remark it purposely, but who in reality was so attentive and thoughtful that it was long before he noticed me. When the reading was over, I said to him:

"So, you two sly personages have laid your sober heads together in order to deceive me; as if I am so silly, so ignorant of peculiarity iu style, as not to discover in an instant the fraud you would impose on me. Thucydides!" said I, "you have read it well; only one could have read it better . . the author himself" . . shaking my head at Pericles.

"O Aspasia!" said our guest, "I confess to you I was always a little too fond of praise, although I have lived in retirement to avoid it until due, wishing to receive the whole sum at once, however long I might wait for it. But never did I expect so much as this: it overturns the scale by its weight."

"O Thucydides!" said Pericles, "I am jealous of Aspasia. No one before ever flattered her so in my presence."

I entreated him to continue to write, and to bring down his history to the present times.

"My reverence for Herodotus," said he, "makes me stand out of his way and look at him from a distance: I was obliged to take another model of style. I hope to continue my work beyond the present day, and to conclude it with some event which shall have exalted our glory and have established our supremacy in Greece."

"Go on," said I; "fear no rivals. Others are writing who fear not even Herodotus, nor greatly, indeed, respect him. They will be less courteous with you, perhaps, whose crown is yet in the garden. The creatures run about and kick and neigh in all directions, with a gadfly on them ever since they left the race-course at Olympia. At one moment they lay the muzzle softly, and languidly, and lovingly upon each other's neck; at another they rear and bite like Python."

"I ought to experience no enmity from them," said he; "before my time comes, theirs will be over."

CXLIV. PERICLES TO ASPASIA.

I am pleased with your little note, and hope you may live to write a commentary on the same author. You speak with your usual judgment, in commending our historian for his discretion in metaphors. Not indeed that his language is without them, but they are rare, impressive, and distinct. History wants them occasionally; in oratory they are nearly as requisite as in poetry; they come opportunely wherever the object is persuasion or intimidation, and no less where delight stands foremost. In writing a letter I would neither seek nor reject one; but I think, if more than one came forward, I might decline its services. If, however, it had come in unawares, I would take no trouble to send it away. But we should accustom ourselves to think always with propriety, in little things as in great, and neither be too solicitous of our dress in the house, nor negligent because we are at home. I think it as improper and indecorous to write a stupid or a silly note to you, as one in a bad hand or on coarse paper. Familiarity ought to have another and worse name, when it relaxes in its attentiveness to please.

We began with metaphors, I will end with one. Do not look back over the letter to see whether I have not already used my privilege of nomination, whether my one is not there. Take, then, a simile instead. It is a pity that they are often lamps which light nothing, and show only the nakedness of the walls they are nailed against.

CXLV. ASPASIA TO CLEONE.

Sophocles left me about an hour ago.

Hearing that he was with Pericles on business, I sent to request he would favor me with a visit when he was disengaged. After he had taken a seat, I entreated him to pardon me, expressing a regret that we hardly ever saw him, knowing, as I did, that no person could so ill withstand the regrets of the ladies.   I added a hope that, as much for my sake as for the sake of Pericles, he would now and then steal an hour from the Muses in our behalf.

"Lady!" said he, "it would only be changing the place of assignation."

"I shall begin with you," said I, "just as if I had a right to be familiar, and desire of you to explain the meaning of a chorus in *King Œdipus*, which, although I have read the tragedy many times, and have never failed to be present at the representation, I do not quite comprehend."

I took up a volume from the table . .

"No," said I, "this is *Electra;* give me the other." We unrolled it together.

"Here it is: what is the meaning of these words about the *Laws ?* "

He looked over them, first, without opening his lips; then he read them in a low voice to himself; and then, placing the palm of his left hand against his forehead:

"Well! I certainly did think I understood it at the time I wrote it."

Cleone! if you could see him you would fall in love with him.   Fifteen Olympiads have not quite run away with all his youth.   What a noble presence! what an open countenance! what a brow! what a mouth! what a rich, harmonious voice! what a heart, full of passion and of poetry!

CXLVI.   REPLY OF PERICLES TO THE ACCUSATION OF CLEON.

There is a race of men (and they appear to have led colonies into many lands) whose courage is always in an inverse ratio to their danger.   There is also a race who deem that a benefit done to another is an injury done to them.   Would you affront them, speak well of their friends; would you deprive them of repose, labor and watch incessantly for their country.

Cleon! in all your experience, in all the territories you

11

have visited, in all the cities and islands you have conquered for us, have you never met with any such people?
And yet, O generous Cleon! I have heard it hinted that
the observation is owing to you.

Were my life a private one, were my services done
toward my friends alone, had my youth been exempt, as
yours hath been, from difficulty and peril, I might never
have displeased you; I might never have been cited to
defend my character against the foulest of imputations.
O Athenians! let me recall your attention to every word
that Cleon has uttered. I know how difficult is the task,
where so much dust is blown about by so much wind.
The valorous Cleon has made your ears tingle and ring
with Harmodius and Aristogiton. I am ignorant which
of the two he would take for imitation, the handsomer or
the braver. He stalks along with great bustle and magnificence, but he shows the dagger too plainly: he neg-
lects to carry it in myrtle.

In your astonishment at this sudden procedure, there
are doubtless many of you who are unable to comprehend
the title of the denunciation. Let me tell you what it is.
"Pericles, son of Xanthippus" . . (may all Greece
hear it! may every herald in every city proclaim it at
every gate!) "Pericles, son of Xanthippus, is accused
of embezzling the public money, collected, reserved, and
set apart, for the building and decoration of the Parthenon. The accuser is Cleon, son of Cleæretus."

The scribe has designated the father of our friend by
this name, in letters very legible, otherwise I should have
suspected it was the son of Cligenes, the parasite of the
wealthy, the oppressor of the poor, the assailer of the
virtuous, and the ridicule of all. Charges more substan-
tial might surely be brought against me, and indeed were
threatened. But never shall I repent of having, by my
advice, a little decreased the revenues of the commonwealth, in lowering the price of admission to the theatres,
and in offering to the more industrious citizens, out of the
public treasury, the trifle requisite for this enjoyment.
In the theatre let them see before them the crimes and
the calamities of Power, the vicissitudes of Fortune, and

the sophistries of the Passions. Let it be there. and there only, that the just man suffers, and that murmurs are heard against the dispensations of the gods.

But I am forgetting the accusation. Will Cleon do me the favor to inform you in what place I have deposited, or in what manner I have spent, the money thus embezzled? Will Cleon tell you that I alone had the custody of it; or that I had anything at all to do in the making up of the accounts? Will Cleon prove to you that I am now richer than I was thirty years ago, excepting in a portion of the spoil won bravely by the armies you decreed I should command; such a portion as the laws allow, and the soldiers carry to their general with triumphant acclamations. Cleon has yet to learn all this : certainly his wealth is derived from no such sources; far other acclamations does Cleon court; those of the idle, the dissolute, the malignant, the cowardly, and the false. But if he seeks them in Athens, and not beyond, his party is small indeed, and your indignation will drown their voices. What need have I of pilfer and peculation? Am I avaricious? am I prodigal? Does the indigent citizen, does the wounded soldier, come to my door and return unsatisfied? Point at me, Cleon! and tell your friends to mark that. Let them mark it; but for imitation, not for calumny; let them hear, for they are idle enough, whence I possess the means of relieving the unfortunate, raising the dejected, and placing men of worth and genius (too often in that number!) where all their fellow-citizens may distinguish them. My father died in my childhood; careful guardians superintended it, managing my affairs with honesty and diligence. The earliest of my ancestors, of whom anything remarkable is recorded, was Cleisthenes, whom your forefathers named general with Solon, ordering them to conquer Cirrha. He devoted his portion of the spoils to the building of a portico. I never have heard that he came by night and robbed the laborers he had paid by day : perhaps Cleon has. He won afterward at the Olympian games : I never have ascertained that he bribed his adversaries. These actions are not in history nor in tradition; but Cleon no doubt has authorities that outvalue tradition and history. Some years afterward, Cleisthenes proclaimed his determination to give in marriage his daughter Agarista to the worthiest man he could find, whether at home or abroad. It is pity that Cleon was not living in those days. Agarista and her father, in default of him, could hear of none worthier than Megacles, son of Alcmæon. Their riches all descended to me, and some, perhaps, of their better possessions. These at least, with Cleon's leave, I would retain; and as much of the other as may be serviceable to my friends, without being dangerous to the commonwealth.

CXLVII. ASPASIA TO CLEONE.

Surely of all our pursuits and speculations, the most instructive is, how the braver pushed back their sufferings, how the weaker bowed their heads and asked for sympathy, how the soldier smote his breast at the fallacies of glory, and how the philosopher paused and trembled at the depths of his discoveries. But the acquirement of such instruction presses us down to the earth. We see the basest and most inert of mankind the tormentors and consumers of the loftiest: the worm at last devours what the lion and tiger paused at and fled from. But Pericles, for the present, is safe and secure; and I am too happy for other thoughts or reflections. Anaxagoras, also, is only doubted: he *may* disbelieve in some mysteries, but he is surely too wise a man to divulge it.

CXLVIII. CLEONE TO ASPASIA.

Now we are quiet and at peace again, I wish you would look into your library for more pieces of poetry. To give you some provocation, I will transcribe a few lines on the old subject, which, like old fountains, is inexhaustible, while those of later discovery are in danger of being cut off at the first turn of the plough.

ERINNA TO LOVE.

Who breathes to thee the holiest prayer,
O Love! is ever least thy care.
Alas! I may not ask thee why 'tis so . .
Because a fiery scroll I see
Hung at the throne of Destiny,
Reason with Love and register with Woe.

Few question thee, for thou art strong,
And, laughing loud at right and wrong,
Seizest, and dashest down, the rich, the poor;
Thy sceptre's iron studs alike
The meaner and the prouder strike,
And wise and simple fear thee and adore.

CXLIX. ASPASIA TO CLEONE.

Among the poems of Sappho I find the following, but written in a different hand from the rest. It pleases me at least as much as any of them; if it is worse, I wish you would tell me in what it is so. How many thoughts might she have turned over and tossed away for it! Odious is the economy in preserving all the scraps of the intellect, and troublesome the idleness of tacking them together. Sappho is fond of seizing, as she runs on, the most prominent and inviting flowers: she never stops to cut and trim them; she throws twenty aside for one that she fixes in her bosom; and what is more singular, her pleasure at their beauty seems never to arise from another's admiration of it. See it or not see it, there it is.

Sweet girls! upon whose breast that god descends
Whom first ye pray to come and next to spare,
O tell me whither now his course he bends,
Tell me what hymn shall thither waft my prayer!
Alas! my voice and lyre alike he flies,
And only in my dreams, nor kindly then, replies.

CL. CLEONE TO ASPASIA.

Instead of expatiating on the merits of the verses you last sent me, or, on the other hand, of looking for any pleasure in taking them to pieces, I venture to hope you will be of my opinion, that these others are of equal authenticity. Neither do I remember them in the copy you possessed when we were together.

SAPPHO TO HESPERUS.

I have beheld thee in the morning hour
  A solitary star, with thankless eyes,
  Ungrateful as I am! who bade thee rise
When sleep all night had wandered from my bower.

  Can it be true that thou art he
  Who shinest now above the sea
Amid a thousand, but more bright?
  Ah yes, the very same art thou
  That heard me then, and hearest now . .
Thou seemest, star of love! to throb with light.

Sappho is not the only poetess who has poured forth her melodies to Hesperus, or who had reason to thank him. I much prefer these of hers to what appear to have been written by some confident man, and (no doubt) on a feigned occasion.

  Hesperus, hail! thy winking light
    Best befriends the lover,
  Whom the sadder Moon for spite
    Gladly would discover.

  Thou art fairer far than she,
    Fairer far, and chaster:
  She may guess who smiled on me,
    I know who embraced her.

  Pan of Arcady . . 'twas Pan,
    In the tamarisk bushes . .
  Bid her tell thee, if she can,
    Where were then her blushes.

  And, were I inclined to tattle,
    I could name a second,
  Whom asleep with sleeping cattle
    To her cave she beckon'd.

  Hesperus, hail! thy friendly ray
    Watches o'er the lover,
  Lest the nodding leaves betray,
    Lest the moon discover.

Phryne heard my kisses given
  Acte's rival bosom . .
'Twas the buds, I swore by heaven,
  Bursting into blossom.

What she heard, and half espied
  By the gleam, she doubted,
And with arms uplifted, cried,
  How they must have sprouted!

Hesperus, hail again! thy light
  Best befriends the lover,
Whom the sadder Moon for spite
  Gladly would discover.

The old poets are contented with narrow couches;
but these couches are not stuffed with chaff which lasts
only for one season. They do not talk to us from them
when they are half asleep; but think it more amusing
to entertain us in our short visit with lively thoughts
and fancies, than to enrich us with a paternal prolixity
of studied and stored-up meditations.

CLI. PERICLES TO ALCIBIADES.

My Alcibiades, if I did not know your good temper
from a whole life's experience, I should be afraid of displeasing you by repeating what I have heard. This is,
that you pronounce in public as well as in private a few
words somewhat differently from our custom. You cannot be aware how much hostility you may excite against
you by such a practice. Remember, we are Athenians;
and do not let us believe that we have finer organs,
quicker perceptions, or more discrimination, than our
neighbors in the city. Every time we pronounce a word
differently from another, we show our disapprobation of
his manner, and accuse him of rusticity. In all common
things we must do as others do. It is more barbarous
to undermine the stability of a language than of an edifice that hath stood as long. This is done by the introduction of changes. Write as others do, but only as the
best of others; and if one eloquent man, forty or fifty

years ago, spoke and wrote differently from the generality of the present, follow him, though alone, rather than the many. But in pronunciation we are not indulged in this latitude of choice; we must pronounce as those do who favor us with their audience. Never hazard a new expression in public; I know not any liberty we can take, even with our nearest friends, more liable to the censure of vanity. Whatever we do we must do from authority or from analogy. A young man, however studious and intelligent, can know, intrinsically and profoundly, but little of the writers who constitute authority. For my part, in this our country, where letters are far more advanced than in any other, I can name no one whatever who has followed up to their origin the derivation of words, or studied with much success their analogy. I do not, I confess, use all the words that others do, but I never use one that others do not. Remember, one great writer may have employed a word which a greater has avoided, or, not having avoided it, may have employed in a somewhat different signification. It would be needless to offer you these remarks, if our language were subject to the capriciousness of courts, the humiliation of sycophants, and the defilement of slaves. Another may suffer but little detriment by the admission of barbarism to its franchises; but ours is Attic, and the words, like the citizens we employ, should at once be popular and select.

CLII. CLEONE TO ASPASIA.

The poetical merits of the unhappy Lesbian are sufficiently well known. Thanks, and more than thanks, if indeed there is anything more on earth, are due for even one scrap from her. But allow me, what is no great delicacy or delight to me, a reprehension, a censure. An admirer can make room for it only when it comes from an admirer. Sappho, in the most celebrated of her Odes, tells us that she sweats profusely. Now surely, no female, however low-born and ill-bred, in short, how-

ever Eolian, could, without indecorousness, speak of
sweating and spitting, or any such things. We never
ought to utter, in relation to ourselves, what we should
be ashamed of being seen in. Writing of war and con-
tention, such an expression is unobjectionable. To avoid
it by circumlocution, or by any other word less expres-
sive and direct, would be the most contemptible and
ludicrous of pedantry ; and, were it anywhere reduced to
practice in the conversation of ordinary life, it would
manifestly designate a coarse-graiued, unpolishable people.
There is nothing in poetry, or indeed in society, so unpleasant as affectation. In poetry it arises from a defi-
ciency of power and a restlessness of pretension ; in
conversation, from insensibility to the Graces, from an
intercourse with bad company, and a misinterpretation
of better.

CLIII. ASPASIA TO CLEONE.

You desire to know what portion of history it is the
intention of Thucydides to undertake. He began with
the earlier settlers of Greece, but he has now resolved
to employ this section as merely the portico to his edifice. The Peloponnesian war appears to him worthier of
the historian than any other. He is of opinion that it
must continue for many years and comprehend many
important events, for Pericles is resolved to wear out the
euergy of the Spartans by protracting it. At present it
has been carried on but few months, with little advantage to either side, and much distress to both. What our
historian has read to us does not contain any part of
these transactions, which, however, he carefully notes
down as they occur. We were much amused by a speech
he selected for recitation, as one delivered by an orator
of the Corinthians to the ephors of Lacedæmon, urging
the justice and necessity of hostilities. Never was the
Athenian character painted in such true and lively
colors. In composition his characteristic is brevity,
yet the first sentence of the volume runs into superfluity.
The words, to the best of my recollection, are these :

"Thucydides of Athens has composed a history of the war between the Peloponnesians and Athenians."

This is enough; yet he adds:

"As conducted by each of the belligerents."

Of course: it could not be conducted by one only.

I observed that in the fourth sentence he went from the third person to the first.

By what I could collect, he thinks the Peloponnesian war more momentous than the Persian; yet had Xerxes prevailed against us, not a vestige would be existing of liberty or civilization in the world. If Sparta should, there will be little enough; and a road will be thrown open to the barbarians of the north, Macedonians, and others with strange names. We have no great reason to fear it; although the policy of Thebes, on whom much depends, is ungenerous and unwise.

He said, moreover, that "transactions of an earlier time are known imperfectly, and were of small importance either in the wars or anything else."

Yet without these wars, or some other of these transactions, our Miletus and Athens, our Pericles and Thucydides, would not be; so much does one thing depend upon another. I am little disposed to overvalue the potency and importance of the eastern monarchies; but surely there is enough to excite our curiosity, and interest our inquiries, in the fall of Chaldæa, the rise of Babylon, and the mysteries of Egypt . . not indeed her mysteries in theology, which are impostures there as elsewhere, but the mysteries in arts and sciences, which will outlive the gods. Barbarians do not hold steadily before us any moral or political lesson; but they serve as graven images, protuberantly eminent and gorgeously uncouth, to support the lamp placed on them by History and Philosophy. If we knew only what they said and did, we should turn away with horror and disgust: but we pound their mummies to color our narratives; and we make them as useful in history as beasts are in fable.

Thucydides shows evidently, by his preliminary observations, that he considers the Trojan war unimportant.

Yet, according to Homer, the Grecian troops amounted
to above a hundred thousand. In reality, so large a
force hath never been assembled in any naval expedition, nor even one half. How was it provisioned at
Aulis? how, on the shores of the Troad? And all these
soldiers, with chariots and horses, were embarked for
Troy a few years after the first ship of war left the
shores of Greece! yes, a very few years indeed; for the
Argo had among her crew the brothers of Helen, who
cannot well be supposed to have been five years older
than herself. It is of rare occurrence, even in the climate of Sparta, that a mother bears children after so
long an interval; and we have no reason to believe that
such a time had elapsed between the brothers and their
sister. Suppose the twins to have been twenty-two
years old (for they had become celebrated for horseman-
ship and boxing), and Helen seventeen, you will find little
space left between the expeditions.

But away with calculation. We make a bad bargain
when we change poetry for truth in the affairs of ancient
times, and by no means a good one in any.

Remarkable men of remote ages are collected together
out of different countries within the same period, and
perform simultaneously the same action. On an accumulation of obscure deeds arises a wild spirit of poetry;
and images and names bu.rst forth and spread themselves,
which carry with them something like enchantment, far
beyond the infancy of nations. What was vague imagination settles at last and is received for history. It is
difficult to effect and idle to attempt the separation; it is
like breaking off a beautiful crystallization from the
vault of some intricate and twilight cavern, out of mere
curiosity to see where the accretion terminates and the
rock begins.

CLIV. ASPASIA TO CLEONE.

We have lost another poet, and have none left beside
the comic. Euripides is gone to the court of Archelaus.
A few years ago he gained the prize against all compet-

itors. He was hailed by the people as a deliverer, for subverting the ascendancy and dominion which Sophocles had acquired over them. The Athenians do not like to trust any man with power for life. Sophocles is now an old man, sixty years of age at the least, and he had then been absolute in the theatre for above a quarter of a century. What enthusiasm! what acclamations! for over-throwing the despot who had so often made them weep and beat their breasts. He came to visit us on the day of his defeat; Euripides was with us at the time.

"Euripides," said he, "we are here alone, excepting our friends Aspasia and Pericles. I must embrace you, now it cannot seem an act of ostentation."

He did so, and most cordially.

"I should be glad to have conquered you," continued he, "it would have been very glorious."

I never saw Pericles more moved. These are the actions that shake his whole frame, and make his eyes glisten. Euripides was less affected. He writes ten-derly, but is not tender. There are hearts that call for imagination; there are others that create it.

I must abstain from all reflections that fall too darkly on the departed. We may see him no more, perhaps; I am sorry for it. He did not come often to visit us, nor indeed is there anything in his conversation to delight or interest me. He has not the fine manners of Sophocles; nor the open unreserved air, which Pericles tells me he admired so much in the soldierly and somewhat proud Æschylus; grave and taciturn, I hear, like himself, unless when something pleased him; and then giving way to ebullitions and bursts of rapture, and filling every one with it round about.

The movers and masters of our souls have surely a right to throw out their limbs as carelessly as they please, on the world that belongs to them, and before the crea-tures they have animated. It is only such insects as petty autocrats that feel oppressed by it, and would sting them for it. Pericles is made of the same clay. He cannot quite overcome his stateliness, but he bends the more gracefully for bending slowly.

When I think of Euripides, I think how short a time
it is since he was hailed as a deliverer, and how odious
he is become for breaking in upon our affections at an
unseasonable hour, and for carrying our hearts into
captivity.   All the writers of the day were resolved to
humble him, and ran about from magistrate to magistrate, to raise money enough for the magnificent representation of his rival . . I have forgotten the man's
name.   Pericles never thwarts the passions and prejudices of the citizens.   In his adolescence he visited the
humble habitation of the venerable Æschylus : throughout life he has been the friend of Sophocles ; he has
comforted Euripides in his defeats, telling him that by
degrees he would teach the people to be better judges :
he rejoiced with him on his first victory, reminding him
of his prophecy, and remarking that they two, of all the
Athenians, had shown the most patience and had been
the best rewarded for it.

We hope he may return.

CLV. ASPASIA TO CLEONE.

The two pieces I am about to transcribe are of styles
very different.   I find them among the collections of
Pericles, but am ignorant of the authors.

> Far from the harp's and from the singer's noise,
>   The bird of Pallas lights on ruin'd towers.
>   I know a wing that flaps o'er girls and boys
> To harp and song and kiss in myrtle bowers ;
> When age is come, I too will sit apart,
> While age is absent, *that* shall fan my heart.

CUPID AND LIGEIA.

> Cupid had played some wicked trick one day
> On sharp Ligeia ; and I heard her say,
> "You little rogue! you ought to be unsext."
> He was as spiteful tho' not quite so vext,
> And said (but held half-shut the folding-doors)
> "Ah then my beard will never grow like yours!"

CLVI. FIRST SPEECH OF PERICLES TO THE ATHENIANS,

On the Declarations of Corinth and Lacedæmon.

The Regency at Lacedæmon has resolved to make an irruption into Attica, if we attempt anything adverse to Potidæa, hearing that, on the declaration of hostilities by Corinth, we ordered the Potidæans, whose infidelity we had detected, to demolish the wall facing Pallene. In reliance on their treason, Perdiccas and the Corinthians had entered into confederacy, and were exciting the defection of our Thracian auxiliaries. Perdiccas prevailed with the Chalcidians to dismantle all their towns upon the sea-side, and to congregate in Olynthos. We made a truce, and afterward a treaty, with Perdiccas: he evacuates the territory he had invaded; we strictly beleaguer the revolted Potidæa. The ephors of Lacedæmon now summon to appear before them not only their allies, but whosoever has any complaint to prefer against the Athenians. Hereupon the Megaræans come forward, and protest that they have been prohibited from our markets, contrary to treaty; and what is worse, that we exclude them from the possession of Potidæa, so convenient for extending their power and authority into Thrace. They appear, in their long oration, to have forgotten nothing, unless that they had murdered our citizens and ambassadors.

By what right, O Athenians, is Lacedæmon our judge? Corinth may impel her into war against us; but Corinth can never place her on the judgment-seat of Greece; nor shall their united voices make us answer to the citation. We will declare, not to her, but to all, our reasons and our rights. The Corcyræans had erected a trophy at Leucimna, and had spared after the victory their Corinthian captives; they had laid waste the territory of Leucas, and they had burnt the arsenal of Cyllene. Meanwhile the Corinthians sent ambassadors to every power in the Peloponnese, and enlisted mariners for their service upon every coast. If valor and skill and constancy could have availed the Corcyræans, they would

have continued to abstain, as they had ever done, from
all alliances. They only sought ours when destruction
was imminent; knowing that, in policy and humanity,
we never could allow the extinction of one Grecian
state, nor consequently the aggrandizement and preponderance of another; and least so when the insolence of
Corinth had threatened our naval ascendancy (by which
all Greece was saved), and the rivalry of Lacedæmon
our equality on land. By our treaty with the Lacedæmonians it is provided that, if any community be not in
alliance with one of the parties, it may confederate with
either, at its discretion; and this compact it was agreed
should be binding not only on the principals, but likewise on the subordinates. In such a predicament stands
Corcyra.

It might behoove us to chastise the inhumanity of a nation which, like Corinth, would devour her own offspring;
but it certainly is most just and most expedient, when,
instead of reasoning or conferring with us on the propriety of our interference, she runs at once to Sparta,
conspiring with her to our degradation, and, if possible,
to our ruin. Satisfactorily to demonstrate our justice
and moderation, I advise that we stipulate with Corcyra
for mutual defence, never for aggression, and admitting
no article which, even by a forced interpretation, may
contravene our treaty with Lacedæmon.

CLVII. SECOND SPEECH OF PERICLES.

The jealousy that Sparta hath ever entertained against
us, was declared most flagrantly, when Leotychides, who
commanded the Grecian forces at Mycale, drew away
with him all the confederates of the Peloponnese. We
continued to assail the barbarians until we drove them
from Sestos, their last hold upon the Hellespont. It was
then, and then only, that the Athenians brought back
again from miserable refuge their wives and children,
and began to rebuild their habitations, and walls for
their defence. Did the Spartans view this constancy and

perseverance with admiration and with pity, as the patri-
otic, the generous, the humane, would do? Did they
send ambassadors to congratulate your fathers on their
valor, their endurance, their prosperous return, their
ultimate security? Ambassadors they sent, indeed, but
insisting that our walls should never rise again from
their ruins. A proposal so unjust and arrogant we
treated with scorn and indignation, when our numbers
were diminished and our wealth exhausted: shall we
bend to their decisions and obey their orders now? If
their power of injuring us were in proportion to their
malice, their valor to their pride, or their judgment to
their ferocity, then were they most formidable indeed;
but turn we to the examination of facts. Having occasion to reduce to obedience a few revolted Helotes in the
city of Ithome, to whom did they apply? to the Athenians; for they themselves were utterly ignorant how to
attack or even to approach a fortress. Even then they
showed their jealousy, rewarding our promptitude to assist them by the ignominious dismissal of our troops.
What was the consequence? a ten years' siege. And
these, O Athenians! are the men who now threaten the
Acropolis and the Piræus!

I can compare the Lacedæmonians to nothing more fitly
than to the heads of spears without the shafts. There
would be abundantly the power of doing mischief, were
there only the means and method of directing it. Where
these are wanting, we have no better cause for apprehension than at the sparks of fire under our horse's hoof, lest
they produce a conflagration; which indeed they might
do, if by their nature they were durable and directable.

Let us see what powerful aid our enemies are expecting; what confederates they are stirring up against us.
The Megaræans, who left their alliance for ours; the
Megaræans, whom we defended against the Coriuthians,
and whose walls we constructed at our own expense from
Megara to Nisæa. Is it on the constancy or on the gratitude of this people that Lacedæmon, in her wisdom, so
confidently relies? No sooner had we landed in Eubæa,
than intelligence was brought us that the Peloponuesians

were about to make an incursion into Attica, and that the Athenian garrison was murdered by the Megaræans, who already had formed a junction with the Corinthians, Sicyonians, and Epidaurians. We sailed homeward, and discomfited the Peloponnesians; returned, and reduced Eubæa. A truce for thirty years was granted to Lacedæmon, restoring to her Nisæa, Calchis, Pegai, and Trœzene. Five years afterward a war broke out between the Samians and Miletus. Justice and our treaties obliged us to rescue that faithful and unfortunate city from the two-fold calamity that impended over her. Many of the Samians were as earnest in imploring our assistance as the Milesians were; for, whatever might be the event of the war, they were sure of being reduced to subjection; if conquered, by a wronged and exasperated enemy; if conquerors, by the king. A rapacious and insolent oligarchy saw no other means of retaining its usurped authority, than by extending it with rigor; and were conscious that it must fall from under them unless the sceptre propped it. Honest men will never seek such aid, and free men will never endure such.

There may be nations monarchal and aristocratical, where the public good is little thought of, and often impeded by restless steps toward personal or family aggrandizement. But there is no man, even among these, so barbarous and inhuman, as to be indifferent to the approbation of some one in his city beloved above all the rest, from whom the happy rush forward for admiration, the less fortunate are gratified with a tear; life, they would tell us, is well lost for either. We Athenians have loftier views, and, I will not say purer, but the same and more ardent aspirations.

In the late brief war, the greater part of you here present have won immortal glory; and let us not believe that those who fell from your ranks in battle are yet insensible to the admiration and gratitude of their countrymen. No one among us, whatever services he may have rendered to Athens, has received such praises, such benedictions, such imperishable rewards, as they have. Happy men! they are beyond the reach of calumny and reverses.

12

There is only one sad reflection resting with them : they can serve their country no more. How high was the value of their lives ! they knew it, and bartered them for renown. We, in this war unjustly waged against us, shall be exposed to fewer dangers, but more privations. In the endurance of these, our manliness will be put severely to the proof, and virtues which have not been called forth in fifty years, virtues which our enemies seem to have forgotten that we possess, must again come into action, as if under the eyes of a Themistocles and an Aristides. We have all done much ; but we have all done less than we can do, ought to do, and will do.

Archidamos, king of Sparta, now about to march against us, is bound to me by by the laws of hospitality. Should he, whether in remembrance of these, or in the design of rendering me suspected, abstain from inflicting on my possessions the violence he is about to inflict on the rest of Attica, let it be understood that henceforth I have no private property in this land, but, in the presence of the gods, make a free donation of it to the commonwealth. Let all withdraw their cattle, corn, and other effects, from the country, and hold Athens as one great citadel, from which the deity who presides over her hath forbidden us to descend.

CLVIII. ORATION OF PERICLES,

On the approach of the Lacedæmonians to Athens.

Long ago, and lately, and in every age intervening, O Athenians! have you experienced the jealousy and insolence of Lacedæmon. She listens now to the complaints of Corinth, because the people of Corcyra will endure no longer her vexations, and because their navy, in which the greater part of the mariners have fought and conquered by the side of ours, seek refuge in the Piræus. A little while ago she dared to insist that we should admit the ships of Megara to our harbor, her merchandise to our markets, when Megara had broken her faith with us, and gone over to the Spartans. Even this indignity we might perhaps have endured. We told the Lacedæmonians that we would admit the Megarœans to that privilege, if the ports of Sparta would admit us and our allies; although we and our allies were never in such relationship with her, and therefore could never have fallen off from her. She disdained to listen to a proposal so reasonable, to a concession so little to be expected from us. Resolved to prove to her that generosity, and not fear, dictated it, we chastised the perfidious Megara.

The king of the Lacedæmonians, Archidamos, a wiser and honester man than any of his people, is forced to obey the passions he would control; and an army of sixty thousand men is marching under his command to ravage Attica. The braver will rather burn their harvests than transfer to a sanguinary and insatiable enemy the means of inflicting evil on their relatives and friends. Few, I trust, are base enough, sacrilegious enough, to treat as guests, those whom you before men and gods denounce as enemies. We will receive within our walls the firm and faithful. And now let the orators who have blamed our expenditure in the fortification of the city, tell us again that it was improvident. They would be flying in dismay had not those bulwarks been raised effectually. Did it require any sagacity to foresee that Athens would be the envy of every state around? Was there any man so ignorant as not to know that he who has lost all his enemies will soon lose all his energy? and that men are no more men when they cease to act, than rivers are rivers when they cease to run? The forces of our assailants must be broken against our walls. Our fleets are our farms henceforward, until the Spartans find that, if they can subsist on little, they cannot so well subsist on stones and ashes. Their forces are vast; but vast forces have never much hurt us. Marathon and Platæa were scarcely wide enough for our trophies; a victorious army, an unvanquished fleet, Militades himself, retired unsuccessful from the rock of Paros. Shall we tremble, then, before a tumultuous multitude, ignorant how cities are defended or assailed? Shall we prevent them from coming to their discomfiture and destruction? Firmly do I believe that the Protectress of our city leads them against it to avenge her cause. They may ravage the lands; they cannot cultivate, they cannot hold them. Mischief they will do, and great; much of our time, much of our patience, much of our perseverance, and something of our courage, are required. At present I do not number this event among our happiest. We must owe our glory partly to ourselves and partly to our enemies. They offer us the means of greatness; let us accept their offer. Brief danger is the price of long security. The countryman, from the mists of the morning, not only foretells the brightness of the day, but discerns in them sources of fertility; and he remembers in his supplications to the immortal gods to thank them alike for both blessings. It is thus, O men of Athens, that you have constantly looked up at calamities. Never have they depressed you; always have they chastened your hearts, always have they exalted your courage. Impelled by the breath of Xerxes, the locusts of Asia consumed your harvests; your habitations crumbled away as they swarmed along: the temples of the gods lay prostrate; the gods themselves bowed and fell; the men of Athens rose higher than ever. They had turned their faces in grief from the scene of devastation and impiety; but they listened to a provident valor, and the myriads of insects that had plagued them were consumed.

There is affront in exhortation. I have spoken.

CLIX. ASPASIA TO CLEONE.

On the shore overlooking the fountain of Arethusa there is a statue of Æschylus. An Athenian who went to visit it, crowned it with bay and ivy, and wrote these verses at the base:

> Stranger! Athenian hands adorn
> A bard thou knowest well.
> Ah! do not ask where he was born,
> For we must blush to tell.

> Proud are we, but we place no pride
>   On good, or wise, or brave;
> Hence what Cephisus had denied
>   'Twas Arethusa gave.

You remember the story of a barbarous king, who
would have kept the Muses in captivity.   His armory fur-
nished an enemy of the poet Lysis with these materials
for skirmishing :

TO LYSIS.

> A curse upon the king of old
>   Who would have kidnapp'd all the Muses!
> Whether to barter them for gold
>   Or keep them for his proper uses.

> Lysis! aware he meant them ill,
>   Birds they became, and flew away . .
> Thy Muse alone continues still
>   A titmouse to this very day.

Do not call me sly and perfidious, if, after tickling you
with this feather, I have not only permitted a wicked
thought to enter my head, but have also devised a place
for it, if possible, in yours.   The lines below are none
of my composition, as you may well imagine from my
character :

> There is in empty kisses a delight;
>   A fragrance of the wine
> Quaff by the happier in the genial night
>   Is there; may these be mine!

> What said I? empty kisses? none are empty.
>   Gods! all the just who give
> That graceful feast from every grief exempt ye!
>   Blest, honor'd, grant they live!

And now I have written them fairly out, I am afraid
of sending them ; for I remember that if ever I uttered
such a word as *kiss*, you wondered at me.   Really and
truly it was as far from wonder as anything could be, and
so it will be now ; but it was very near a slight displeasure, which now it must not be.

CLX. ASPASIA TO CLEONE.

After an interval of nearly three years, Comedy may reappear on the stage. It is reported that Pericles obtained this indulgence from the archons; and in consequence of it he is now represented by the dramatists as a Jupiter, who lightens and thunders, and what not. Before he became a Jupiter, I believe he was represented as the enemy of that god, and most of the others; aud the people having no public amusement, no diversion to carry off their ill-humors, listened gloomily to such discourses. Pericles noted it, and turned them into their fold again, and had them piped to; but not before the fly entered the fleece.

CLXI. ASPASIA TO CLEONE.

Twenty days, O Cleone, twenty days are not elapsed, since Anaxagoras told me that he was about to leave Attica for the Propontis. I urged him to alter his resolution. He affirmed that his presence in the house of Pericles had brought a cloud over it, which would only disappear by his absence. "Of late," said he, "I have received so much kindness from the philosophers, that I begin to suspect a change of fortune, by no means in my favor. I must fly while the weather is temperate, as the swallows do."

He mixes not with the people, he converses with none of them, and yet he appears to have penetrated into the deepest and darkest recesses of their souls.

Pericles has lost their favor; Anaxagoras is banished; Aspasia . . but what is Aspasia? Yours; and therefore you must hear about her.

We have all been accused of impiety; Anaxagoras and myself have been brought to trial for the offence. Diopeithes is the name of our accuser. He began with Anaxagoras; and having proved by three witnesses that he in their hearing had declared his opinion, that lightning and thunder were the effect of some combustion and concussion in the clouds, and that they often happened when Jupiter was in perfectly good-humor, not thinking at all about the Athenians, there was instantly such a rage and consternation in the whole assembly, that the judges were called upon from every quarter to condemn them for impiety; sentence, death.

Pericles rose. He for the first time in his life was silenced by the clamorous indignation of the people. All parties, all classes, men, women, children, priests, sailors, tavern-keepers, diviners, slave-merchants, threatened, raved, foamed.

"Pericles! you yourself will soon be cited before this august tribunal," said Diopeithes. The clamor now began to subside. Curiosity, wonder, apprehension of consequences, divided the assembly; and, when Pericles lifted up his arm, the agitation, the murmurs, and the whispers, ceased.

" O men of Athens! " said he, calmly, " I wish it had pleased the gods that the vengeance of Diopeithes had taken its first aim against me, whom you have heard so often, known so long, and trusted so implicitly. But Diopeithes hath skulked from his ambush and seized upon the unsuspecting Anaxagoras, in the hope that, few knowing him, few can love him. The calculation of Diopeithes is correct: they who love him are but those few. They, however, who esteem and reverence him, can only be numbered by him who possesses a register of all the wise and all the virtuous men in Greece."

Anaxagoras stepped forward, saying:

" You, O Athenians! want defenders, and will want them more : I look for protection to no mortal arm ; I look for it to that divine power, the existence of which my accuser tells you I deny."

"He shirks the thunder," said one.

" He sticks to the blind side of Jupiter," said another.

Such were the observations of the pious and malicious, who thought to expiate all their sins by throwing them on his shoulders, and driving him out of the city. He was condemned by a majority of voices. Pericles followed him through the gates, beyond the fury of his persecutors.

CLXII. ASPASIA TO CLEONE.

Three days after the banishment of Anaxagoras, the threat of Diopeithes was carried into effect; not against the person of Pericles, but against your Aspasia. Diopeithes had himself denounced me, on the same count as Anaxagoras; and Hermippos, whose entire life has been (they tell me) one sluggish stream of gross impurities, impeached me as a corruptress of the public morals.

You will imagine, my Cleone, that something loose and lascivious was brought forward in accusation against me. No such thing. Nothing of the kind is considered as having any concern with public morals here in Athens. My crime was, seducing young men from their parents and friends; retaining them in conversation at our house; encouraging them to study the sciences in preference to the machinations of sophists; to leave the declaimers an empty room for the benefit of their voices, and to adhere more closely to logic before they venture upon rhetoric.

You will now perceive, that all who have the most interest and the most exercise in the various artifices of deception, were my enemies. I feared lest Pericles should run further into the danger of losing his popularity by undertaking my defence, and resolved to be my own pleader. The hour had been appointed for opening the trial: I told him it was one hour later. When it was nearly at hand, I went out of the house unobserved, and took my place before the assembly of the people. My words were these:

"If any of the accusations brought against me were well founded, they would have been known to Pericles. It would be strange were he indifferent to any offence of mine against the laws, especially such as you accuse me of, unless he is, as the accusation would imply, insensible to honor, propriety, and decency. Is this his character? He never has had an enemy bold and false enough to say it: I wonder at this; yet he never has."

The people, who had been silent, now began to favor me, when Diopeithes asked me whether I could deny my conversations with Anaxagoras, and my adherence to his tenets.

Love of truth, pity for Anaxagoras, and pride (it may be) in the strength of mind he had given me, and in the rejection of unworthy notions on the gods, urged me to say :

" I deny no conversation I ever had with him, no tenet I ever received, no duty I ever learnt from him. He taught me veneration for the gods ; and I pray them to render me grateful for it."

Pericles at this moment stood at my side. Indignation that he should have followed Anaxagoras out of the gates, and should have embraced him affectionately at parting, turned many furious faces, furious cries, and furious gestures against him. He looked round disdainfully, and said aloud :

" Respect the laws and the unfortunate, you who revere the gods !

" It was not the condemned man I followed out of the city : it was age, which would have sunk under blows ; it was rectitude, which feared not death ; it was friendship, which, if I cannot make you esteem, I will not implore you to pardon.

" At last, O Athenians ! my enemies and yours have persuaded you to assemble in this place, and to witness the humiliation and affliction of one who never failed to succor the unfortunate, and who has been the solace of my existence many years. Am I, of all in Athens, the man who should mistake crimes for virtues ; the man pointed out from among the rest as the most insensible to his dignity ? How widely, then, have you erred in calling me to your counsels ! how long, how wilfully, how pertinaciously ! Is it not easier to believe that two or three are mistaken now, than that you all, together with your fathers and best friends, whose natal days, and days of departure from us, you still keep holy, have been always so ? "

Hermippos and Diopeithes, seeing that many were moved, interrupted him furiously.

" O Pericles ! " cried Hermippos, " we are aware that

this woman of Ionia, this Milesian, this Aspasia, entertains the same opinions as yourself."

"Highly criminal!" answered Pericles, with a smile;
"I hope no other Athenian is cursed with a wife liable
to so grievous an accusation."

"Scoffer!" cried Diopeithes; "dare you deny that in
the summer of this very year, when you was sailing to
lay waste the coasts of the Peloponnese, you attempted to
pervert the religion of the sailors? The sun was suddenly bedimmed; darkness came over the sea, as far
even as unto our city! the pilot fell upon his face and
prayed: and did not you, O Pericles! raise him up with
one hand, and, throwing your mantle over his eyes with
the other, ask whether he found anything dreadful in it?
And when he answered, in his piety, ' It is not *that*,' did
not you reply:

" ' The other darkness is no otherwise different than in
its greater extent, and produced by somewhat larger than
my mantle '?"

"Proceed to interrogate," said Pericles.

"Answer that first, O sacrilegious man!" exclaimed
Diopeithes.

"Athenians!" said Pericles, "many of you here present were with me in the expedition. Do assure Diopeithes that it was not my mantle which darkened the sea
and sun, that to your certain knowledge both sun and sea
were dark before I took it off. So that the gods, if they
were angry at all, were angry earlier in the day. And
not only did the sun shine out again, bright and serene
as ever, but the winds were favorable, the voyage prosperous, the expedition successful.

"It appears to me that the gods are the most angry
when they permit the malicious and the false to prevail
over the generous and simple-hearted; when they permit
the best affections to be violated, and the worst to rise up
in disorder to our ruin. Nor do I believe that they are
very well pleased at hearing their actions and motives
called in question; or at winks and intimations that they
want discernment to find out offenders, and power and
justice to punish them."

"In spite of philosophers," cried Diopeithes, "we still have our gods in Athens!"

"And our men too," replied he, "or these before me must only be the shadows of those who, but lately under my command, won eternal renown in Samos."

Tears rose into his eyes: they were for me; but he said in a low voice, audible, however, in the silence that had succeeded to a loud and almost universal acclamation:

"At least for our lost comrades a few tears are not forbidden us."

The people struck their breasts; the judges unanimously acquitted me, surrounded Pericles, and followed us home with enthusiastical congratulations.

CLXIII. ASPASIA TO CLEONE.

Never did our house receive so many visitors as on my acquittal. Not only our friends and acquaintances, but every one who had fought under Pericles, came forward to offer his felicitations and his services. I was forgotten . . the danger, the insult, seemed his. When they had all retired to dinner, he, too, left me with my music, and I did not see him again until late the next morning. It was evident he had slept but little. He came up to me, and, pressing my hand, said:

"Aspasia, I have gained a great victory; the greatest, the most glorious, and the only one not subject to a reverse."

I thought his words related to his defence of me: I was mistaken.

"It was yesterday, for the first time," said he, "that I knew the extent of my power. I could have demolished the houses of my adversaries; I could have exiled them from the city; I could have been their master: I am more; I am my own.

"Great injuries create great power; no feeble virtues are necessary to its rejection. In polity," continued he, "the humble may rise, but not the fallen. States live

but once. Had I no Aspasia, no children, I am ignorant what support I could have found against the impulses
of ambition. Many who seize upon kingly power are
the more desirous of possessing it, because they have
sons to succeed them. Imprudent men! they expose
those sons to infinite dangers, and create no new advantages for them. If they provided for their security, they
would abdicate their power, when about to be taken away
by death from those over whom they exercised it. If
they provided for their glory, they would not subject
them to the reproach, always merited, of possessing less
activity and sagacity than their father. Do they care
about their wisdom or their virtue? they will not cast
them among idlers and sycophants, nor abandon them on
a solitary island, where many sing and none discourse.
What life is wretcheder? what state more abject?"

"Yours, my dear Pericles!" said I, "is far happier,
but by no means enviable."

"True!" answered he; "I am subject to threats,
curses, denunciations, ostracism, and hemlock; but I
glory in the glory of the state, and I know that I can
maintain it."

I was listening with attention, when he said to me with
an air of playfulness:

"Am I not a boaster? am I not proud of my command? am I not over-fond of it, when I am resolved not
to transmit it hereditarily to another?"

"Rightly judged, dear Pericles!" said I; "you
always act judiciously and kindly."

"Political men, like goats," continued he, " usually
thrive best among inequalities. I have chosen the
meadow; and not, on the whole, imprudently. My life
has been employed in making it more pleasurable, more
even, more productive. The shepherds have often quar-
relled with me; and but now the sheep, too, in their wisdom, turned their heads against me."

We went into the air, and saw Alcibiades walking in
the garden. He, not observing us, strode along rapidly,
striking with his cane every tree in the alley. When we
came up nearer, he was repeating:

"The fanatical knaves! I would knock the heads off all their Mercuries.

"Noisy demagogues! I would lead them into the midst of the enemy . . I would drag them on by the ears . . not fifty should return. *They*, in their audacity, impeach Aspasia! *they* bring tears into the eyes of Pericles! I will bring more into theirs, by holy Jupiter!"

He started at our approach. My husband laid his hands upon the youth's shoulder, and said to him:

"But, Alcibiades! if you do not lead fifty back, where will you leave the captives?"

He sprang to the neck of his guardian, and, turning his face toward me, blushed and whispered:

"Did she, too, hear me?"

CLXIV. ASPASIA TO PERICLES.

I would not disturb you, my beloved Pericles! but let not anything else! Why are you so busy now the danger is over? why do so many come to you, with countenances so earnest when they enter, and so different from composed when they go away? You never break your resolutions, otherwise I should fear they might lead you above the place of fellow-citizen. Then farewell happiness, farewell manliness, security, sincerity, affection, honor.

O Pericles! descend from the car of Victory on the course itself. In abandoning power and station, what do you abandon but inquietude and ingratitude?

CLXV. PERICLES TO ASPASIA.

We never alight from a carriage while it is going down a hill, but always at the top or at the bottom. There is less danger in being shaken out than there is in leaping out.

Were I at this juncture to abdicate my authority, I should appear to the people to confess a fault, and to myself to commit one.

I must defend those who would have defended me.
Rely on my firmness in all things; on Pericles, one,
immutable.

CLXVI. ASPASIA TO CLEONE.

Alcibiades will one time or other bring us all into peril
by his recklessness and precipitation.

When he heard I was arraigned and Pericles threatened, he ran from house to house among the officers of
the army, embraced them, knelt before them, adjured
them to save their general from ignominy, his wife from
insult, the city from mourning, and themselves from in-
activity. He swore that if they would not, he would:
that two thousand of the same age, or rather older, would
join him and obey him, and that he would throw judges,
accusers, applauders, listeners, over the Piræus. Not a
soldier did he pass without a kiss, without a pressure of
the hand, without a promise; not a girl in Athens that
was not his sister, not a matron that was not his mother.

Within an hour, in every part of the city there were
cries :

"The Lacedæmonians have none of these rogues
among them."

"No accusers there; no judges there."

"Archidamos is wise; Pericles is wiser; shall the one
be a king, the other a culprit?"

"Shall his war-horse," cried a soldier, "carry pan-
niers?"

"Fore-foot and hind-foot say I," cried another, "against
these market-place swine, these black-muzzled asses!"

"Out upon them! what have they won for us?" cried
another.

"And what have we not won for them?" roared the
next.

"What was all the stir about?" asked one more
quiet.

"They dared to accuse our general of denying their
dues to the gods. Liars! he gives every man his due."
A laugh arose. "No laughing here! I uphold it, we

soldiers can take as good care of the gods as they can.
Who believes they ever were in danger? Pericles might
have cracked them by the dozen: he has left them all
standing; not a head missing. Save him, comrades,
from the cowards, the poisoners."

On all sides of the city the soldiers ran to their officers,
and then toward the house of Pericles. It was with difficulty he could dissuade them from their resolution to
confer upon him the same authority and station as Archidamos holds among the Spartans.

"We shall then meet the enemy upon equal terms,"
said they; "ay, more than equal; affability for moroseness, liberality for parsimony."

The greater part of the citizens would have followed:
the turbulent for change, the peaceable for tranquillity.

My husband has allayed the tempest: his ambition is
higher. Nothing can be taken from the name of Pericles,
and what is added to it must be of baser metal.

CLXVII. ASPASIA TO CLEONE.

The poet Hermippos will be remembered for the malignity of his accusation against me, when all the poetry
he has ever written, even the worst of it, is forgotten.
At what a price would many men purchase the silence
of futurity! Hermippos will procure it reasonably, excepting two memorable words, *Prosecutor* of *Aspasia*.
Such people show me only the more clearly to the world,
by throwing their torches at me. Pallas hath whispered
in my ear, both dreaming and awake, that distant times
shall recognize me, never perhaps alone, but sometimes
by the side of Pericles, and sometimes on the bosom of
Cleone.

CLXVIII. ASPASIA TO PERICLES.

What but the late outrages, or rather, what but the
ascendancy you have obtained in consequence, could have
brought the aristocratical party to offer you their services,

in helping to keep down the ferocity of the populace? It might indeed be well to unite them, were it possible; but not being possible, I would rather place the more confidence in the less ignorant and turbulent.

CLXIX. PERICLES TO ASPASIA.

Aspasia! as you are cautious not to look earnestly at a handsome man, but rather turn your eyes another way, so must I do in regard to Aristocracy. It is not proper that I should discover any charms in her.

Among the losses I sustained by the flight of youth, I ought to regret my vanity. I had not enough of it for a robe, but I had enough for a vest; enough to keep me warm and comfortable. Not a remnant have I now. Why be ashamed of our worthy party? Did I espouse it for its virtues? Was it ever in high repute for its fidelity? What is it to me whether a couple or two of housed pards bite one another's tails off or not, excepting that they lie down the quieter for it afterward? They have still heads and necks to be led along by. We have only to walk up to them firmly, to look at them steadily, speak to them boldly, lay the hand upon them confidently as their masters, and grasp them with a tenacity that neither relaxes nor hurts. He who does this, and there are some who can do it, may go forth and catch other beasts with them, and feast all his friends in the city.

CLXX. ASPASIA TO PERICLES.

There is irritation in your irony, O Pericles! your spirit is not at rest. Unworthily, for the first time since I knew you, have you thought and spoken! *Thought!* no, Pericles! passion is not thought. Contumely has produced this bitterness; it left you with the words.

CLXXI. PERICLES TO ASPASIA.

Aspasia! you have looked into my heart, and purified it. Your indignities sometimes rise up before me ; and it is only when I am prompted to do wrong by others, that I recover all my firmness. Athens has a right to my solicitude and devotion. I will forget no favor she has ever shown me, and remember no enmity.

CLXXII. ASPASIA TO CLEONE.

Peace is at all times a blessing ; and war, even the most prosperous, a curse. In war extremely few of men's desires are gratified, and those the most hateful ; in peace many, and those the kindliest. Were it possible to limit the duration of hostilities, the most adverse nations, in the enjoyment of a long security, would find time enough for the cultivation of the social affections, and for the interchange of hospitality and other friendly offices. As some bodily diseases, if they can only be deferred for a certain time, terminate altogether, so might the worst of social diseases, war. I do not much wonder that no statesman ever upheld this truth ; but I do greatly that it is to be found among the tenets of no philosopher. We women, who are liable to the worst outrages, and are framed by nature to the greatest susceptibility of fears, usually love war the most, until it enters our houses. We are delighted at the sound and at the spectacle from afar ; and no music is more pleasing to our ears than that which is the prelude to the cries of agony and death. The Spartans are now ravaging all the country round about us. Will they never let me visit their celebrated city? Must I never fancy I am a Helen while I am bathing in the Eurotas or the Tiasa? I am curious to see their Skeias,* and to compare it with our Hecatompedon

---

* " It was of a cirular form, with a roof like an umbrella, and erected about 760 years B. C." — *St. John's Ancient Greece.* The most learned, the most comprehensive, and the most judicious work ever written about the manners, the institutions, and the localities of that country.

13

It would interest me the more, because in this edifice the
lyre of our countryman Timotheus is suspended. It was
forfeited, you know, for his having added four strings.
Woe betide those improvident creatures who add anything
to our delights ! But surely poor Timotheus must have
fallen among the poets.

CLXXIII. ASPASIA TO PERICLES.

When the war is over, as surely it must be in another
year, let us sail among the islands of the Ægæan, and be
young as ever. O that it were permitted us to pass
together the remainder of our lives in privacy and retirement ! This is never to be hoped for in Athens.

I inherit from my mother a small yet beautiful house
in Tenos : I remember it well. Water, clear and cold,
ran before the vestibule ; a sycamore shaded the whole
building. I think Tenos must be nearer to Athens than
to Miletus. Could we not go now for a few days ? How
temperate was the air, how serene the sky, how beautiful
the country ! the people how quiet, how gentle, how
kind-hearted !

Is there any station so happy as an uncontested place
in a small community, where manners are simple, where
wants are few, where respect is the tribute of probity,
and love is the guerdon of beneficence ? O Pericles ! let
us go ; we can return at any time.

CLXXIV. ANAXAGORAS TO ASPASIA.

The gratitude and love I owe to Pericles induces me to
write the very day I have landed at Lampsacos. You
are prudent, Aspasia ! and your prudence is of the best
quality ; instinctive delicacy. But I am older than you,
or than Pericles, although than Pericles by only six years ;
and, having no other pretext to counsel you, will rest
upon this. Do not press him to abstain from public
business ; for, supposing he is by nature no obstinate

man, yet the long possession of authority has accustomed
him to grasp the tighter what is touched; as shell-fish
contract the claws at an atom.   The simile is not an
elegant one, but I offer it as the most apposite.   He
might believe that you fear for him, and that you wish
him to fear; this alone would make him pertinacious.
Let everything take its season with him.   Perhaps it is
necessary that he should control the multitude : if it is,
he will know it; even you could not stir him, and would
only molest him by the attempt.   Age is coming on.
This will not loosen his tenacity of power . . it usually
has quite the contrary effect . . but it will induce him to
give up more of his time to the studies he has always delighted in, which, however, were insufficient for the full
activity of his mind.   Mine is a sluggard; I have surrendered it entirely to philosophy, and it has made little
or no progress; it has dwelt pleased with hardly anything
it has embraced, and has often run back again from foud
prepossessions to startling doubts : it could not help it.

But as we sometimes find one thing while we are looking for another, so, if truth escaped me, happiness and
contentment fell in my way, and have accompanied me
even to Lampsacos.

Be cautious, O Aspasia! of discoursing on philosophy.
Is it not in philosophy as in love? the more we have of
it, and the less we talk about it, the better.   Never touch
upon religion with anybody.   The irreligious are incurable
and insensible; the religious are morbid and irritable;
the former would scorn, the latter would strangle you.
It appears to me to be not only a dangerous, but, what
is worse, an indelicate thing, to place ourselves where
we are likely to see fevers and frenzies, writhings and
distortions, debilities and deformities.   Religion at Athens is like a fountain near Dodona, which extinguishes a
lighted torch, and which gives a flame of its own to an
unlighted one held down to it.   Keep yours in your
chamber; and let the people run about with theirs; but
remember, it is rather apt to catch the skirts.   Believe
me, I am happy : I am not deprived of my friends.   Imagination is little less strong in our later years than in

our earlier. True, it alights on fewer objects, but it rests longer on them, and sees them better. Pericles first, and then you, and then Meton, occupy my thoughts. I am with you still; I study with you, just as before, although nobody talks aloud in the school-room.

This is the pleasantest part of life. Oblivion throws her light coverlet over our infancy; and, soon after we are out of the cradle, we forget how soundly we had been slumbering, and how delightful were our dreams. Toil and pleasure contend for us almost the instant we rise from it; and weariness follows whichever has carried us away. We stop awhile, look around us, wonder to find we have completed the circle of existence, fold our arms, and fall asleep again.

CLXXV. ANAXAGORAS TO ASPASIA.

Proxenos, a native of Massilia, is lately come over to visit his relations and correspondents. The Phocæaus, you know, were the founders of Lampsacos, long before they were driven by the invasion of Cyrus into Italy and Gaul. Like the generality of mercantile men, Proxenos is little attached to any system of philosophy, but appears to hold in some esteem the name and institutions of Pythagoras. Formerly we have conversed together with Pericles on this extraordinary man, regretting that so little is known of him in the midst of his celebrity. Hardly a century hath elapsed since he left his native Samos, and settled on the peaceful shores of Italy. His presence, his precepts, his authority, his example, were unavailing to the preservation of that tranquillity, which the beauty of the climate, the fertility of the soil, and the freedom of the institutions, ought to have established and perpetuated. But it is in the regions of the earth as in the regions of the air; the warm and genial are absorbed by the cold and void, and tempests and storms ensue. The happiness of thousands is the happiness of too many, in the close calculation of some inexpert contriver : and he spoils the honey by smoking the hive. No sooner is a nation at ease, than he who should be the first to participate in the blessing, is the most uneasy; and, when at last he has found a place to his mind, before he lies down he scratches a hole in it, as the dogs do.   Such had been the case at Samos, and such was likewise the case at Croton.   The difference lay merely in this.   Polycrates was a man of abilities, and capable of holding the government in his single hand : he loved power, he loved pleasure, he contented the populace, and he reconciled the wise : Croton was subject to the discretion of an oligarchy, incompetent, arrogant, jealous, and unjust.   It is untrue that Pythagoras was ever at enmity with him, or was treated by him with disrespect.   The one was as fond of authority as the other, and neither was willing to divide it.   Whatever could be done to promote the studies of the philosopher was done spontaneously by the chief magistrate, who gave him letters of recommendation to the king of Egypt.   By these, and perhaps by these only, could he ever have penetrated into the innermost recesses of the priesthood.   Conversing with them, and observing their power over the people, he lost nothing of his inclination to possess the same, and added much to the means of acquiring it.   Epimenides the Cretan was perhaps the exemplar he had resolved to follow, but with mitigated severity.   Solon, with all his wisdom, and never had mortal more, was unable to bring back the Athenians to the simplicity and equity of their forefathers.   Knowing well their propensity to superstition, which always acts with its greatest intensity on the cruel and the loose, he invited Epimenides to come and overawe them by his sanctity and his sacrifices.   We cannot doubt that he left the whole management of their conversion to the discretion of the stranger.   An Epimenides, in all ages of the world, will possess more influence than a Solon.   Lustrations and sacrifices followed prodigies and omens; and among the marvels and miracles which the Cretan seer displayed, the last was the greatest in the eyes of Athens.   He announced his determination to return home, and refused all the honors and riches the people would have lavished on him.   Epi-

menides wanted nothing: the gods were less moderate;
they required a human victim.   Cratinos was too happy
in devoting his blood at the altar; Ctesibias, on the
bosom of his friend.

Proxenos is come in by appointment, and has broken
off an old story which you know as well as I do.   I will
give you his; but not without an account from you in
return, of what is going on among the craft at Athens.

CLXXVI. ASPASIA TO ANAXAGORAS.

Secrecy and mystery drive the uninitiated into suspicion and distrust: an honest man never will propose, and
a prudent man never will comply with, the condition.
What is equitable and proper lies wide open on the plain,
and is accessible to all, without an entrance through lab-
yrinth or defile.   I do not love Pythagoras nor Epimenides, nor indeed my friend Socrates so much as perhaps
I should, who, however, beside his cleverness, has many
good qualities.   He, like Pythagoras, is endowed with
an extraordinary share of intellect; but neither of them
has attained the fixed and measured scope of true philosophy: the one being in perpetual motion to display his
surprising tricks of rhetorical ingenuity, which tend only
to the confusion of truth and falsehood, and consequently
to indifference in the choice of them; the other was no
less active and restless in the acquisition and mainte-
nance of power.   The business of philosophy is to ex-
amine and estimate all those things which come within
the cognizance of the understanding.   Speculations on
any that lie beyond, are only pleasant dreams, leaving
the mind to the lassitude of disappointment.   They are
easier than geometry and dialectics; they are easier than
the efforts of a well-regulated imagination in the structure
of a poem.   These are usually held forth by them as
feathers and thistle-down; yet condescend they nevertheless to employ them; numerals as matter and mind;
harmony as flute and fiddle-strings to the dances of the
stars   In their compositions they adopt the phraseology

and courtesy to the cadences of poetry. Look nearer; and what do you see before you? the limbs of Orpheus, bloodless, broken, swollen, and palpitating on the cold and misty waters of the Hebrus. Such are the rhapsodical scraps in their visionary lucubrations. They would poison Homer, the purest and soundest of moralists, the most ancient and venerable of philosophers, not out of any ill-will to him, but out of love to the human race. There is often an enchantment in their sentences, by which the ear is captivated, and against which the intellectual powers are disinclined to struggle; and there is sometimes, but very rarely, a simplicity of manner, which wins like truth. But when ambition leads them toward the poetical, they fall flat upon thorny ground. No writer of florid prose ever was more than a secondary poet. Poetry, in her high estate, is delighted with exuberant abundance, but imposes on her worshipper a severity of selection. She has not only her days of festival, but also her days of abstinence, and, unless upon some that are set apart, prefers the graces of sedateness to the revelry of enthusiam. She rejects, as inharmonious and barbarous, the mimicry of her voice and manner by obstreperous sophists and argute grammarians, and she scatters to the winds the loose fragments of the schools.

Socrates and his disciples run about the streets, pick up every young person they meet with, carry him away with them, and prove to him that everything he ever heard is false, and everything he ever said is foolish. He must love his father and mother in their way, or not at all. The only questions they ask him are those which they know he cannot answer, and the only doctrines they inculcate are those which it is impossible he should understand. He has now fairly reached sublimity, and looks of wonder are interchanged at his progress. Is it sublime to strain our vision into a fog? and must we fancy we see far because we are looking where nobody can see farther?

CLXXVII. ANAXAGORAS TO ASPASIA.

The Massilian is intelligent and communicative. Some matters which he related at our conference you will perhaps remember in Herodotus : others are his own story ; so let him tell the whole in his own manner.

" The unbroken force of Persia was brought under the walls of Phocæa. Harpagos, equally wise and generous, offered to our citizens the most favorable terms of surrender. They requested one day for deliberation. Aware of their intentions, he dissembled his knowledge, and allowed them to freight their ships, embark, and sail away. His clemency was, however, no security to his garrison. Within a few days the expatriated citizens landed again, slew every Persian within the walls, then, casting a mass of iron into the sea, swore they would never return a second time until it rose and floated on the surface. Some historians would persuade us that, after this cruel vengeance, this voluntary and unanimous oath, the greater part returned. Such a tale is idle and absurd. The Persians would too surely have inflicted due vengeance on their perfidy. Some, however, did indeed separate from the main body of the emigration, and came to reside here in Lampsacos, which their ancestors had founded, and where they continued on the most hospitable terms by frequent intermarriages. The bulk of the expedition reached Alalia, a colony of theirs, led recently into Corsica. Here they continued to reside but a little time unmolested by the jealousy of the Carthaginians and Tyrrhenians. Undaunted by the coalition against them, and by the loss of many ships in a battle with the united fleet of the confederates, they sailed to the neighborhood of the more ancient Grecian cities, and founded Elea, near Poseidonia. And now probably they first became acquainted with the disciples of Pythagoras. He himself, it is said, retired to Metapouton, and died there. When he went from Samos to Croton, he was in the vigor of life ; and not many years elapsed ere he beheld the overthrow of his institutions. He is reported by some to have attained an extreme old age, which his tranquillity and temperance render probable. Even without this supposition, he may, perhaps, have visited the coast of Gaul, before or after the arrival of the Phocæans. Collecting, we may imagine, additional forces from the many Ionians whom the generals of Cyrus had expelled, they began to build the city of Massilia, not long after the settlement at Elea, which the vicinity of powerful states, and its incapacity and insecurity for the mooring of a navy, rendered ineligible as the seat of government, or as a constant station."

Thus much I had collected from Proxenos, when he began to give me information on anchorages and harbors, imports and exports ; I could not in common civility interrupt him, or ask anything better than what it pleased him to bestow on me. As our acquaintance strengthens, I will draw more unreservedly from his stores.

CLXXVIII. ANAXAGORAS TO ASPASIA.

Proxenos runs into some errors both in regard to facts and motives. It is false that Pythagoras, on returning from his voyage in Egypt, was indignant at finding a tyrant in his native city. Polycrates was in possession of the supreme power when the philosopher left the island, and used it with clemency and discretion. The traveller might have gone and might have returned with discontent, but indignation is averse to favors, and these he was by no means reluctant to accept. Finding he could not be the principal man among his fellow-citizens, he résolved to attain that rank where the supremacy was yet unoccupied. He had seen enough of the Egyptian and heard enough of the Indian priesthood, to convince him that, by a system somewhat similar to theirs, absolute power was more attainable and more safe. He took lessons and precautions ; and wherever there was a celebrated and ancient temple, he visited its priests, and explored the origin and conduct of their institutions and authority. In recompense for these, he is reported to have raised his tunic to the holy ones at Olympia, and to have displayed a golden thigh. Nothing so royal, so godlike, had been seen since the reign of Pelops. A golden thigh is worth an ivory shoulder. Such a miracle, we may be sure, was not altogether lost upon the prophetess at Delphi, the fair Themistocleia, who promulgated to him her secrets in return.

His doctrines were kept within his own circle, under the safeguard of an oath. This in all countries is and ought to be forbidden, as being the prerogative of the magistracy. Love of supremacy was the motive in all his injunctions and in all his actions. He avoided the trouble of office and the danger of responsibility ; he excluded the commons, and called to him the nobles, who alone were deemed worthy of serving him. Among these he established an equality, which, together with the regularity and frugality of their living, must have tended to conciliate and gratify in some measure the poorer citizens. Certain kinds of animal food were forbidden, as in India, and other countries less remote, but, contrary to what we have often heard asserted, no species of pulse or vegetable. *" Abstain from the bean "* signified *" abstain from elections to political employments."* The teacher was in the place of parent to his disciples, who appear to have renounced all the natural affections that had sprung up before they entered the society. His regimen was mild and generous : its principal merit was, however, the repression of loquacity, — common in the ardor of youth after its chase in the fields of knowledge ; commoner, and more unbecoming, in the morose repose of an arrogant philosophy. The history of Pythagoras, forasmuch as he interests us in being the leader of a sect and of a party, is neither long nor obscure. The commons of Croton soon began to perceive that, under his management, the sons of the aristocracy would be no better inclined than their fathers had been to concede them an equal share in the government ; and the rulers themselves, day after day, lost somewhat of authority in their families. During the whole time that he had resided in Italy, the people of nearly all the Greek cities heaved indignantly under oppressive oligarchies.   Sybaris, whose health they were absorbing in more than Circæan luxuries, rose first upon her feet, and expelled the council of five hundred.   They retired for refuge to the lords of Croton ; and, when the Sybarites called for justice on them, the demand was voted an affront.   And now, indeed, the veil of sanctity and se-clusion was violently rent by the disciples of the Samian. He incited them to maintain peace and good government ; pointed out to them the phantom of Freedom, how it blasted every region it passed over ; and adjured them to the defence of their rulers by the purity of their religion. They marched, fought a battle, won it, and Sybaris was swept from the earth.

Discord, I suspect, O Aspasia ! is the readiest of all the deities to appear at our invocation.   The oligarchs of Croton, long accustomed to uncontrolled power and irresponsible injustice, refused to the army, now compre-hending all the active citizens, even the smallest portion of the spoils.   Again did the Crotoniats cry to arms ; and again, and in a better cause, were conquerors.   Pyth-agoras * and his disciples fled before them, and the hall in which they assembled was reduced to ashes.

It is only a free city that is strong ; for it is only in a free city that the mass of the people can be armed.

CLXXIX. ASPASIA TO ANAXAGORAS.

Men of powerful minds, although they never give up Philosophy, yet cease by degrees to make their professions in form, and lay ultimately the presents they have received from her at the feet of History.   Thus did Herodotus, thus did Hecatæus, and thus, let me hope, will Anax-agoras.   The deeds of past ages are signally reflected on the advancing clouds of the future : here insurrections and wrecks and conflagrations ; here the ascending, there the drooping diadem ; the mighty host, the mightier man before it ; and, in the serener line on the horizon, the

* Pythagoras was a Præ-jesuit.

emersion of cities and citadels over far-off seas. There are those who know in what quarter to look for them; but it is rarely to their hands the power of promoting the good, or averting the evil, is intrusted. Yet, O Anax-agoras! all is not hideous in the past, all is not gloomy in the future. There are communities where the best and wisest are not utterly cast aside, and where the robe of Philosophy is no impediment to the steps of men. Idly do our sages cry out against the poets for mistuning the heart and misgoverning the intellect. Meanwhile they themselves are occupied in selfish vanities on the side of the affections; and, on the side of the understanding, in fruitless, frivolous, indefinite, interminable disquisitions. If our thoughts are to be reduced to powder, I would rather it were for an ingredient in a love-potion, to soften with sympathies the human heart, than a charm for raising up spectres to contract and to coerce it. If dust is to be thrown into our eyes, let it be dust from under a bright enlivening sun, and not the effect of frost and wind

CLXXX. ANAXAGORAS TO ASPASIA.

Philosophy is but dry bread: men will not live upon it, however wholesome; they require the succulent food and exciting cup of Religion. We differ in bodily strength, in compactness of bone, and elasticity of sinew; but we all are subject to the same softness, and nearly to the same distemperature, in the nobler animators of the frame, the brain and blood. Thus it is in creeds: the sage and sim-ple, the ardent enthusiast and the patient investigator, fall into and embrace with equal pertinacity the most absurd and revolting tenets. There are as many wise men who have venerated the ibis and cat, as there are who have bent their heads before Zeus and Pallas. No extrav-agance in devotion but is defended by some other tower-ing above it; no falsehood but whose features are composed to the semblance of truth. By some people those things are adored that eat them; by others, those

that they eat.   Men must rest here ; superstition, satiated
and gorged, can go no farther.

The progression of souls is not unreasonable, the
transmigration is.   That we shall pass hereafter into
many states of successive existence is credible enough ;
but not upon earth, not with earthly passions.   Yet
Pythagoras was so resolute and so unguarded, that he
asserted to himself a series of lives here among men, by
the peculiar and especial favor of the gods, with a perfect consciousness of every change he had undergone.
Others became dogs, wolves, bears, or, peradventure,
men again ; but knowing as little of what had happened.
Nevertheless, he pretended that these transmigrations
were punishments and rewards.   Which is punished? the
dead creature or the living? the criminal man or the
guiltless animal?   Some believe they can throw their sins
into a fox ; others (in Africa for instance) into a priest.
Now the priest may have received what he esteems an
equivalent ; the fox is at once a creditor and a debtor,
with little hope, on either side, of indemnity or balance.
It is only when you or Pericles were my audience, that I
ever was inclined to press hard against the inconsistencies
of philosophers.   But we must trace things to their origin
where we can.   The greater part of those now prevalent
are ascribable to the school of Samos.   Numerals were
considered by the teacher as materials, and not only as
the components, but as the elements, of the world.   He
misunderstood his own theory : the reason is, he made it
his own by theft.   The young persons who are hearers
of the warier Socrates, catch at it in the playground, and
the ill-compacted cake crumbles under their hands.

Unfavorable as my evidence must appear, and is, I am
fortunate in being able to lay before you another and
comelier representation of a philosopher so enriched by
genius.   1 have always, in all companies, and upon all
occasions, been sparing of my questions, and have exerted
the uttermost ingenuity I am master of, in drawing the
truth on, without such an instrument of torture.   Probably I have lost by age a part of my dexterity, or presence

of mind, or determination ; for Proxenos, at the close of
our conference, said aloud and sharply :

"You shall never make *that* out. I think him a very
honest man ; and I think nobody an honest man who
thinks otherwise."

" Fair Proxenos !" I replied, "you are now greatly
more than a philosopher. Some favorite god alone could
have inspired all this enthusiam. In the vigorous expression of that terse apothegm is there not somewhat
more of the poet than of the Pythagorean ?"

" I believe there may be," replied he, " I was always
much given to poetry."

He grew instantly calm upon my compliment, and said,
with the most polite complacency :

" Well ! I am not a match for you Half-Athenians ;
but read this little volume by my friend Psyllos of Metapouton ; it will open your eyes, I warrant it."

" Blessings upon it, then !" said I, bending over and
taking it with due reverence ; " many of late have done
quite the contrary."

CLXXXI. PSYLLOS TO PISANDER OF ELEA,

On the Lawgiver of the Gauls, forwarded to CLEONE.

"Pisander ! when last we met, I promised you I would
make farther inquiries into the subject of our conversation at the house of Euryalos, and that I doubted not of
success in attempting to prove the identity of Pythagoras
and Samotes. Strange, that the idea should have occurred to no one else in the course of many generations.
Was it not sufficiently clear for the follower of truth? or
was it not sufficiently dark and intricate for the lover of
mystery and paradox? I imagine it stood between both,
at an equal distance from the road of each, and thus it
was passed unnoticed.

" There is nobody then who can explain to me what was
the religion of the Gauls at the time of the Phocæan emigration. Samotes is recorded as their legislator. Leg-

islation here includes, as it necessarily must in ages of barbarism, not only the civil institutions of the people, but likewise the religious. Yet neither the character nor the tenets, neither the period nor the country, nor indeed the existence of Samotes, have ever been ascertained. Ask the people who he was, and they will tell you that he came to them *over the sea*, long ago. Computation of time, past and future, never occupies, never occurs to, the barbarian. It was long ago that the old tree, against which his cabin leans, sprang up; long ago since the cabin was built; long ago since he was a child. Whatever is not visible to him, or was not, has feeble hold on his memory, and never enters into his calculation. As lawgiver of the Gauls, Samotes is acknowledged to have instructed them both in the ceremony of human oblations and in the creed of the metempsychosis; for these are mentioned together in the first opening of their history. But it appears to me that the metempsychosis, which is generally held as the basis of druidism, is adventitious. We shall find that this institution is composed of two extremely different and obstinately discordant parts. One, the result of ferocity, varies but little from what exists in the early state of most nations; which diversity may be accounted for, from their climate, their wants, their habits, and pursuits. The other is ingrafted on its savage stock, by the steady but not sufficiently impressive hand of a gentle and provident philosophy. You ask me when? by whom? One word will solve both questions: by Samotes; by the man of Samos. Do you doubt that he ever was in Gaul? And do you think it probable that, with his fondness for travelling, his alacrity in inquiry, he would have resided many years in Italy, and have never once visited a country so near to him, a country so singular in its customs, at least in the combination of them, *if such customs then existed,* a country on whose shores the most valiant of his own countrymen were landing? If at this early epoch the tribes of Gaul believed in the metempsychosis, would not sympathy, would not admiration, have impelled him thither? But if, on the contrary, the doctrine did not prevail, who introduced it? what author of greater weight? I am curious to learn his name or his country. Perhaps by knowing the one, we may guess the other, since the ideas he impressed and left behind him are stamped with a peculiar mark. It may be argued that, able to inculcate lastingly on the mind of his Gallic proselytes a dogma which seems to have been received but partially, and to have soon disappeared, where he lived in the full exercise of authority, he still was unable to abolish, as he would wish to do, their sanguinary rites. He was: for it is easier to learn than to unlearn what incessantly works and excites and agitates our passions. The advantages of the metempsychosis were perhaps the most striking of any that could be presented to warlike minds; to which minds, you must have remarked, O Pisander, advantages will present themselves more readily than disadvantages. Beside, the Druids, whom we cannot well consider at any time a very enlightened order, or likely to see every consequence, every contingency, had no direct interest in suppressing such a doctrine. New colonies were endeavoring to establish themselves in their country; and colonies are the unfailing seed of wars. For, if they flourish, they require an accession of territory; if they do not flourish, they either turn into vagabonds and robbers, or employ violence to remove the obstacles that impede their industry. Something great, then, and something new was wanting, since the danger that impended was both new and great. Immolations before them on one side, and the sublime view of the metempsychosis on the other, what could either shake the confidence or abate the courage of the Gauls? A new body was new armor, beautiful, strong, in which they would elude the rage and laugh at the impotence of War. It was delightful to try other scenes of existence, to extinguish their burning wounds in the blood of their enemies, and to mount from the shields of their comrades into fresh life and glory.

"A religion thus compounded is absurd and contradic-

tory, but contradiction and absurdity in religion are not
peculiar to barbarians.   The sacrifice of a human victim
was deemed the most solemn and important duty, and
they would rather abandon any other ceremony than
this.   They were savage ; we are civilized ; they fought,
and their adversaries were to share their immortality ;
we fight to make others as abject as ourselves.   They
had leaders of proud spirit who raised them to the
heavens ; we have heavy oligarchs who bend us to the
earth.

" Rituals, in even the less ardent and intractable, are
not soon, nor easily, nor all at once, resigned.   We must
cease, then, to marvel that the most impressive, the most
awful, and perhaps the most universal of devotions, human sacrifice, should not have been overthrown by the
declining years of Pythagoras.   It is true he retained his
faculties to the last ; he retained also the energy of his
mind ; but the voluntary exile of Samos was purely a
lawgiver in philosophy.   His religion was not intolerant
nor intrusive, but mainly adapted to the humbler offices
of temperance and peace.   Beyond this, little is known,
and much is feigned of him.   It would have been well if
historians had related to us more of what he did, and
less of what he did not.   If, instead of the story of his
dying in a bean-field, through horror of its impurity, they
had carefully traced and pointed out his travels, they
would neither have mentioned his voyage to India* nor
have omitted his voyage to Gaul.   The priests on
the Nile were at all times well acquainted with their
brethren on the Indus and Ganges ; and indeed I believe
that all the great temples of the world have secret com-
munications.   Do not lift up your hands, my good Pisander ! not underground, not magical, but opened from
time to time, in cases of difficulty and danger, through
confidential agents.†

---

* If Pythagoras had visited India, the learned men who accompanied Alexander would have inquired after him, and would
have given the result.

† The use of gunpowder, for instance, if not of guns, was
known to the priests in countries the most distant and of the

14

"All religions in which there is no craft nor cruelty, are pleasing to the immortal gods; because all acknowledge their power, invoke their presence, exhibit our dependence, and exhort our gratitude.   Therefore, let us never be remiss in our duty of veneration to those holy men, who not only manifest their good-will toward such as think and worship with them, but also toward the stranger at the steps of other altars.   While orators, and poets, and philosophers too, are riotous and quarrelsome, malicious and vindictive, Religion leads to herself, and calls her own, the priests of all persuasions, who extend their hands one to another from a distance, unrestricted by jealousy and undefiled by blood.

"How great, O my friend, is our consolation in the certainty that our prayers and sacrifices are accepted! so long as the priests in our country and around us live fraternally, let us likewise be of the household.   But if any devastating religion should spring up, any which rouses strife and spreads distrust, any which sunders man from man, *that* religion must be rejected by the gods as wicked, and renounced by their worshippers as ineffectual.   The claimants of such an imposition shall never have from me white flour or salt.   Should you question why the milder creed had little effect in Gaul,— why the golden rules are not valued by the people as the precious relics of a departed master.— I reply, that in such a state of society it was impossible to bring them bodily into use.   The priests alone (and it is not every priest who will readily sit down to be instructed) could profit by his knowledge of geometry, or would apply to practice or speculation his theory of numbers.   A few of them are not utterly ignorant of either; and it is hence that the trickling may be traced.   Men living in a state of barbarism and warfare would entertain but small respect for injunctions to abstain from any obvious and palatable food.   Silence, forbearance, quietude, it cannot be ex-

most different religions.   The army of the Macedonians was smitten by its lightnings under the walls of the Oxydracians; the Gauls, and afterward the Persians, under the temple of Delphi.

pected should be the inmates of a camp. Soldiers without regular supplies (in which consists the main difficulty and on which depend the main advantages in the science of war) must subsist on whatever they can seize; and men without regular government (by which I can intend no other than of magistrates chosen by the people) would, if we consider the bean as employed in ballot, be ignorant of the lax and foreign interpretation.

"As the fountains of the most celebrated rivers are neither easily discoverable nor large, so it often happens that things of the greatest moment, in the political and moral world, are derived from an obscure, from a remote, and from a slender origin. I have given you my opinion on the cause of the supposition ; but, having heard another, however less probable, I will report it.*

"In the south of Italy, where Pythagoras resided, are several cities, Tarentum in particular, of Lacedæmonian foundation. One festival of this people, whose ancestors were distinguished for frugality, was, nevertheless, even in the midst of primitive Lacedæmon, even in the bosom of Temperance herself, deformed with foul excess. It was called *The Feast of the Nurses.* They carried male infants to the Temple of Diana, and, after exposing themselves among the tents where the populace was assembled, fed them with the entrails of swine, which had been sacrificed, and with figs, vetches, and *beans.* Their morals, we may believe, were not rendered more austere by the fertility and invitations of a delicious climate. At a distance from Taygetos and Cithæron, they were (allow me the expression) beyond the latitudes of checking breezes from the headlands of bluff morality ; and the voice of the Syrens sounded in ears sealed only to the call of reprehension and reproof. The hunter of Laconia would have smiled to hear them imitate his shout, and tell the trembling Sybarite, their neighbor, that such were the shouts of Spartans. He would have wondered that terror should be excited in another by that which excited

---

Query, whether any author now extant, excepting Psyllos, in his epistle, mentions this.

only ridicule in himself; he would have stared not a little at the start from the couch, and the rustle of roses on the marble floor.

"Pythagoras could not say, Abstain from the city, abstain from the fellowship of the Tarentines; it would have exasperated them against him; but he might have heard related to him some instance of sensuality which happened at this festival, and might have said briefly, yet significantly, Abstain from beans. Ordinances have often been observed and commemorated far beyond the intent and expectation of their founder. Certain it is that, formerly as at present, in the popular states of Italy, the election and rejection of magistrates were signified by beans; and no less evidently was it the interest of the philosophical stranger to dissuade his auditors from the concerns of state. This, while it procured toleration and conciliated esteem, introduced them to such habitudes of close reflection, as withheld them from being the agitators, and fitted them to become, by just degrees, the leaders of the commonwealth. After all, if they pursued any other line of conduct, *he* at least would escape uncensured, and might complete without juridical, or, what he would more have deprecated, popular molestation, his scheme of general reform.

" 'Abstain from beans' we have considered in a moral and political, but also in a religious point; it may easily be defended, by high authorities. However, I must express my doubts whether in the lifetime of Pythagoras his followers abstained from this article of food. Is it not probable that those who came after him took the letter for the spirit, as we know it to have happened in some other doctrines, and within a century from the founder's death? To abstain with rigor from things indifferent (and from some indeed they did abstain), may not appear consistent with the exercise of reason. Arrogant it may be thought in him who commanded, and infantine in those who obeyed. But, in the religions which have continued the longest, certain foods (it is said) are prohibited; and the observance of such prohibition is the moral cause of their duration. He who will not obey in what is easy

will not obey in what is difficult ; but the subjects of these
theocratical governments are every day refreshed with
the exercise of salutary compliance. At the moment
when a sense of duty is liable to be extinguished in others,
in them it is sure to be excited : there is piety if they
fast ; if they satisfy their hunger there is piety. It appears to me, that the wisest and most provident of ori-
ental legislators are in nothing more worthy of our esteem
and veneration, than in the ordinance of these prohibi-
tions. Can we ascertain what nations have, or what
nations have not, been cannibals? Why does it revolt
more strongly against our senses to eat a man than to kill
one? The crime in itself is surely not so great. Nature
has fixed certain barriers, of which many seem fancifully
chosen and arranged, against the irruption of our appetites. There are animals never brought upon our tables,
although the flesh is said to be wholesome and the flavor
grateful. It is needless to seek how first it happened
that man violated the semblance of himself and of his
gods. Was it war, was it fanaticism, or was it famine,
that impelled him to the accursed sacrifice? Pisander !
Pisander ! he had tasted the fatness of the lamb that he
carried in his bosom ; he had tempted the fawn by ca-
resses from afar ; it had licked his hand, and he had shed
its blood !

" Cannibals have been found where food was plentiful ;
and the savage does not loathe for its ugliness the hugest
serpent. There must be something, and it must be in
the brute creation, which he shall fear to consume for
the impiety of the deed.

" The sacrifice of a human victim can only be performed
with the concurrence of prince or magistracy. Of course
Pythagoras could not oppose it, consistently with his
profession of abstaining from their concerns. Nevertheless he was at liberty to introduce a doctrine which, as
the day of cultivation advanced, would undermine the
pyre and release the victim. The Druids were, and are,
and always will be, barbarous. Their order has not existed long, and will soon terminate, the Gauls being not
only the most ferocious of mankind, but the most suspi-

cious and acute; they are also the most versatile, the most inconstant, and (what makes sad work with solemnities), on the detection of halt or blemish, men of irrepressible mimicry and unquenchable derision. Those in the vicinity of Massilia are free already from the furies of fanaticism. Intercourse with the Tyrrheuians and Ligurians has humanized them greatly, and the softer voice of Ionia has now persuaded them, that the gods can take us when they want us, without wicker-baskets; and that the harp and dance are as pleasant to them as the cries and agonies of dying men."

Thus ends the epistle of Psyllos; and at least in the end of it I think we shall agree. His comfits will sweeten my pomegranate.

CLXXXII. ASPASIA TO ANAXAGORAS.

Whatever may be the partiality of your Massilian to Pythagoras, it is evident enough that the philosopher of Samos, possessing great acquired intelligence, and gifted with extraordinary powers of mind, was an intriguer and an impostor. And truly, O Anaxagoras, it is much to be desired that others now living were exempt from a certain part of such an imputation. Our friend Socrates, I am sorry to say, intimates to his friends in private that he has a kind of Genius always at his ear, who forewarns him in affairs apparently the most indifferent. If we consider it well, we shall be of opinion that there are few things so indifferent as they seem to us; few, the consequence of which may not, visibly or invisibly, act with grave importance on the future. But if a Genius, a superhuman power, were to influence the actions of any man, surely it would be those which must necessarily put in motion the levers and regulators of a commonwealth. We are all under the guidance of a deity if we will let him act on us; but it is as easy to slip from under his guidance, as it is difficult to escape from the penalties of our error. Already there are some who are jealous of Socrates and his Genius; and who perhaps may try hereafter whether the Genius will help him to elude the laws. For novelties in religion, as you know, are not held guiltless ; and a Genius that renders a man wiser or better is indeed an innovator. As they cannot catch him, I fear they may lay their hands upon our Socrates.

CLXXXIII. ANAXAGORAS TO PERICLES.

It is easier to answer the questions than the kindnesses of your letter. I will begin, then.

We have not two factions ; aristocracy has kept aloof from Lampsacos. The people find themselves so secure and comfortable under the ancient laws, that they would no more hazard any innovation, than they would alter their course at sea when they were sailing with a favorable wind. They hardly can be brought to believe that any nation hath abrogated two laws in twenty or thirty years, or hath been obliged by prosperity or adversity to enact so many in so brief a space of time. Miletus was always just to her colonies. She has founded more than sixty ; and not a single one has ever had reason to complain of her exactions or restrictions. All the great empires that have existed in the world, Chaldæa, Babylonia, Media, Persia, all these taken together, have not sent out the hundredth part of what has gone forth from the bosom of Miletus. Surely, of political glory this is the highest : to rear carefully a numerous family, educate it honestly, protect it bravely, and provide for it plenteously and independently. Her citizens have more reason to be proud of this section in their polity, than some others who are much powerfuller. Would not every mother wish to see her own features in her daughter? her own constitutional strength, her own character, her own prosperity? What inconsistency then, what folly, what madness, for the metropolis to wish otherwise in regard to her colony! Is the right arm stronger by rendering the left weaker? Gain we any vantage-ground against our enemy by standing on the prostrate body of our child?

To whom am I writing? to Pericles? yes, to him; to
the man who best knows that the strongest reasons of
state proceed from the mouth of Justice.

And now let me loose again. Seldom have I written,
and never have I spoken, so long at a time on such a
subject. Could you ever draw from me even an opinion
on these matters, in a city where (excepting myself) you
alone preserved in them your calmness, equanimity, and
composure? Even Aspasia, who unites the wisdom of
the heart to the wisdom of the understanding, and has
more in both than any one else in either, was sometimes
in perturbation at politics, and sometimes in grief.

A while since I sent her a dozen or more of such
verses as our young people, and others who should know
better, are idle enough to compose in the open air. My
neighbor, Proxenos the Massilian, has been employed
in making a collection from the gardens round about.
The greater part, he tells me, are upon love and flowers,
dews and suns, stars and moons, evenings and mornings,
springs and autumns. He observes that summer is
rather out of favor with the poets; and that where
winter is mentioned, he has often found the whole composition scored across with a nail, or with a piece of tile,
or defaced in some other way as nigh at hand. Proxenos
is no poet, and therefore it is the more amusing to hear
him discourse on poetry.

"I am sated with flowers," said he. "The Muses
ought to keep out of the market; if they must come into
it, let them not come as green-grocers. See, what a large
proportion in my collection is upon flowers and foliage,
with here and there a solitary turtle-dove, and a nightingale deplorably belimed. A few pious men, indeed, have
written in reverence of the tutelary god, and have done
all they could to repress the licentiousness of the young
and thoughtless. The best inscription I have found
among them is in the garden of Mnestheus; and this, perhaps, is worth preservation rather for its grave admonition
and religious sentiment, than its poetry."

So far Proxenos. I do not remember what were those

verses I sent to Aspasia; there may be more good sense
in these:

INSCRIPTION ON A PLINTH IN THE GARDEN OF MNESTHEMUS AT LAMPSACOS.

Youngsters! who write false names, and slink behind
The honest garden-god to hide yourselves,
Take heed unto your ways! the worshipful
Requires from all upright straightforwardness.
Away, away then subterfuge with him!
I would not chide severely; nor would he,
Unless ye thwart him; for alike we know
Ye are not childisher than elder folk,
Who piously (in doing ill) believe
That every god sees every man . . but one.

CLXXXIV. ASPASIA TO ANAXAGORAS.

The style of your Psyllos is, I presume, Massiliau.
He walks heavily through high-stemmed leafy flowers.
Does he not deserve now this little piece of imitation?

Forbear to call it mockery; for mockery is always rude
and inhumane.

Our friend Socrates has taken a wife. In every danger
he has been thought singularly brave; and, if she is what
she is represented, the action proves it. He retains his
custom of sitting in the porticos, and beckoning to pass-
ers, and conversing on loveliness, and commending equanimity, and driving the school-men mad. Yet among the
Epithalamions, the cleverest is one which celebrates him
for the quality most remote from his character. Thales
and Pherecydes and Pythagoras, and some few more,
would really have made Philosophy domestic. Our epitha-
lamiast, intending nothing satirical, tells Socrates (whom
neither celibacy nor marriage have detained at home, and
who never could resist an opportunity of wrangling, while
a sophist or a straw was before him) that he first brought
Philosophy from heaven into private houses! I hope he
will find her in his own as often as he wants her; but if
he is resolved to bring her down into ours, such as we

have seen her lately, the city will be all in a bustle with
the double-bolting of doors.

Let the archons look to it.

CLXXXV. ASPASIA TO CLEONE.

I have been exhorting Pericles to leave Attica for a
while, and to enjoy with me the pleasures of retirement
in the little isle of Tenos. He listened to my entreaty
with his usual attention and interest, and soon began to
expatiate on the charms, on the benefits, on the necessity,
of retirement. Without a question I fancied I had persuaded him to compliance, when, with an air of sadness
so attempered with sweetness as it never was in any other
man, he said to me : " Aspasia ! you can create in me as
many wishes as spring up in the bosom of a child : and it
is partly by planting the slips of your own in mine, and
partly by the warmth of your eloquence. What then
must be my sense of duty to my country, if, after all
these representations, and after all my fatigues and injuries, my determination is fixed to remain some time longer
in the city. Hereafter we may visit Tenos ; hereafter I
may drink of the limpid brook, before the house, whose
cold water has reddened this hand when you were little.
We will build our navies on it ; we will follow them along
the bank, and applaud them as they clash. Even I foresee
a perfidy in Aspasia ; she will pretend to run as fast as
she can, and yet let Pericles outrun her. No, no ; that
kiss shall not obviate such duplicity. Have I no reason
for the suspicion, when you often have let me get the better of you in argument? Another and easier life may
await us there, when this political one is uncoiled from
us. But our child must associate with the children of the
Athenians ; he must love his father's friends ; he must
overcome and pardon his father's adversaries. We ought
never to buy happiness with our children's fortunes ; but
happiness is not the commodity ; it is desertion, it is eva-
sion, it is sloth. However, there is at last a time when
we may hang up our armor, and claim the stipend of re-

tirement and repose. Meanwhile let us fix our eyes on Tenos."

Whether, O Cleone, we regard the moral or the material world, there is a silent serenity in the highest elevation. Pericles appears the greater when seen on his solitary eminence against the sky. Power has rendered him only more gracious and compliant, more calm and taciturn.

CLXXXVI. ANAXAGORAS TO ASPASIA.

Pericles tells me that you are less tranquil than you were formerly, and that he apprehends you are affected not a little by the calumnies of your enemies.

If it is true that there can be no calumny without malice, it is equally so that there can be no malice without some desirable quality to excite it. Make up your mind, Aspasia, to pay the double rate of rank and genius. It is much to be the wife of Pericles; it is more to be Aspasia. Names that lie upon the ground are not easily set on fire by the torch of Envy, but those quickly catch it which are raised up by fame, or wave to the breeze of prosperity. Every one that passes is ready to give them a shake and a rip; for there are few either so busy or so idle as not to lend a hand at undoing.

You, Pericles, and myself, have a world of our own, into which no Athenian can enter without our permission. Study, philosophize, write poetry. These things I know are difficult when there is a noise in the brain; but begin, and the noise ceases. The mind, slow in its ascent at first, accelerates every moment, and is soon above the hearing of frogs and the sight of brambles.

CLXXXVII. ASPASIA TO CLEONE.

A pestilence has broken out in the city, so virulent in its character, so rapid in its progress, so intractable to medicine, that Pericles, in despite of my remonstrances and prayers, insisted on my departure. He told me that,

if I delayed it a single day, his influence might be insufficient to obtain me a reception in any town, or any ham-
let, throughout the whole of Greece. He has promised
to write to me daily, but he declared he could not assure
me that his letters would come regularly, although he pur-
poses to send them secretly by the shepherds, fumigated
and dipped in oil before they depart from Athens. He
has several farms in Thessaly, under Mount Ossa, near
Sicurion. Here I am, a few stadions from the walls.
Never did I breathe so pure an air, so refreshing in the
midst of summer. And the lips of my little Pericles are
ruddier and softer and sweeter than before. Nothing is
wanting, but that he were less like me and more like his
father. He would have all my thoughts to himself, were
Pericles not absent.

CLXXXVIII. CLEONE TO ASPASIA

Aspasia! I will not allow either the little Pericles, or the
great one, or both together, to possess all your thoughts.
Nay, your letter itself contradicts you. Cleone and the
plague must intercept and divide them occasionally.

Pestilences are maladies that rage with more violence
than others, but, like all violent things, soon pass away.
The worst effects of them are the seditions, and other sad
irregularities, that always burst forth when the banner of
Death is unfurled in a populous city. But it is mostly the
intemperate that are swept away.

Alas! I must not dissemble the magnitude of the danger; for I know your resolution, I might say rashness.
What I have written is true; but I am most afraid that
you will not fear enough. Keep up your courage where
you are; do not exert it anywhere else.

CLXXXIX. ASPASIA TO CLEONE.

Cleone! Cleone! if you could but see Athens, you
would find it a ditch to throw all your dogmas into. The

pestilence has not only seized the intemperate, but, like that which Chryses imprecated on the Greeks before Troy, smitten nobler heads after the viler.   Pericles himself has not escaped it.   He refused to abstain from appearing in the assemblies of the people, and among the consultations to regulate (as far as might be) the burial and burning of the dead.   His temperance and courage, the most efficacious preservatives against contagion, failed at length in the effect.   The fever seized him, and although he has risen from his bed free from all symptoms of the distemper, his strength is impaired, and many years (he tells me) seem to have crowded into a few days.

CXC. ANAXAGORAS TO ASPASIA.

Behold, O Aspasia ! I send you verses.   They certainly are less valuable than some in your collection, but, to make up the difference, I enclose a cockle-shell :

> Beauty ! thou art a wanderer on the earth,
>   And hast no temple in the fairest isle
> Or city over-sea, where Wealth and Mirth
>   And all the Graces, all the Muses, smile.
>
> Yet these have always nurst thee, with such fond,
>   Such lasting love, that they have followed up
> Thy steps thro' every land, and placed beyond
>   The reach of thirsty Time thy nectar-cup.
>
> Thou art a wanderer, Beauty ! like the rays
>   That now upon the platan, now upon
> The sleepy lake, glance quick or idly gaze,
>   And now are manifold and now are none.
>
> I have call'd, panting, after thee, and thou
>   Hast turn'd and look'd and said some pretty word,
> Parting the hair, perhaps, upon my brow,
>   And telling me none ever was preferr'd.
>
> In more than one bright form hast thou appear'd,
>   In more than one sweet dialect hast spoken :
> Beauty ! thy spells the heart within me heard,
>   Griev'd that they bound it, grieves that they are broken.

All the verbiage which you will find below I found rudely scrawled on a stone-table, in the garden of my next neighbor Parmenio. I perceive it to be of little worth by this; it has found an imitator, or rather a correspondent; yet, as he writes angrily, it may not be much amiss.

These are scratched under the preceding :

> I have some merit too, old man!
> And show me greater if you can.
> I always took what Beauty gave,
> Nor, when she snatch'd it back, look'd grave.
> Us modest youths it most beseems
> To drink from out the running streams :
> Love on their banks delights to dwell . .
> The bucket of the household well
> He never tugs at, thinking fit
> Only to quench his torch in it.
> Shameless old fellow! do you boast
> Of conquests upon every coast?
> I, O ye gods! should be content
> (Yea, after all the sighs I've spent,
> The sighs, and, what is yet more hard,
> The minas, talents, gone in nard!)
> With only one : I would confine
> Meekly this home-sick heart of mine
> 'Twixt Lampsacos and Hammon's shrine.

CXCI. ASPASIA TO ANAXAGORAS.

It is really odd enough that no temple or altar was ever dedicated to Beauty. Vengeance and other such person ages, whom *we*, Anaxagoras, venture occasionally to call allegorical, have altars enow, and more than enow of worshippers.

Whatever, in your satirical mood, you may think about the cockle-shell, I shall always value it, as much nearly as the verses, and I have ordered it to be made into a clasp for them. Taunt me, then, as often as you please : it will be like girls pelting with roses; if there is any harm done, it is only to the fingers of the pelter.

CXCII. ASPASIA TO PERICLES.

Now the fever is raging, and we are separated, my comfort and delight is in our little Pericles. The letters you send me come less frequently, but I know you write whenever your duties will allow you, and whenever men are found courageous enough to take charge of them. Although you preserved with little care the speeches you delivered formerly, yet you promised me a copy of the latter, and as many of the earlier as you could collect among your friends. Let me have them as soon as possible. Whatever bears the traces of your hand is precious to me : how greatly more precious what is imprest with your genius, what you have meditated and spoken ! I shall see your calm thoughtful face while I am reading, and will be cautious not to read aloud lest I lose the illusion of your voice.

CXCIII. PERICLES TO ASPASIA.

Aspasia ! do you know what you have asked of me ? Would you accept it, if you thought it might make you love me less ? Must your affections be thus loosened from me, that the separation, which the pestilence may render an eternal one, may be somewhat mitigated ? I send you the papers. The value will be small to you, and indeed would be small to others, were it possible that they could fall into any hands but yours. Remember the situation in which my birth and breeding and bent of mind have placed me ; remember the powerful rivals I have had to contend with, their celebrity, their popularity, their genius, and their perseverance. You know how often I have regretted the necessity of obtaining the banishment of Cimon, a man more similar to myself than any other. I doubt whether he had quite the same management of his thoughts and words, but he was adorned with every grace, every virtue. and invested by Nature with every high function of the soul. We happened to be placed by our fellow-citizens at the head of two adverse factions. Son of the greatest man in our annals, he was courted and promoted by the aristocracy; I, of a family no less distinguished, was opposed to him by the body of the people. You must have observed, Aspasia, that although one of the populace may in turbulent times be the possessor of great power, it rarely has happened that he retained it long, or without many sanguinary struggles. Moroseness is the evening of turbulence. Every man after a while begins to think himself as capable of governing as one (whoever he may be) taken from his own rank. Amid all the claims and pretensions of the ignorant and discontented, the eyes of a few begin to be turned complacently toward the more courteous demeanor of some well-born citizen, who presently has an opportunity of conciliating many more, by affability, liberality, eloquence, commiseration, diffidence, and disinterestedness. Part of these must be real, part may not be. Shortly afterward he gains nearly all the rest of the citizens by deserting his order for theirs : his own party will not be left behind, but adheres to him bravely, to prove they are not ashamed of their choice, and to avoid the imputation of inconsistency.

Aspasia! I have done with these cares, with these reflections. Little of life is remaining, but my happiness will be coetaneous with it, and my renown will survive it ; for there is no example of any who has governed a state so long, without a single act of revenge or malice, of cruelty or severity. In the thirty-seven years of my administration I have caused no citizen to put on mourning. On this rock, O Aspasia! stand my Propylæa and my Parthenon.

CXCIV. ASPASIA TO PERICLES.

Gratitude to the immortal gods overpowers every other impulse of my breast. You are safe.

Pericles! O my Pericles! come into this purer air! live life over again in the smiles of your child, in the devotion

of your Aspasia! Why did you fear for me the plague
within the city, the Spartans round it? why did you exact
the vow at parting, that nothing but your command should
recall me again to Athens? Why did I ever make it?
Cruel! to refuse me the full enjoyment of your recovered
health! crueller to keep me in ignorance of its decline!
The happiest of pillows is not that which Love first
presses; it is that which Death has frowned on and passed
over.

CXCV. ANAXAGORAS TO ASPASIA.

Have you never observed, O most observant Aspasia,
that there are many things which we can say in writing,
and which we cannot so well deliver in speech, even to
our nearest friend? During all the time of my residence
with you and Pericles, intimate as was our familiarity
from the commencement, never once did either of you
express a wish to hear the reason why I left my countrymen for strangers. The dislike I always had to relate
my concerns, and to present my features for inspection,
withheld me from the narrative; and delicacy withheld
you from inquiry.

Come, I will live over with you now that portion of my
life which I did not live with you before. I would not
escape for refuge into crowds; I would not repair my fortune by hammering on the anvil in the Agora; I would
not (pardon my application of our proverb at Clazomenai) make my purse of swine's ears. Such is the occupation of those who intend to profit by a public auditory.

Often had I been solicited by the worthier of the citizens to appear in public, and to take a part, if not in the
administration of affairs, at least in the debates. It ill
suited my temper and turn of mind. Ours, like most
free cities, was divided into two factions, the aristocratical and democratical. While others were making their
way forward to the head of them, I sat quietly at home,
and, to relax my mind occasionally from its sustained
and fixed position for loftier and purer speculations, meditated on the advantages and disadvantages of each govern-

15

ment. No small quantity had I written at last of remarks and aphorisms; behold a specimen: "In most cities the majority is composed of the ignorant, the idle, and the profligate. In most cities, after a time, there are enough of bad citizens to subvert good laws. Immoral life in one leader of the people is more pernicious than a whole streetful of impurities in the lower quarters of the community, seeing that streams, foul or fair, cannot flow upward."

Be sure, Aspasia, I never promulgated such perilous doctrines. To prove that I was erroneous in the two first positions, the citizens would have poisoned or stoned me, and their orators would clearly show my unfitness to give advice, in my attempting to demonstrate no more important or novel a truth than that water cannot run up a mountain. Such is the employment, such the ingenuity and sincerity of eloquence.

I was inclined to the democracy, because I knew that all government ought to be chiefly for the advantage of the many; but when I considered long and attentively its operations and effects, I began to doubt whether the people are more likely to know their interests than the aristocracy are to promote them. Immovable property is the only sure pledge for political equity, and the holders are not at all times ready to offer it. Merchants are the worst of adventurers and gamesters, because their native land is not their country. They are the sucklings of an alien, and love her best who gives them nutriment. Their preponderance in a state will invariably be its subversion.

I intended to speak of myself, but you see I cannot keep to my theme; it soon tires me . . soon escapes me. The scanty streamlet has run but a little way, and is lost among the sands. A few words more, however. Before I left my country, I offered some brief observations on important matters, then in discussion, to persons in authority. Do I much over-estimate my solidity of intellect, my range of comprehension, or my clearness of discernment, in believing that all these qualities in me, however imperfect, are somewhat more than equivalent to theirs? I concealed this truth from them, if truth it be, and told them only what I thought it was their interest, and would surely be their intention, to perform. They rewarded me by suffering me to depart in peace, unanswered and unnoticed. We might imagine that advice, like manure, is only good and applicable when it has lain a long while by. He reasons ill who reasons with a bad reasoner . . he walks on chaff, and tires himself without progress and without impression. I never expostulate with the self-sufficient; but on this occasion I desired a friend of theirs to inquire of them whether they thought a conflagration in Clazomenai would only warm their baths and cook their dinners. Had I been willing to abuse my faculties, it would have been an easy matter for me to have swept them from their places, and to have assumed the highest; for the rapacious has no hold upon the people, and vulgar manners in the candidate for office are no recommendation even to vulgar men.

Here ended my life in my own country.

CXCVI. CLEONE TO ASPASIA.

It has been wisely said that Virtue hath only to be seen to be beloved : but unwisely, that Vice hath only to be seen to be hated. Certain it is that the more habituated we are to the contemplation of a pure and placid life, the more do we delight in it. I wish it were equally so that every glance at Vice loosens a feather from her plumage, and that on a nearer approach and more stedfast observation she grows hideous. Proofs to the contrary come before us every day.

Eupolis, and Mnesilochos, and Callias, and Cratinos, like most other authors, are indifferent to any result from their writings but popularity and emolument. And we are informed here at Miletus that several of your philosophers are now employing a language, on the powers and provinces of love, far more seductive to the passions of their youthful auditors than the most indecent of theatrical ribaldry. For surely there is little seductive in a boisterous jocularity, that seizes and holds down the hand from the painfully blushing forehead, and forces the eyes to

see what they would shun.   Ionian manners, I am afraid,
are as licentious as the Athenian : but ours are become
so by our intercourse with the Persians, the Athenian by
theirs with the Philosophers.   It is only of late that such
poisonous perfumery has had this influence on the brain ;
it is only since the departure of the sedate, unostentatious
Anaxagoras, that syllogists have snapped their fingers at
experiment.   Against such men the arrows of ridicule
are well directed : but these arrows fall harmlessly from
flowing robes ; and, indeed, the purple dye is everywhere
a panacea.

CXCVII. ANAXAGORAS TO PERICLES.

Thanks, O Pericles, for your provident care of me !
Provident do I say? no, anything but that ; kind, generous, profuse ; but if you really saw the extent of my
wants, you would only send me notice that you and those
about you are well and happy.

The fever which has broken out in your city will certainly spare you if you reside in the Acropolis ; and yet
you tell me that you are resolved on taking no such pre-
caution, lest you should appear to claim an exemption
from the common peril.

What prudent men were my enemies in Athens, to send
me back hither ! they would not let me live nor die among
them !

You have little curiosity to know anything about private men and retired places.   Nevertheless, I will tell you
and Aspasia what is Lampsacos.

Shrimps and oysters are the lower order of the inhabitants ; and these, it is pretended, have reason to complain of the aristocracy above them.   The aristocracy on
their side contend that such complaints are idle and unfounded ; that they are well fed and well clothed, and that
the worst that ever happens to them is to be taken out of
their beds, and to be banded, marshalled, and embarked,
in the service of their country.   In few more words, we
all are either fishermen or vine-dressers.   I myself am a

chief proprietor; my tenement is small, but my vineyard
is as spacious as any about. It is nearly a hundred of
my paces broad; its length I cannot tell you, for in this
direction it is too steep for me to walk up it. My neighbors have informed me that there is a fine spacious view
of the Hellespont and headlands from the summit. I only
know that there is a noble god, a century old at the least ..
he who protects our gardens and vines. An image of him
stands either at the top or the bottom of every avenue in the
vicinity. He frowns in many of them; yet, amid all his
threats, there is in his good-humored gravity something
like a half-invitation. The boys and girls write verses
under him, very derogatory to his power and dignity.
They usually write them, I understand, in one another's
name; just as if he could not find them out, and would
not punish them in due season. Enough of this: I have
somewhat less to say about myself. The people love me,
for I am no philosopher here, and have scarcely a book
in the house. I begin to find that eyes are valuables and
books utensils. Sitting at my door, I am amused at the
whistle of curlews, and at their contentions and evolu-
tions, for a better possession than a rabble's ear. Sometimes I go down, and enjoy a slumber on the soft deep
sands; an unexpected whisper and gentle flap on the face
from the passing breeze awakens me, or a startling plash
from the cumbersome wave as it approaches nearer. Idleness is as dear to me, reflection as intense, and friendship as warm as ever. Yes, Pericles! Friendship may
pause, may question, may agonize, but her semblance
alone can perish.

My moon is in the last quarter, and my days ought
now to be serene; they are so. Be yours no less; yours
and Aspasia's!

CXCVIII. PERICLES TO ASPASIA.

One true and solid blessing I owe to my popularity.
Seldom is it that popularity has afforded any man more
than a fallacious one. Late wisdom, and dearly bought,

is mine. Aspasia! But I am delaying your delight, at one moment by the hurry of my spirits, at another by the intensity of my reflections. Our Pericles is Athenian in privileges as in birth. I have obtained a law to revoke a former one enforced by me .. and felt no shame. If I could hope that other statesmen would take example from my faults, if I could hope that at any future time they would cease to be opinionative, imperious, and self-willed, mistaking the eminence of station for the supremacy of wisdom, I would entreat them to urge no measure in which might be traced the faintest sign of malice or resentment, whether in regard to parties or private men. But alas! the inferior part of man is the stronger; we cannot cut the centaur in twain; we must take him as we find him composed, and derive all the advantage we can both from his strength and his weakness.

I am growing the politician again, when I should be the husband and father.

The odious law, the weight of which I drew upon my own head,* is abrogated. The children of women not Athenian are declared free citizens. Many good men, many good mothers, have mourned the degradation of theirs through my severity.

How dear, above the sweetest of Spring, are the blos-

---

* It is stated in every *Life of Pericles* that he obtained the enactment of it. This is incorrect. The law was an ancient one, and required fresh vigor and vigilant observance at a time when hostilities were imminent, and when many thousands were residing in the city who would otherwise have claimed a right to vote as citizens, while their connections were to be found among the inveterate enemies or the seceding allies of Athens. Long antecedently to the administration of Pericles, it appears that at a certain age the illegitimate were assembled at Cynosarges, in the wrestling-ring dedicated to Hercules, who himself was in that predicament; and these alone entered it. On which occasion Themistocles, his mother being a Thracian, gave the earliest proof of his astuteness, by inviting some of unmixed blood and aristocratical lineage to wrestle with him. It is far from improbable that Pericles insisted the rather on the execution of this law in opposition to Cimon, whose father, Miltiades, had married the daughter of Oloros, a prince of Thrace, and who himself was descended also from a ruler of that nation.

soms that appear in the less genial hours of winter! how dear, above earth, above all things upon earth (Aspasia will pardon this, whether true or false), is our little Pericles! Am I dreaming when I imagine I see this beautiful boy, with Health and Hope beside him, kneeling on the border of the tomb, and raising up from it a whole family, in long perspective! We were gone, I thought, we were lost forever. The powerful father merged his whole progeny in utter darkness; an infant shall reclaim it.

No longer is there a cloud upon my brow! no longer is there, I am apt to think, a pestilence in Athens.

CXCIX. ASPASIA TO PERICLES.

Blessings on the generosity of the Athenians! blessings a thousandfold on the paternal heart of Pericles!

O Pericles! how wrong are all who do not forever follow Love, under one form or other! There is no god but he, the framer, the preserver of the world, the pure Intelligence! All wisdom that is not enlightened and guided by him is perturbed and perverted. He will shed, O my husband, his brightest tints over our autumnal days. Were we ever happy until now? Ah yes, we were .. but undeserving. A fresh fountain opens before us, subject to no droughts, no overflowings. How gladly, how gratefully, do I offer to immortal Love the first libation!

Come hither, my sweet child! come hither to my heart! thou art man, thou art Athenian, thou art free. We are now beyond the reach, beyond the uttermost scope and vision, of Calamity.

CC. ASPASIA TO CLEONE.

Alcibiades is grown up to the highest beauty of adolescence. I think I should be enamored of him were I a girl, and disengaged. No, Cleone! the so easy mention of him proves to me that I never should be. He is pet-

ulant, arrogant, impetuous, and inconsistent. Pericles
was always desirous that he should study oratory, in order
that it might keep him at home, gratify his vanity the most
perfectly and compendiously, and render him master of
his own thoughts and those of others. He plainly told
Pericles that he could learn little from him except dissimulation.

"Even that," replied Pericles, "is useful and necessary ; it proceeds from self-command. Simulation, on the
contrary, is falsehood, and easily acquired by the meanest
intellect. A powerful man often dissembles ; he stands
erect in the course of glory, with open brow but with
breath supprest ; the feebler mind is ready to take refuge
in its poverty, under the sordid garb of whining simulation."

He then remarked to Pericles that his oratory was somewhat like his economy, wanting in copiousness and display.

"Alcibiades!" said my husband, "it is particularly
this part of it which I could wish you to adopt. In oratory there are few who can afford to be frugal ; in economy
there are few who can afford to act otherwise than fru-
gally. I am a public man, and it little becomes me to
leave room for suspicion that, by managing ill my own
small affairs, I may be negligent in the greater of the
commonwealth. There are kingdoms in Thrace and
Asia, where the cares of government are consigned to
ministers or satraps, and where it shall be thought honorable and glorious in one of these functionaries to die in
debt, after managing the treasury. But surely there is in
this no proof whatever that he managed it discreetly ;
there is a fair presumption that, neglecting his household,
he left the community in worse disorder. Unquestionably
he was a dishonest man, to incur a debt beyond the extent of his estate. Forbearance from accumulation in
his own house, is hardly to be deemed a merit by the most
inconsiderate, in one who can unlock the treasury to every
relative, every friend, every associate, and every dependent.
Such persons will generally be found to have been gamesters and prodigals, and to have intrusted the subordinate
branches of public concerns to servants, as unfaithful and

improvident as those menials who admiuistered their own ; and the reigns of the princes who employed them, if recorded at all, are recorded as prodigies of expenditure, profligacy, and disaster.

"Aristides died poor ; but Aristides never was rich ; he threw away nothing but his good example. And was his the fault there? He was frugal, he was provident ; every action he performed, every word he uttered, will excite, inform, and direct, remotest generations. Thus indeed it cannot properly be said that, however now neglected, his example was thrown away. Like the seeds of plants which a beneficent God hath scattered throughout the earth, although many fail to come up soon after the season of their sowing, yet do they not decay and perish, but germinate in the sterilest soils many ages later. Aristides will be forefather to many brave and honest men not descended from his lineage nor his country ; he will be founder of more than nations ; he will give body, vitality, and activity, to sound principles. Had he merely been a philosopher, he could effect little of this ; commander as he was, imperial Persia served only for a mirror to reflect his features from Attica on the world."

Alcibiades, in several parts of this discourse, had given signs of weariness and impatience. Pericles perceived it, and reverted to Aristides. At every word that was now spoken he grew more and more auimated ; at the close he sprang up, seized the hand of Pericles, and told him he would listen as long as he went on in that manner.

"Speak to the purpose, as you have begun to do, and about Aristides, and I shall like you better than Aspasia. I think, after all, I may perhaps let you be my teacher." He said this laughing.

My husband replied :

" I will not undertake it, Alcibiades ! Peradventure I may offer you, from time to time, a little at once, some serviceable observations, some fruits of my experience ; but it is only to grace and beauty that your restless, intractable mind is obedient for an hour."

" Call me anything, do anything, or nothing," said the youth, "if you will only give me such a smile again."

"Go and ride into the country," said my husband, as he was rising. "If you retain your high opinion of me on your return, you will find me at leisure to continue. I leave you, for the present, with Aristides."

Away he went, without a word more to either of us. When he was out of the apartment, Pericles said, after a thoughtful and serious pause :

"He is as beautiful, playful, and uncertain, as any half-tamed young tiger, feasted and caressed on the royal carpets of Persepolis ; not even Aspasia will ever quite subdue him."

CCI. CLEONE TO ASPASIA.

I shall never more be in fear about you, my Aspasia ! Frolicsome and giddy as you once appeared to me, at no time of your life could Alcibiades have interested your affections. You will be angry with me when I declare to you that I do not believe you ever were in love. The re-nown and genius of Pericles won your imagination ; his preference, his fondness, his constancy, hold, and will forever hold, your heart. The very beautiful rarely love at all. Those precious images are placed above the reach of the Passions : Time alone is permitted to efface them ; Time, the father of the gods, and even *their* consumer.

CCII. ASPASIA TO CLEONE.

Angry ! yes indeed, very angry am I ; but let me lay all my anger in the right place. I was often jealous of your beauty, and I have told you so a thousand times. Nobody for many years ever called me so beautiful as Cleone ; and when some people did begin to call me so, I could not believe them. Few will allow the first to be first ; but the second and third are universal favorites. We are all insurgents against the despotism of excellence.

Ah Cleone ! if I could divide my happiness with you, I do think I should have much to give you. I would demand a good deal of your sound judgment for it ; but you should have it.   We both of us value our beauty, I suspect, less than we used to do, which is certainly wrong; for whatever we may be told, or may tell ourselves, we have rather a scantier store of it.   However, we are not yet come to the last loaf in the citadel.

I did not see Alcibiades again, that day or the following.   When he came to me, he told me he was ashamed of having said an uncivil thing.

" Of which are you ashamed?" said I, " O Alcibiades! for there were several not distinguished for courtesy."

" As usual, in good humor, which always punishes me," said he.   "But I remember I made a rude observation on what lies within your department."

" Economy?" said I.

Before he could answer me, Pericles, informed that Alcibiades had inquired for him, entered the apartment.

"I am glad you are come in," cried he, " for, although I have taken two days to collect my courage and words, I think I shall have more of both, now you are present."

He then began his apology, which Pericles thus interrupted :

" Be prepared for chastisement ; I shall impose a heavy mulct on your patience ; I shall render an account to you of my administration, and I hope you will permit it to pass.

" I have a son, as you know, in whose character parsimony is not among the more prominent qualities.   I am unwilling to shock him by it, which is always apt to occasion a rebound to the opposite side ; and I am equally unwilling to offer an example or pretext for luxury and expense.   My own character will permit neither.   I never gave a splendid feast ; I never gave a sparing entertainment ; I never closed my dining-room to a man of elegant manners or of sound information.   I have not the ample fortune of our cousin Cimon, who always used it magnificently ; and glad am I that I have it not ; for it would oblige me to receive many who must disgust me, and who would occupy more hours of my leisure than I can spare.   My system of domestic life has produced me contentment and happiness. May yours, my dear Alcibiades, whether like it or unlike it, do the same!"

"Thank you!" said he carelessly, and added: "but your manner of speaking, which we first began to talk about, the other day, is proper only for yourself; in any other man it would be ridiculous. Were I to employ it, people would believe I assumed the character of Jupiter or Hermes walking among mortals. Aspasia's is good enough for me. Many think her language as pure and elegant as yours; and I have never known it enrage and terrify men as yours does."

"Study, then, Aspasia in preference," said he. "You possess already some of her advantages. A beautiful mouth is always eloquent; its defects are taken for tropes and figures. Let us try together which can imitate her best. Neither of us hath ever seen her out of temper, or forgetful what argument to urge first and most forcibly. When we have much to say, the chief difficulty is to hold back some favorite thought, which presses to come on before its time, and thereby makes a confusion in the rest. If you are master of your temper, and conscious of your superiority, the words and thoughts will keep their ranks, and will come into action with all their energy, compactness, and weight. Never attempt to alter your natural tone of voice; never raise it above its pitch; let it at first be somewhat low and slow. This appears like diffidence; and men are obliged to listen the more attentively, that they may hear it. Beginning with attention, they will retain it during the whole speech; but attention is with difficulty caught in the course of one.

"I am intruding a little on the province of Aspasia. If she approves of my advice, pursue it; if she disapproves, be sure I have spoken inconsiderately; although I fancy I have observed such effects on several occasions."

He ceased: I enforced as well as I could his admonition. But Alcibiades, with grace nearly equal, wants his gravity; and, if ever he should be his successor in the administration of the republic, he must become so by other methods.

CCIII. ANAXAGORAS TO ASPASIA.

Proxenos is sailing back to Massilia. Before he left us, he collected a large cargo of *Inscriptions*, chiefly poetical. In Massilia these matters are curiosities. The people, who cannot have them fresh, are glad to accept them dry, although, according to Proxenos, they are little acute in relishing or distinguishing them.

In his last conversation with me, he gave evidence that, should he ever fail as a merchant, he hopes to make his fortune as a critic. Among his remarks was this:

" I cannot for my life imagine why Zephyr is such a favorite with the poets."

I answered that we Ionians were always shy of him; but that in other parts, and especially toward Gaul and Italy, he certainly was better behaved.

"Better behaved!" cried Proxenos. "By the Twins! he hath split my sail more than once."

To comfort him, I replied: "He has done that with his best friends, O Proxenos!"

" And no longer ago," continued he, " than last Boedromion, he carried off my nether garment that was drying upon deck."

" Ah! there," said I, " mischievous as he is, he could not do the same to them without homicide; few of them have one to spare."

At the recollection of his superior wealth and dignity, he grew composed again. The gods grant him a prosperous voyage! Ere this letter shall reach Athens, he must be almost as far as Cythera. What labors and perils do seafaring men undergo! What marvels are ships! They travel in a month farther than the fleetest horse can do; to such perfection have they been brought, and such confidence is there now in human courage and skill. As there hath been but little or no improvement in them for some centuries, we may suppose that, contrary to all other inventions, the ingenuity of mortals can do nothing more for them.

I forgot to mention of Proxenos, what mayhe it were

better not to mention at all, that he is reported to have broken off the extremity of a leaf or two on some curious old vases, and a particle of a volute* from a small column at the corner of a lane.   Nothing can so distinctly prove, say the Lampsacenes, that Proxenos has a few drops of barbarian blood in him.   Genuine Greeks may travel through all the world, and see every vase, every column, every statue, worth seeing in its whole circumference, without a thought of mutilation.   Those people who cannot keep their hands from violating the purest works of ancient days, ought, if there are not too many of them, to be confined in separate cages, among the untamable specimens of zoölogy.

The Lampsacenes, you see by this, are not averse to protect the Arts.

CCIV. CLEONE TO ASPASIA.

I have found eight verses, of which I send you only the four last.   So entirely do they express what I have felt, it seems as if I myself had composed them.

They who tell us that love and grief are without fancy and invention, never knew invention and fancy, never felt grief and love.

> The thorns that pierce most deep are prest
> Only the closer to the breast:
> To dwell on them is now relief,
> And tears alone are balm to grief!

* One Eyles Irwin, who was not poor nor quite uneducated, tells us in his *Travels* that he broke off a volute *as a relic* from what was called Pompey's Pillar.   This happened so lately as the last century.   We are, it seems, about to remove from Egypt the obelisk named Cleopatra's Needle.   Do we believe that Egypt is never to come to life again?   It may be some hundreds, it may be some thousands of years : but these are to the glories of Egypt as pounds are to our national debt . . itself so glorious, and of which the formation has constituted our glorious men! Are we sure that the Genius who created these eternal works derives no portion of his beatitude from the hourly contemplation of them, in the country where they were formed and fixed?

You perhaps will like these better, Aspasia! though very unlike in sentiment and expression.

> Pyrrha! your smiles are gleams of sun
> That after one another run
> Incessantly, and think it fun.
>
> Pyrrha! your tears are short sweet rain
> That glimmering on the flower-lit plain
> Zephyrs kiss back to heaven again.
>
> Pyrrah! both anguish me; do please
> To shed but (if you wish me ease)
> Twenty of those, and two of these.

CCV. ANAXAGORAS TO ASPASIA.

Ships are passing and repassing through the Hellespont all hours of the day; some of them from the Piræus, urging the allies of Athens to come forward in her defence; others from the Peloponnese, inciting them to rise up in arms, and at once to throw off allegiance.

Would there be half this solicitude in either of the belligerents to be virtuous and happy, supposing it possible to persuade the one or the other that she might be, and without an effort? supposing it, in other words, to be quite as easy and pleasant to receive a truth as an untruth. Would these mariners and soldiers, and those statesmen who send them out, exert half the anxiety, half the energy and prowess, to extinguish the conflagration of a friend's house in the neighborhood, as they are exerting now to lay in ashes all the habitations that lie beyond it? And such are brave men, such are wise men, such are the rulers of the world! Well hath it been said by some old poet:

> Men let themselves slide onward by degrees
> Into the depths of madness; one bold spring
> Back from the verge, had saved them; but it seems
> There dwells rare joy within it! O thou Sire
> Of gods and mortals, let the blighting cloud
> Pass over me! O grant me wholesome rest
> And innocent uprisings, although call'd
> The only madman on thy reeling earth!

CCVI. ANAXAGORAS TO ASPASIA.

It is well that you are removed from the city, and that the enemies of Athens pay respect either to your birth-place or your wisdom, either to your celebrity or your confidence. I remember that, speaking of the human form and countenance, both as existing in life and repre-sented in the ideal, you remarked that the perfection of beauty is what is farthest from all similitude to the brutes. Surely then, in like manner, the perfection of our moral nature is in our remoteness from all similitude to their propensities. Now the worst propensity of the worst beasts is bloodshed, for which we pursue them as nearly as we can to extermination, but which they never commit with so little urgency, or to so great an extent, as we do. Until we bring ourselves at least to an equality with them, we can hardly be said to have made much progress in wisdom. It will appear wonderful and perhaps incredible to future generations, that what are now considered the two highest gifts of man, oratory and poetry, should be employed, the one chiefly in exciting, the other in embla-zoning, deeds of slaughter and devastation. If we could see, in the nature of things, a child capable of forming a live tiger, and found him exercising his power of doing it, I think we should say to him :
" You might employ your time better, child ! "
But then, Aspasia, we must not be orators nor poets, nor hope for any estimation in the state. Beware how you divulge this odd opinion ; or you may be accused, as before, of crimes against the purity of morals, against the customs of our forefathers, and against the established and due veneration of the gods. I hardly know what I am treading on, when I make a single step toward phil-osophy. On sand I fear it is ; and, whether the impres-ion be shallow or profound, the eternal tide of human passions will cover and efface it. There are many who would be vexed and angry at this, and would say, in the bitterness of their hearts, that they have spent their time in vain. Aspasia ! Aspasia ! they have indeed, if they are angry or vext about it.

CCVII. ANAXAGORAS TO ASPASIA.

Did I tell you, O Aspasia, we were free and remote
from the calamities of war? we were.   The flute and the
timbrel and the harp alone were heard along our streets ;
and the pavement was bestrewn with cistus and lavender
and myrtle, which grow profusely on the rocks behind us.
Melanthos had arrived from the Chersonese to marry
Eurycleia ; and his friend Sosigenes of Corinth had determined to be united on the same day with her sister
Phanera.

Those who have seen them, say that they were the
prettiest girls in the city: they were also the happiest ;
but less happy than their lovers, who, however, owed at
present but a part of the happiness to either.   They were
sworn friends from early youth, and had not met since,
but always had corresponded.

Why cannot men draw a line against war as against
plague, and shut up the infected? Instead of which, they
are proud of being like the dogs in the worst feature ;
rushing forth into every affray, and taking part in it instantly with equal animosity.   I wish we had arrived at
such a degree of docility, and had advanced so many
steps in improvement, that by degrees we might hope to
acquire anything better of these good creatures.   We
have the worst of every beast, and the best of none.

This is not, O Aspasia! my usual tone of thinking and
discoursing ; nor is what has happened here among the
usual occurrences of my life.   The generous heart needs
little to be reminded what are the embraces of young and
ardent friends ; and the withered one could ill represent
them.

Eurycleia, in the silence of fondness, in the fulness of
content, was holding the hand of her Melanthos.   Love
has few moments more sweet, Philosophy none more calm.
That moment was interrupted by the entrance of Sosigenes ; and composure was exchanged for rapture by the
friendly soul of Melanthos.   Yes, yes, Aspasia! friend-

ship, even in the young, may be more animated than love
itself.   It was not long, however.

" Where is Phanera?"

" I will call her," said Eurycleia, and went out.

Phanera, fond of ornament, it may be, and ambitious
to surpass her sister and enchant her lover, came not
speedily, nor indeed did Eurycleia very soon, for it was
not at first that she could find her.   Conversation had
begun in the meanwhile about the war.   Melanthos was
a little more vehement than the mildness of his nature,
it is said, ever allowed him before, and blamed the Corinthians for inciting so many states to hostility.   Often
had Sosigenes been looking toward the door, expecting
his Phanera, and now began to grow impatient.   The
words of Melanthos, who felt the cruelty of war chiefly
because it would separate the two sisters and the two
friends, touched the pride of Sosigenes.   Unable to moderate his temper, now excited by the absence of Phanera
after the sister had some time returned, he said, fiercely:

" It is well to blame the citizens of the noblest city
upon earth, for not enduring an indignity.   It is well;
but in slaves alone, or viler dependents."

" Sosigenes ! Sosigenes !" cried Melanthos, starting up
and rushing toward him.   At that instant the impetuous
Sosigenes, believing violence was about to follow affront,
struck him with his dagger to the heart.

" I could not then calm thy anger with an embrace !
my too unhappy friend !" while the blood gurgled through
the words, sobbed forth Melanthos.

CCVIII. ALCIBIADES TO PERICLES.

You commanded me, O Pericles, that I should write to
you, whenever I found an opportunity on land.   Phormio
cast anchor before Naupactos : we command the Gulf of
Crissa and check the movements of the Corinthians.
The business of blockading is little to my mind.   Writing
is almost as insufferable : it is the only thing I do not
willingly undertake when my friends desire it.   Beside, I

have nothing in the world to write about. We have done little but sink a few vessels and burn a few villages. It is really a hard matter to find a table to write upon, so quick and so complete is the devastation. I fancied war had something in it more animating and splendid. The people of the Peloponnese are brave, however. They sometimes ask for their children (if very young) but never for their lives. Why cannot we think them as little worth taking as they of giving?

I am heartily tired of this warfare; and Phormio has told me, in plain words, he is heartily tired of *me*. Upon this, I requested his permission to join without delay our army before Potidæa. I expected not only an uncivil refusal, but a sharp rebuke.

"The gods have begun to favor us!" cried Phormio. "This offer is better than the luckiest omen. Alcibiades! thou art the whitest of white birds; and thy flight, whichever wind it float upon, is worth a victory."

I would have been angry, but laughter sprang uppermost; so, throwing my arms round old Phormio's neck. I almost pulled him down with it.

"How now, stripling!" cried he, as willing to be angry as I was; "all this buffoonery before the commander of the fleet!"

CCIX. ALCIBIADES TO PERICLES.

Hardly could it have been expected that "the whitest of white birds" should have been so speedily on the wing. The day had not closed when Phormio told me, that, knowing my fickleness, he had given orders for my voyage back. Every voyage is prosperous that brings me within sight of an enemy worth seeing. Brave fellows these Potidæans! They never lose their appetite, even in the greatest want of air and exercise. You, who hear everything, must know that they eat one another rather than surrender. I have been but three days in the camp, where, to my delight, I found the brave and kindly Socrates. Do you disapprove of my renewing my intimacy with Philosophy in the midst of battles? Let Philosophy then stand aside; and behold in her place the defender of his country and the savior of his friend.

The morning after my arrival, the Potidæans burst forth with incredible bravery from their gates, overthrowing all opposition. Now was my time. The heavy-armed in general, being old soldiers, were somewhat slower; and many of the enemy were assailing me when they came up; nor indeed was it then in sufficient force. I was wounded and overthrown, and, at the beginning, stunned; but presently I fancied I heard the sound of a brisk sword on armor over me, and felt something heavy fall on my legs. I was drawn forcibly from under the last of my antagonists. Socrates raised me up, and defended me from the weapons of not a few, unwilling to retire, and irresolute to renew the engagement.

I write now, because I am so wounded I can do nothing else.

CCX. PERICLES TO ALCIBIADES.

You are courageous, my Alcibiades, to a degree which I hardly ever observed in another. This alone induces me to doubt whether you will become, so soon as we both of us wished it, an accomplished and perfect soldier. To rush against the enemy before your comrades, is not, indeed, quite so unseemly as to lag behind; yet it may be even more detrimental in an officer. With old troops, who know their duty, it is always so: with younger alone, who want encouragement, it may not be. Socrates deserved the first honors in the action; his modesty and his affection transferred them to the imprudent and the vanquished, whom he rescued from the shame of rashness and the wretchedness of captivity. With all my fondness for you, I could not have given you my vote; and, had I commanded against Potidæa, I must have reproved you in presence of the army.

Never, O Alcibiades, inflict on me the misery of passing so severe a sentence. I praised you before others did; I condemn you after them. Your high spirit deserved its reward; your temerity its rebuke. I, who have been the careful guardian of your fortune, am the more anxious one of your safety and of your fame. In my former letter I gave unobstructed way to the more pleasurable emotions ; and, in every one that I shall have occasion to write to you hereafter, I am confident of the same enjoyment. Reply to me as your friend, your comrade, the partaker of your pains and pleasures, and at most the director of your studies. But here, my Alcibiades, we must be grave and serious : I must, for once, not guide, but dictate ; no answer is here admissible, excepting the answer of a soldier to his general.

CCXI. ASPASIA TO CLEONE.

You know that to Niconöe was awarded by her judge Priapos the prize of beauty in the Kallisteia. In return for this favorable decision, she dedicated to him a golden ewer and a fawn-skin. Under his image a poet, who perhaps was her admirer, and who was grateful to the arbiter, wrote this epigram :

> Niconöe is inclined to deck
> Thy ruddy shoulder and thick neck
>   With her own fawn-skin, Lampsacene !
> Beside, she brings a golden ewer
> To cool thy hands in, very sure
>   Among what herbage they have been.
>
> Ah ! thou hast wicked leering eyes,
> And any maiden were unwise
>   Who should invest thee face to face ;
> Therefore she does it from behind,
> And blesses thee, so just and kind
>   In giving her the prize for grace.

Here are some others, I believe by Erinna herself, but I find inscribed on them *Address to Erinna.*

> Ay, shun the dance and shun the grape,
> Erinna ! thou shalt not escape.
> Idle the musing maid who thinks
> To lie unseen by sharp-eyed lynx

Where Bacchus, god of joy and truth,
Hunts with him, hunts for bashful youth.
So take the thyrsus if you please,
And come and join the Mœnades.

CCXII. ANAXAGORAS TO ASPASIA.

We are now so near winter that there may not be, after the vessel which is about to sail, any more of them bound for Athens, all the remainder of the year. And who knows what another may bring or take away?

I remain in health, but feeble. Life slips from me softly and imperceptibly. I am unwilling to tire myself by blowing a fire which must soon go out, whether I blow it or not. Had I any species of curiosity to send you, were it pebble, sea-weed, or new book, I would send it; not (for it is idle to talk so) as a memorial of me. If the friend is likely to be forgotten, can we believe that anything he has about him will repose a longer time on the memory?

Thus far had I written, when my strength failed me. Stesicles and Apollodoros have told me I must prepare for a voyage. The passage is neither so broad nor so stormy as the Hellespont.

I was resolved not to go until I had looked in my garden for some anemonies, which I recollected to have seen blossoming the other day. It occurred to me that usually they appear in spring; so does poetry. I will present to you a little of both; for the first time. They are of equal value; and are worth about as much as the pebble, or the sea-weed, or the new book.

Where are the blooms of many dyes
That used in every path to rise?
  Whither are gone the lighter hours?
What leave they? I can only send
My wisest, loveliest, latest friend
  These weather-worn and formless flowers.

Think me happy that I am away from Athens; I, who always lose my composure in the presence of crime or calamity.   If any one should note to you my singularities, remembering me a year hence, as I trust you and Pericles will do, add to them, but not aloud, a singularity of felicity, " *He neither lived nor died with the multitude.*" There are, however, some Clazomenians who know that Anaxagoras was of Clazomenai.

CCXIII. ALCIBIADES TO PERICLES.

Pericles! I did wrong and rashly.   The praises of the Athenians are to me as the hum of insects : they linger in my ear, but are senseless and unexciting.   I swear to you I will do better ; but I must see you before I go.

Aspasia, whose letter you have sent me since, is even more severe than you have been ; and she has neither right nor reason.   She is the only woman upon earth that ever railed at rashness, the only one that could distinguish it from fortitude.   But every man must be rash once : it saves him from as much inconvenience and mischief as being oftener rash would incur.

Do not consider this nonsense as vindication or reply ; and let it not stand in the way of your pardon.

CCXIV. ASPASIA TO ALCIBIADES.

Are you not ashamed, young man, to leave the aged behind you, with all their wounds, merely to show how dexterous you are become in the management of your sword?   Unworthy Alcibiades!   Never expect that the Athenians, whatever be their levity and inconsiderateness, will award to you the honor of superiority in valor. Socrates well deserved it ; not for saving a life which on the next ocasion will be thrown away, but for giving to every one capable of profiting by it, an example of steadiness and constancy.   Pericles, I hope, will not allow you to disembark, until you have acquired the rudiments of discipline, in the only art in which you ever seemed likely to excel.   Have you forgotten, too, that the pestilence

is raging in the city? O rash Alcibiades! the sight of
Pericles himself, to you at least, could hardly have been
worth so desperate a hazard. But Pericles will reprove
you, confident boy! Let me hear no more of you until
I have heard that he has granted you his forgiveness.

CCXV. ASPASIA TO PERICLES.

Censure not too severely, O my Pericles, your inconsiderate cousin! In these days, when so many of your
adherents are fallen, some by the fever, some by war, we
must be parsimonious in the treasury of friendship, at all
times far from inexhaustible.

A hundred men of more wisdom and more virtue than
Alcibiades would prevail much less with the multitude,
should anything sinister befall you. May the gods avert
it! but I always fear something; and, what certainly is
more foolish, I fancy my presence could avert from you
any calamity. I wish I were persuaded that the Immortals hear us; I would then so perpetually pray for you
as hardly to give myself time to read your letters; and
you should quarrel with the shortness of mine. But
reason, which strengthens our religion, weakens our devotion. Happy are those who have retained throughout
life their infantine simplicity, which nurses a tractable
idol in an unsuspicious bosom, is assured it knows and
heeds the voice addressing it, and shuts it up again with
a throb of joy, and keeps it warm. For this, the mind
must be nurtured to the last with the same milky food as
in childhood; the gods must have their tangible images,
and must laugh to us out of ivy and flowers.

Thinking of you, I had forgotten that I began to write
in favor of Alcibiades. Lest, by taxing him with impetuosity and imprudence, you should alienate his fickle
mind, I myself have written to him with quite enough
severity; at least I think so: you shall judge for yourself. When you have perused it, let it go to him instantly; for here we are uncertain at what point the
troops will land from Potidæa. I shall be grieved if

anything happens to him. He has more life in him than is enough to animate a city; yet the point of an arrow may extinguish it in an instant. With however long experience before us, we yet might wonder that what is so animated should ever cease at all. You men often talk of glorious death, of death met bravely for your country: I too have been warmed by the bright idea in oratory and poetry; but ah! my dear Pericles! I would rather read it on an ancient tomb than on a recent one.

CCXVI. PERICLES TO ASPASIA.

I had already warned Alcibiades of his imprudence and irregularity; but your letter will insure his correction. The reply he sent me is worthy of a man formed for command. We must watch over him: he will do great good or great evil. Those who are most capable of both, always end miserably; for, although they may have done many things well, yet the first or second that they do badly is their ruin. They know not whom to choose as their follower up the scaling-ladder, nor when to loosen their grasp of the pinnacle. Intractable as you may think Alcibiades, there is not a youth in Athens so easily led away by a weaker judgment than his own. He wishes to excel in everything, and succeeds: but this wish brings him into contact with too many; and he cannot at present push them off far enough from him to see plainly and distinctly what they are. He will soon stand above them, and know them better.

I must leave off: the dying call me forth. Blessings on my Aspasia and her little Athenian!

CCXVII. ASPASIA TO CLEONE.

The verses I shall presently write out for you, at the bottom of my letter, are composed, as you will perceive, in the broadest Dorian, on the extraordinary death of Æschylus. Probably the unhappy poet was murdered

by some enemy or some robber.   He was found with his
skull fractured, and, maybe, with a tortoise near him.
But who in the world can believe that an eagle dropped
it from above? that the quickest in sight of all animals
mistook a bald head for a rock?   And did ever man walk
in the fields of Sicily with his head uncovered?   If he
did, his death might easily be accounted for, without a
tortoise or eagle ; a sunbeam is stronger and surer.
Whenever I find a book containing this gross absurdity,
I instantly throw it aside, as the effusion of an idle and
silly writer, and am well assured it must be incapable
of instructing or interesting me.

The petulant author of the verses you will find below,
is evidently a disappointed poet.   Hiero and Theron
could never treat Æschylus with neglect or with indifference.   Little as may be our regard and our respect for
royalty, we hardly can suppose any king, who knows
Greek, so barbarous and stupid as to fancy in himself a
nobility more exalted than in Æschylus, or gifted by the
gods with a higher office, than stewardship to the greatest
of men among whom he himself is the richest.

> Bard of Eleusis ! art thou dead
>   So strangely ! can it be
> An eagle dropt upon thy head
>   A tortoise ? no, not he.
>
> They who devised the fable, marr'd
>   The moral of their song :
> They meant the eagle by the bard,
>   But placed the creature wrong.
>
> Quickest in courts those ever move
>   Whom nature made most slow :
> Tortoise wears plumes and springs above
>   While eagle moults below.

I have room enough for another short piece, which
carries with it somewhat more than the dialect for a
testimonial of its Atticism.   They who are ill-trained in
the course of poetry, *puff and blow*, as the trainers express
it, at short distances ; they who are trained better, move

with little difficulty, and no appearance of exertion.
Strength does not lie in varicose veins.   This is, however,
a subject which requires grace only.   You like to drink
water ; but you like to drink it from a silver cup.

To Love.

Where is my heart, perfidious boy?
  Give it, O give it, back again!
I ask no more for hours of joy;
  Lift but thy hand and burst my chain.

Love's Reply.

Fond man! the heart we rashly gave
  She values not, yet won't restore:
She passes on from slave to slave;
  Go, go; thy heart is thine no more.

CCXVIII.   CLEONE TO ASPASIA.

The Athenians, my dear Aspasia, are reported to be a
religious people ; yet I have often wondered at their freedom and boldness, in depriving the immortal gods of
their power on some occasions, and on others in accost-
ing them with familiarity and disrespect.   It would have
been satisfactory to me if you had related what befell the
unhappy man who presumed to call *perfidious* and *boy*
one of the most powerful.   Certainly we are inspired by
our holy religion to believe that Love is youthful ; but
Anacreon is the only poet who represents him as a child.
There is an absurdity in making him appear younger
than we ourselves are when we begin to be under the influence of the passion.   But the graver fault is in calling
him (what I tremble to write) perfidious!   You will relieve my mind of some anxiety by assuring me that nothing sinister has befallen so captious and irreverential a
votary.   If his fault is recent, and if he is yet living, it
would be wise and considerate in him to implore the
blessed mother of this almighty deity, that she may be
pleased to avert his anger, should he not have forgotten
the offence.   I say it, because the most experienced and

the most pious are of opinion that he is oftener oblivious.
Was not he both wiser and more pious who wrote a
poem in a very different spirit, and, whether more or
less Attic, fuller of thought, consistency, and reflection.
If you have forgotten it, let me bring it back again, and
fix it as firmly as may be in your memory :

Ah! what a blessed privilege it is
To stand upon this insulated rock
On the north side of youth! I see below
Many at labor, many at a game
Than labor more laborious, wanting breath
And crying *help!* What now! what vexes them?
Only a laughing maid and winged boy,
Obstinate boy indeed, who will not shoot
His other arrow, having shot the first.
Where is the harm in this? yet they meanwhile
Make all the air about them pant with sobs,
And with one name weary poor Echo down.

Aspasia! I too have suffered; and Love knows it; yet
I dare not even tell him that he knows it. To remind
him would be indelicate; to complain would be irreligious. And what could all his power do for me now?
But this, believe me, is not the reason why I endure in
silence, and bend in submission to the arbitrament of the
gods. Surely, too surely, whoever has breathed has
sighed. When we have lost, O Aspasia! those we love,
whether by impassable distance or any other dispensa-
tion of the gods, youth is less happy than age, and age
than death.

CCXIX. ASPASIA TO CLEONE.

Youth, like the aloe, blossoms but once, and its flower
springs from the midst of thorns; but see with what
strength and to what height the aloe-flower rises over
them; be not surpassed by it.

On love, on grief, on every human thing,
Time sprinkles Lethe's water with his wing.

If I continue to reason, or to moralize, or to versify, you will begin to doubt my sincerity, or at least the warmth of my affection. I am induced to believe, O Cleone! that the Deity you venerate so profoundly and solemnly, is far from unforgiving. In the verses I now send you, there appears to be a proof of it; for the writer seems to have treated him not only as a child, but a child much addicted to mischief; yet never was man treated in return with more benignity. I should tremble at the manner in which the Fates are mentioned, if matters were left at their arbitration. But we know the contrary: we know positively that they can spin only what is on their distaffs, and not a thread can be turned to a new pattern.

I would be grave, Cleone! I would indeed; but really there is no harm in laughing at children and old women, gods or not. We know they have a good deal to do in the affairs of this world, however; and it is unwise to laugh at those who are as capable of extinguishing our laughter as of exciting it.

> "What art thou doing with those shears?"
> I shouted in an urchin's ears,
> Who notched them and who made them grate,
> While three old women near him sate,
> And scowl'd at every scratch they heard,
> But never said a single word.
> In a dark corner thus all three
> Sate with an elbow on the knee,
> And three blue fingers held their tips
> Imprest on three still bluer lips.
> Although the froward boy I chid
> Did not (boys will not) what was bid,
> His countenance was not malign
> As that was of the elder trine.
> "Look at those frightful ones!" he said,
> And each one shook her thin-hair'd head.
> "Nay, never fear the angry crones" . .
> Said he; and each replied with groans.
> "They are all vicious; for they knew
> That what I did I did for you,
> Contemplating the fairest maid
> That ever with my bow has play'd.
> Crones! by my help your shears have got
> A set of teeth, which you have not.

Come! come! Death's bridemaids! snip as fast
As snip ye may, her years shall last
In spite of you, her beauty bloom
On this side and beyond the tomb:
I swear by Styx."
                    "And I by thee,"
Cried I, " that what thou sayst shall be."

CCXX. ALCIBIADES TO PERICLES.

Pray why did you tell Phanomachos to station some confidential one near me, who should be an eternal check on me? There is little chance that I should do anything extravagant, unless the Potidæans invite me to dinner and I accept the invitation. I will not allow any man to defend me before I stand in need of defence, and before I have deserved to save my life by proving it worth something. I should quarrel with Socrates himself, much more with another, presuming to take what belongs to me, of danger or of glory. It is not kind in you, nor open, nor prudent. Would you wish any one to say, " Pericles takes care of his own relatives!" This ought only to be said of the vilest men in the worst governments; and of you, until now, it never could be. You have given no such orders in regard to Xanthippos. He may be as rash and violent as he pleases. Even here he dares to call me *Neaniskos* and *Kouridion* and *Ta paidika.** By Castor! if he were not the son of Pericles, his being my cousin should not save from a stroke of the sabre that fierce disdainful visage. I promise you it shall soon be seen which of us is the braver and the better man. I would not say this to you unless that you might let him know my sentiments. I have no words, written or spoken, for the contumelious: my complaints are for the ear of those only who are kind to me.

* This expression was usually reproachful; not always, as we see in Plato.

CCXXI. PERICLES TO ALCIBIADES.

Do not think, my Alcibiades, that I recommended you to the guardianship of Phanomachos, in order that he should exercise over you a troublesome vigilance of control, or indulge toward you an unmilitary partiality. But I am more intimate with him than I am with Xenophon or Aristoclides or Hestiodoros ;* and having sons, he knows that restraints are often necessary on the impatience of military ardor.

Your letter is a proof that I judged rightly. My praises of your valor are lost amid those of the army and of the city ; but the delight it has given me is, I am confident, one among the thoughts that have assuaged your wounds. On your return, the citizens will express their sense of your conduct.

Endeavor to prove, now that you are acknowledged to be the first in bravery, that you are more discreet than Xanthippos. Many in every army are so nearly on an equality in courage, that any attempt of theirs to show a superiority is ineffectual. Unbecoming language can neither prove nor disprove it, but must detract from its worth and merit. Discretion, on the contrary, is the sure sign of that presence of mind without which valor strikes untimely and impotently. Judgment alone makes courage available, and conciliates power with genius. Consider that you never will have attained the scope of your ambition, until you lead and govern those men against whom your passions now exasperate you ; and, unless you do conciliate them, you never can induce them to acknowledge your superiority, much less submit to your governance. It is best the germs of power should spring forth early, that they may have time enough for gaining strength ; therefore I write to you, no longer as a youth in pupilage, but as a candidate for the highest offices of the commonwealth.

* These three were appointed to commands with Phanomachos.

Try whether your forbearance may not produce a better effect on Xanthippos than my remonstrances. I write to you rather than to him, because I rely more firmly on your affection. Be worthy of such a secret, O Alcibiades! and think how highly I must esteem your prudence and manliness, when I delegate to you, who are the younger, the power of correcting in him the faults which I have been unable to eradicate or suppress. Go, and, in the spirit with which I send it, give my love to Xanthippos. He may neglect it, he may despise it, he may cast it away, but I will gather it all up again for him: you must help me.

CCXXII. ALCIBIADES TO PERICLES.

Pericles, I was much edified by your letter; but, pardon me, when I came to the close of it I thought you rather mad.

"What!" said I, "beard this panther!"

However, when I had considered a little more and a little better on it, I went to him and delivered your love. He stared at me, and then desired to see the direction. "Ay," said he, "I remember the handwriting. He oftener writes to me than I to him. I suppose he has less to do and less to think of."

The few other words he added are hardly worth the trouble of repetition; in fact, they were not very filial. Dear Pericles! I would love him, were it only out of perversity. But, beside all other rights over me, you have made me more disposed than ever to obey you, in making me more contented with myself, as you have by this commission. I may do something yet, if we can but fumigate or pray away the plague. Of two thousand four hundred soldiers, who landed but forty days before me from the Bosphorus, under the command of Agnon, son of Nikias, one thousand and fifty are already dead. I shall have nobody to persuade or manage, or even to fight with, if we go on so.

CCXXIII. ALCIBIADES TO PERICLES.

Potidæa has surrendered. The dead of the city are scarcely more shadows than the living, and yet how bravely they fought to the last! I should have been sorry for them a few months ago; but I have now learnt what it is to be a soldier. We must rise superior to pain, and then take another flight, farther afield, and rise superior to pity. Beside, the Potidæans were traitors; and next, they were against us; and furthermore, they were so wicked as to eat one another rather than submit. This shows their malice. Now we have done nothing half so bad toward them; and I assure you, if others are disposed to such cruelty, I will take no part in it; for who would ever kiss me afterward?

CCXXIV. PERICLES TO ALCIBIADES.

The remembrance of past days that were happy, increases the gloominess of those that are not, and intercepts the benefits of those that would be.

In the midst of the plague this reflection strikes me, on the intelligence I have received from Lampsacos. You likewise will be sorry, O Alcibiades! to hear that Anaxagoras is dying. Although he seldom conversed with you, and seldom commended you in private, believe me, he never omitted an occasion of pointing out to your friends any sign you had manifested of ability or virtue. He declined the character of teacher, yet few have taught so much, wherever his wisdom was accessible. Philosophers there have been indeed, at Athens and elsewhere, earnest in the discovery and in the dissemination of truth; but, excepting Thales and Pherecydes, none among them has been free from ostentation, or from desire of obtaining the absolute and exclusive possession of weak and ductile minds. Now the desire of great influence over others is praiseworthy only where great good to the community may arise from it. To domineer in the arbi-

17

trary sway of a dogmatical and grasping, yet loose and
empty-handed philosophy, which never bears upon inventions and uses, nor elevates nor tranquillizes the mind, and
to look upon ourselves with a sweet complacency from
so petty an eminence, is worse than boyish ambition.
To call idlers and stragglers to us, and to sit among
them and regale on their wonder, is the selfishness of an
indigent and ill-appointed mind. Anaxagoras was subject to none of these weaknesses, nor to the greater of
condescending to reprove, or to argue with, those who
are. He made every due allowance for our infirmities
of understanding, and variations of temper, the effect
of them; and he was no less friendly toward those who
differed widely in opinion from him, than toward those
who quite agreed. When a friend of his was admiring
and praising him for it, he interrupted him, saying:

"Why not? Is it not too self-evident for language,
that, if I had taken the same road, I should have gone
in the same direction? and would not the same direction
have led to the same conclusion?"

Yes, Alcibiades! it is indeed self-evident, and, were it
spoken unwarily, it would be reprehended for being so;
and yet scarcely one man in ten millions acts consistently
upon it.

There are humanities, my friend, which require our
perpetual recollection, and are needful to compensate, in
some measure, for those many others we must resign to
the necessities and exactions of war.

CCXXV. ASPASIA TO CLEONE.

Serene and beautiful are our autumnal days in Thessaly. We have many woods about us, and many wood-
land sounds among them. In this season of the year I
am more inclined to poetry than in any other; and I
want it now more than ever to flow among my thoughts,
and to bear up the heavier.

I hesitate, O Cleone! to send you what I have been
writing. You will say it is a strange fancy of mine, and

fitter for me in those earlier hours of life when we were reposing in the Island.

Nothing, I must confess, would be more ill-placed than a *Drama* or *Dialogue* in the world below; at least if the Shades entered into captious disquisitions or frivolous pleasantries. But we believe that our affections outlive us, and that Love is not a stranger in Elysium. Humors, the idioms of life, are lost in the transition, or are generalized in the concourse and convergency of innumerable races; passions, the universal speech, are throughout intelligible.

The Genius of Homer is never to be gainsaid by us; and he shows us how heroes, and women worthy of heroes, felt and reasoned. A long dialogue, a formal drama, would be insupportable; but perhaps a single scene may win attention and favor from my own Cleone.

I imagine then Agamemnon to descend from his horrible death, and to meet instantly his daughter. By the nature of things, by the suddenness of the event, Iphigeneia can have heard nothing of her mother's double crime, adultery and murder.

I suspend my pen. Although I promised you in the morning my short Acherusian scene, I am almost ready to retract my words. Everybody has found out that I am deficient in tenderness. While I was writing I could not but shed tears . . just as priests do libations, you will say, to save other people the trouble.

THE SHADES OF AGAMEMNON AND OF IPHIGENEIA.

Iphigeneia. Father! I now may lean upon your breast,
And you with unreverted eyes will grasp
Iphigeneia's hand.
        We are not shades
Surely! for yours throbs yet.
        And did my blood
Win Troy for Greece?
        Ah! 'twas ill done to shrink,
But the sword gleam'd so sharp, and the good priest
Trembled, and Pallas frown'd above, severe.
  Agamemnon. Daughter!
  Iphigeneia. Beloved father! is the blade
Again to pierce my bosom? 'tis unfit

For sacrifice; no blood is in its veins;
No god requires it here; here are no wrongs
To vindicate, no realms to overthrow.
You are standing as at Aulis in the fane,
With face averted, holding (as before)
My hand; but yours burns not, as then it burn'd;
This alone shows me we are with the Blest,
Nor subject to the sufferings we have borne.
I will win back past kindness.

                              Tell me then,
Tell how my mother fares who loved me so,
And griev'd, as 'twere for you, to see me part.
Frown not, but pardon me for tarrying
Amid too idle words, nor asking how
She prais'd us both (which most?) for what we did.

    Agamemnon. Ye gods who govern here! do human pangs
Reach the pure soul thus far below? do tears
Spring in these meadows?

    Iphigeneia.   No, sweet father, no . .
I could have answered that; why ask the gods?

    Agamemnon. Iphigeneia! O my child! the Earth
Has gendered crimes unheard-of heretofore.
And Nature may have changed in her last depths,
Together with the gods and all their laws.

    Iphigeneia. Father! we must not let you here condemn;
Not, were the day less joyful: recollect
We have no wicked here; no king to judge.
Poseidon, we have heard, with bitter rage
Lashes his foaming steeds against the skies,
And, laughing with loud yell at winged fire
Innoxious to his fields and palaces,
Affrights the eagle from the sceptered hand;
While Pluto, gentlest brother of the three
And happiest in obedience, views sedate
His tranquil realm, nor envies theirs above.
No change have we, not even day for night
Nor spring for summer.

                       All things are serene,
Serene too be your spirit! None on earth
Ever was half so kindly in his house,
And so compliant, even to a child.
Never was snatch'd your robe away from me,
Though going to the council. The blind man
Knew his good king was leading him indoors
Before he heard the voice that marshall'd Greece.
Therefore all prais'd you.

                     Proudest men themselves
In others praise humility, and most
Admire it in the sceptre and the sword.

What then can make you speak thus rapidly
And briefly? in your step thus hesitate?
Are you afraid to meet among the good
Incestuous Helen here?

   Agamemnon.   O! gods of Hell!

   Iphigeneia. She hath not past the river.

                        We may walk
With our hands link'd nor feel our house's shame.

   Agamemnon. Never mayst thou, Iphigeneia, feel it!
Aulis had no sharp sword, thou wouldst exclaim,
Greece no avenger . . I, her chief so late,
Through Erebos, through Elysium, writhe beneath it.

   Iphigeneia. Come, I have better diadems than those
Of Argos and Mycenai: come away,
And I will weave them for you on the bank.
You will not look so pale when you have walk'd
A little in the grove, and have told all
Those sweet fond words the widow sent her child.

   Agamemnon. O Earth! I suffered less upon thy shores!
(*Aside.*) The bath that bubbled with my blood, the blows
That spilt it (O worse torture!) must she know?
Ah! the first woman coming from Mycenai
Will pine to pour this poison in her ear,
Taunting sad Charon for his slow advance.
Iphigeneia!

   Iphigeneia.   Why thus turn away?
Calling me with such fondness! I am here,
Father! and where you are, will ever be.

   Agamemnon. Thou art my child; yes, yes, thou art my child.
All was not once what all now is! Come on,
Idol of love and truth! my child! my child!
(*Alone.*) Fell woman! ever false! false was thy last
Denunciation, as thy bridal vow:
And yet even that found faith with me! The dirk
Which sever'd flesh from flesh, where this hand rests,
Severs not, as thou boastedst in thy scoffs,
Iphigeneia's love from Agamemnon:
The wife's a spark may light, a straw consume,
The daughter's not her heart's whole fount hath quench'd,
'Tis worthy of the gods, and lives forever.

   Iphigeneia. What spake my father to the gods above?
Unworthy am I then to join in prayer?
If, on the last, or any day before,
Of my brief course on earth, I did amiss,
Say it at once, and let me be unblest;
But, O my faultless father! why should you?
And shun so my embraces?

                      Am I wild
And wandering in my fondness?

We are shades!
Groan not thus deeply; blight not thus the season
Of full-orb'd gladness!   Shades we are indeed,
But mingled, let us feel it, with the blest.
I knew it, but forgot it suddenly,
Altho' I felt it all at your approach.
Look on me; smile with me at my illusion . .
You are so like what you have ever been
(Except in sorrow!) I might well forget
I could not win you as I used to do.
It was the first embrace since my descent
I ever aim'd at : those who love me live,
Save one, who loves me most, and now would chide me.
  Agamemnon. We want not, O Iphigeneia, we
Want not embrace, nor kiss that cools the heart
With purity, nor words that more and more
Teach what we know from those we know, and sink
Often most deeply where they fall most light.
Time was when for the faintest breath of thine
Kingdom and life were little.
  Iphigeneia.   Value them
As little now.
  Agamemnon. Were life and kingdom all!
  Iphigeneia. Ah! by our death many are sad who loved us.
The little fond Electra, and Orestes
So childish and so bold!   O that mad boy!
They will be happy too.
                        Cheer! king of men!
Cheer! there are voices, songs . . Cheer! arms advance.
  Agamemnon. Come to me, soul of peace! These, these
      alone,
These are not false embraces.
  Iphigeneia.   Both are happy!
  Agamemnon. Freshness breathes round me from some
      breeze above.
What are ye, winged ones! with golden urns?

            The Hours (descending).

  The Hours.   To each an urn we bring.
            Earth's purest gold
            Alone can hold
  The lymph of the Lethèan spring.

  We, son of Atreus! we divide
  The dulcet from the bitter tide
      That runs athwart the paths of men.
  No more our pinions shalt thou see.
  Take comfort! We have done with thee,
      And must away to earth again.

(Ascending.)

Where thou art, thou
Of braided brow,
Thou cull'd too soon from Argive bow'rs,
Where thy sweet voice is heard among
The shades that thrill with choral song,
None can regret the parted Hours.

Chorus of Argives.

Maiden! be thou the spirit that breathes
   Triumph and joy into our song!
Wear and bestow these amaranth-wreaths,
   Iphigeneia! they belong
To none but thee and her who reigns
(Less chaunted) on our bosky plains.

Semichorus.

Iphigeneia! 'tis to thee
Glory we owe and victory.
Clash, men of Argos, clash your arms
To martial worth and virgin charms.

Other Semichorus.

Ye men of Argos! it was sweet
To roll the fruits of conquest at the feet
Whose whispering sound made bravest hearts beat fast.
   This we have known at home,
   But hither we are come
To crown the king who ruled us first and last.

Chorus.

Father of Argos! king of men!
   We chaunt the hymn of praise to thee.
In serried ranks we stand again,
   Our glory safe, our country free.
Clash, clash the arms we bravely bore
Against Scamander's God-defended shore.

Semichorus.

Blessed art thou who hast repell'd
Battle's wild fury, Ocean's whelming foam;
   Blessed o'er all, to have beheld
Wife, children, house avenged, and peaceful home!

Other Semichorus.

We too, thou seest, are now
Among the happy, though the aged brow
From sorrow for us we could not protect,

Nor, on the polisht granite of the well
Folding our arms, of spoils and perils tell,
Nor lift the vase on the lov'd head erect.

Semichorus.

What whirling wheels are those behind?
What plumes come flaring through the wind,
    Nearer and nearer?   From his car
He who defied the heaven-born Powers of war
    Pelides springs!   Dust, dust are we
    To him, O king, who bends the knee,
Proud only to be first in reverent praise of thee.

Other Semichorus.

Clash, clash the arms!   None other race
Shall see such heroes face to face.
We too have fought; and they have seen
Nor sea-sand gray nor meadow green
Where Dardans stood against their men . .
Clash!   Io Pæan!   clash again!
Repinings for lost days repress . .
The flames of Troy had cheer'd us less.

Chorus.

Hark!   from afar more war-steeds neigh,
Thousands o'er thousands rush this way.
Ajax is yonder!   ay, behold
The radiant arms of Lycian gold!
Arms from admiring valor won,
Tydeus!   and worthy of thy son.
'Tis Ajax wears them now;   for he
Rules over Adria's stormy sea.

He threw them to the friend who lost
(By the dim judgment of the host)
Those wet with tears which Thetis gave
The youth most beauteous of the brave.
In vain!   the insatiate soul would go
For comfort to his peers below.
Clash!   ere we leave them all the plain,
Clash!   Io Pæan!   once again!

Hide these things away, Cleone!   I dare never show
them to any but Pericles.   I can reach no further than a
chorus; hardly that.   Tragedy is quite above me: I
want the strength, the pathos, the right language.   Fie!
when there are so many who would teach me.   Concede,

that the shades were not happy at once in Elysium ; and that the Hours are not more shadowy than they. Æschylus brings into *our* world Beings as allegorical ; and where shall we fix a boundary between the allegorical and divine?

CCXXVI. CLEONE TO ASPASIA.

You build your nest, Aspasia, like the swallow,
Bringing a little on the bill at once,
And fixing it attentively and fondly,
And trying it, and then from your soft breast
Warming it with the inmost of the plumage.
Nests there are many, of this very year
Many the nests are, which the winds shall shake,
The rains run through, and other birds beat down ;
Yours, O Aspasia ! rests against the temple
Of heavenly love, and thence inviolate,
It shall not fall this winter, nor the next.

CCXXVII. ASPASIA TO CLEONE.

You have encouraged me to proceed in the most difficult tract of poetry. Had I openly protested that the concluding act of *Agamemnon*, the *Electra* of our tragedian, dissatisfies me, he alone of the Athenians would have pardoned my presumption. But Electra was of a character to be softened rather than exasperated by grief. An affectionate daughter is affectionate even to an unworthy mother ; and female resentment (as all resentment should do) throws itself down inert at the entrance of the tomb. Hate with me, if you can hate anything, my Cleone ! the vengeance that rises above piety, above sorrow ; the vengeance that gloats upon its prostrate victim. Compunction and pity should outlive it ; and the child's tears should blind her to the parent's guilt. I have restored to my Electra such a heart as Nature had given her ; torn by suffering, but large and alive with tenderness. In her veneration for the father's memory, with his recent blood before her eyes, she was vehement in urging the punishment of the murderess. The gods had

commanded it at the hands of their only son. When it
was accomplished, he himself was abhorrent of the deed,
but defended it as a duty ; she in her agony cast the whole
on her own head. If character is redeemed and restored ;
if Nature, who always is consistent, is shown so ; if pity
and terror are concentrated at the close ; I have merited
a small portion of what my too generous Cleone bestowed
on me in advance.

THE DEATH OF CLYTEMNESTRA.

Orestes and Electra.

Electra. Pass on, my brother! she awaits the wretch,
Dishonorer, despoiler, murderer . . .
None other name shall name him . . . she awaits
As would a lover . .
     Heavenly gods! what poison
O'erflows my lips!
     Adultress! husband-slayer!
Strike her, the tigress!
     Think upon our father . .
Give the sword scope . . think what a man was he,
How fond of her! how kind to all about,
That he might gladden and teach *us* . . how proud
Of thee, Orestes! tossing thee above
His joyous head and calling thee his crown.
Ah! boys remember not what melts our hearts
And marks them evermore!
     Bite not thy lip,
Nor tramp as an unsteady colt the ground,
Nor stare against the wall, but think again
How better than all fathers was our father.
Go . .
 Orestes. Loose me then! for this white hand, Electra,
Hath fastened upon mine with fiercer grasp
Than mine can grasp the sword.
 Electra.   Go, sweet Orestes!
I knew not I was holding thee . . Avenge him!
(*Alone.*) How he sprang from me!
     . . Sure, he now has reacht
The room before the bath . .
     The bath-door creaks!
. . It hath creakt thus since he . . since thou, O father!
Ever since thou didst loosen its strong valves,
Either with all thy dying weight, or strength
Agonized with her stabs . .

What plunge was that?

Ah me!

.. What groans are those?

Orestes (returning).　　　　They sound through hell
Rejoicing the Eumenides.*

She slew
Our father; she made thee the scorn of slaves;
Me (son of him who ruled this land and more)
She made an outcast . . .

Would I had been so
Forever! ere such vengeance . . .

Electra.　　　　　　　　O that Zeus
Had let thy arm fall sooner at thy side
Without those drops! list! they are audible . .
For they are many . . from the sword's point falling,
And down from the mid blade!

Too rash Orestes!
Couldst thou then not have spared our wretched mother?

Orestes. The gods could not.

Electra.　　　　　　　　She was not theirs, Orestes.

Orestes. And didst not thou . .

Electra.　　　　　　'Twas I, 'twas I, who did it;
Of our unhappiest house the most unhappy!
Under this roof, by every god accurst,
There is no grief, there is no guilt, but mine.

Orestes. Electra! no!

'Tis now my time to suffer . .
Mine be, with all its pangs, the righteous deed.

CCXXVIII. CLEONE TO ASPASIA.

I will never praise you again until you complete the
tragedy. This is the time for it, now all the dramatic
poets of your country are dead or silent. Not that I
would invite you to have it represented or published : but,

---

*An ancient scholiast has recorded that the name of Eumenides
was given to these goddesses after the expiation of Orestes.
But Catullus (called the *learned* by his countrymen) represents
Ariadne invoking them by this appellation long before the
Trojan war. The verses are the most majestic in the Roman
language.

　　　Eumenides! quarum anguineis redimita capillis
　　　Frons expirantes præportat pectoris iras,
　　　Huc, huc adventate! etc.

believe me, the exertion of poetical power, in these elevations, throws off many of the mind's diseases.   Little or
nothing of the sort can be effected by slenderer and more
desultory attempts.   A bushel of garnets and amethysts
and topazes is not worth a single ruby the size of the
smallest ; and yet they are pretty things enough, and attract as many people.   One single act of such a tragedy
as you are able to compose, outvalues a thousand pieces
of less cohesive and infrangible materials.   Let others
expatiate on trivial objects, ordinary characters, and uninteresting events ; let them be called poets by themselves
and by their households ; but remember, O Aspasia ! that
you have Athenians for judges, and that the progeny of
heroes and gods is about to plead before them.

Again, I declare it, I will never praise you until you
comply with me ; I will only love you ; and hardly that.

CCXXIX. ASPASIA TO CLEONE.

I will never take so many steps up the heights of
poetry, as to make any poet doubt whether he can over-
take me.   There is not enough honey in my cells to attract the wasps ; nor shall there be.   If you really think
I have done better in some parts than the generality,
keep the secret ; at least from others ; and if you desire
to see the tragedy completed . . finish it yourself.   You
have often done work for me greatly more difficult.   I
never could work anything with the needle ; and it was
not because I feared its roughening my fingers, as you
were pleased to say after you had finished it.   I do not
like any labor of the hands ; that is the matter of fact ;
not even so little as the writing out of a tragedy.   I will,
however, on this one occasion, give you a little assistance.

THE MADNESS OF ORESTES.

Orestes and Electra.

Orestes. Heavy and murderous dreams, O my Electra,
Have dragged me from myself.

Is this Mycenai?
Are we . . . are all who should be . . . in our house?
Living? unhurt? our father here? our mother?
Why that deep gasp? for 'twas not sigh nor groan.
She then . . . 'twas she who fell! when? how? beware!
No, no, speak out at once, that my full heart
May meet it, and may share with thee in all . .
In all . . . but that one thing.
                                It was a dream.
We may share all.
                        They live? both live?
O say it!
 Electra. The gods have placed them from us, and there rolls
Between us that dark river . . .
 Orestes.   Blood! blood! blood!
I see it roll; I see the hand above it,
Imploring; I see *her.*
                        Hiss me not back,
Ye snake-hair'd maids! I will look on; I will
Hear the words gurgle thro' that cursed stream,
And catch that hand . . that hand . . which slew my father!
It cannot be . . . . how could it slay my father?
Death to the slave who spoke it! . . . slay my father!
It tost me up to him to earn a smile;
And was a smile then such a precious boon,
And royal state and proud affection nothing?
Ay, and thee too, Electra, she once taught
To take the sceptre from him at the door . .
Not the bath-door, not the bath-door, mind that! . .
And place it in the vestibule, against
The spear of Pallas, where it used to stand.
Where is it now? methinks I missed it there.
How we have trembled to be seen to move it!
Both looking up, lest that stern face should frown
Which always gazed on Zeus right opposite.
O! could but one tear more fall from my eyes,
It would shake off those horrid visages,
And melt them into air.
                        I am not yours,
Fell goddesses! A just and generous Power,
A bright-hair'd god, directed me.
                                And thus
Abased is he whom such a god inspired!
                (*After a pause.*)
Into whose kingdom went they? did they go
Together?
 Electra.   Oh! they were not long apart.
 Orestes. I know why thou art pale; I know whose head
Thy flower-like hands have garlanded; I know

For whom thou hast unbraided all thy love.
He well deserves it . . . . he shall have it all.
Glory and love shall crown thee, my brave sister!

    Electra. I am not she of Sparta. Let me live
(If live I must, Orestes!) not unnamed,
Nor named too often. Speak no more of love,
Ill-omen'd and opprobrious in this house . .
A mother should have had, a father had it,
O may a brother let it dwell with him,
Unchangeable, unquestioned, solitary,
Strengthened and hallowed in the depths of grief!
Gaze not so angrily . . I dare not see thee,
I dare not look where comfort should be found.

    Orestes. I dare and do behold them all day long,
And, were that face away so like my mother's,
I would advance and question and compel them . .
They hear me and they know it.

    Electra.   Hear me too,
Ye mighty ones! to me invisible!
And spare him! spare him! for without the gods
He wrought not what he wrought: And are not ye
Partakers of their counsels and their power?
O spare the son of him whom ye and they
Sent against Ilion, to perform your will
And bid the rulers of the earth be just.

    Orestes. And dare they frighten thee too? frighten thee?
And bend thee into prayer?

                      Off, hateful eyes!
Look upon me, not her.

                  Ay, thus; 'tis well.
Cheer, cheer thee, my Electra!

                    I am strong,
Stronger than ever . . steel, fire, adamant . .
But cannot bear thy brow upon my neck,
Cannot bear these wild writhings, these loud sobs.
By all the gods! I think thou art half mad . . .
I must away . . follow me not . . stand there!

Here is the Prayer of Orestes, in his madness, to
Apollo; and there follows, what is not immediately con-
nected with it, the Reply of the Priestess.

    Orestes. O king Apollo! god Apollo! god
Powerful to smite and powerful to preserve!
If there is blood upon me, as there seems,
Purify that black stain (thou only canst)
With every rill that bubbles from these caves
Audibly; and come willing to the work.

No; 'tis not they; 'tis blood; 'tis blood again
That bubbles in my ear, that shakes the shades
Of thy dark groves, and lets in hateful gleams,
Bringing me .. what dread sight! what sounds abhorr'd!
What screams! They are my mother's: 'tis her eye
That through the snakes of those three furies glares,
And makes them hold their peace that she may speak.
Has thy voice bidden them all forth? There slink
Some that would hide away, but must turn back,
And others like blue lightnings bound along
From rock to rock; and many hiss at me
As they draw nearer. Earth, fire, water, all
Abominate the deed the gods commanded!
Alas! I came to pray, not to complain;
And lo! my speech is impious as my deed!

Priestess of Apollo.

Take refuge here amid our Delphian shades,
    O troubled breast!
Here the most pious of Mycenai's maids
    Shall watch thy rest
And wave the cooling laurel o'er thy brow,
    Nor insect swarm
Shall ever break thy slumbers, nor shalt thou
    Start at the alarm
Of boys infesting (as they do) the street
    With mocking songs,
Stopping and importuning all they meet,
    And heaping wrongs
Upon thy diadem'd and sacred head,
    Worse than when base
Œgisthus (shudder not!) his toils outspread
    Around thy race.
Altho' even in this fane the fitful blast
    Thou may'st hear roar,
Thy name among our highest rocks shall last
    For evermore.

Orestes. A calm comes over me: life brings it not
With any of its tides: my end is near.
O Priestess of the purifying god,
Receive her! * and when she hath closed mine eyes,
Do thou (weep not, my father's child!) close hers.

* Pointing to his sister.

CCXXX. ASPASIA TO CLEONE.

Many are now recovering from the fever, which no longer can be called a pestilence. Pericles, though he tells me he is weak in body and altered in appearance, will soon overcome his fears about me. We shall presently meet again. And so, Cleone, you really have ventured at last to accept the invitation of Euphorbia. If she talked to you of her son she was imprudent and indiscreet; perhaps in her earlier invitations she was hardly less so. But who can foresee the end of sorrow, or would foresee the end of happiness? It usually is nearer at hand. When we enter a place whence the beloved has been long absent, part of the presence seems to be left behind. Again we draw back from the window as we did before, because then we were told people were coming. Foolish! foolish! I am representing my own sensations in times past: girlish sensations, which never were Cleone's, even in girlhood. Ah, Cleone! the beautiful smooth dove's plumage is hard and cold externally; but what throbbing, what warmth, what ardor, what tenderness, deep within! We must neither of us prefix *ah!* to anything in future; we must be the happiest of the happy. Here are two pieces of verse for you. That on Dirce was sent to me by Pericles; to prove that his Athenians can sport with Charon even now. The last quaternion seems the production of an elderly man; and some of the ladies, on whom it was not written, and to whom it is not applicable, cry shame on him, beyond a a doubt.

> Stand close around, ye Stygian set,
>   With Dirce in one boat convey'd,
> Or Charon, seeing, may forget
>   That he is old, and she a shade.

> Love ran with me, then walkt, then sate,
> Then said, *Come! come! it grows too late.*
> And then he would have gone, but . . no . .
> You caught his eye: he could not go.

CCXXXI. ASPASIA TO CLEONE.

Where on earth is there so much society as in a beloved child? He accompanies me in my walks, gazes into my eyes for what I am gathering from books, tells me more and better things than they do, and asks me often what neither I nor they can answer. When he is absent I am filled with reflections; when he is present I have room for none beside what I receive from him. The charms of his childhood bring me back to the delights of mine, and I fancy I hear my own words in a sweeter voice. Will he (O how I tremble at the mute oracle of futurity!), will he ever be as happy as I have been? Alas! and must he ever be as subject to fears and apprehensions? No; thanks to the gods! never, never. He carries his father's heart within his breast: I see him already an orator and a leader. I try to teach him daily some of his father's looks and gestures, and I never smile but at his docility and gravity. How his father will love him! the little thunderer! the winner of cities! the vanquisher of Cleone!

CCXXXII. CLEONE TO ASPASIA.

The Lacedæmonions, we hear, have occupied not only all Attica, but are about to enter, if they have not entered already, the territory of their confederates the Thebans, and to join their forces. Whither will you go, my Aspasia? Thessaly is almost as perilous as Bœotia. It is worse than criminal to be so nearly allied to the greatest man on earth, who must always have the greatest enemies. There are more who will forgive injury than there are who will forgive station; and those who assail in vain the power of Pericles, will exert their abilities in diminishing his equanimity and happiness. I fear your fondness will have induced you again to enter the city, that you may assuage and divide those cares which must weigh heavily on his wisdom and patriotism; and the

18

more, since his health has been underminded by the pestilence. I dare not advise you to forego a duty; but
remember he has commanded you to remain away. Your
return would afflict him. I am quite incapable of judg-
ing for you. Were I with you, then, perhaps I might
know many things which should influence your decision.

And can two years have passed over since this evil
entered your city, without my flying to comfort you?
Two years have indeed passed over; but my house has
also had its days of mourning. The prayers of my father
were heard: he died contentedly, and even joyfully. He
told me he had implored of the gods that they would
bestow on me a life as long and happy as his own, and
was assured they would. Until we have seen some one
grown old, our existence seems stationary. When we feel
certain of having seen it (which is not early) the earth
begins a little to loosen from us. Nothing now can detain
me at Miletus, although when I have visited you I shall
return. You must return with me, which you can do
from any region but Attica. Pericles will not refuse, for
you have already conciliated me his favor. In the meanwhile, do not think yourself bound by the offices of
humanity to bestow those cares on others which are all
required for your own family. Do not be so imprudent
as to let the most intimate of your friends persuade you
to visit them. You have a child, you have a husband,
and, without your presence, you possess the means of
procuring every human aid for the infected. O that I
were with you! to snatch you away from the approach
of the distemper. But I sadly fear I should grow hard-
hearted toward others, in your danger.

I must be with my Aspasia; and very soon.

O Athens! Athens! are there not too many of the
dead within thy walls already? and are none there who
never should have been? *

* This seems to refer to Xeniades.

CCXXXIII. ASPASIA TO PERICLES.

Never tell me, O my Pericles! that you are suddenly changed in appearance. May every change of your figure and countenance be gradual, so that I shall not perceive it; but if you really are altered to such a degree as you describe, I must transfer my affection . . from the first Pericles to the second. Are you jealous! if you are, it is I who am to be pitied, whose heart is destined to fly from the one to the other incessantly. In the end it will rest, it shall, it must, on the nearest. I would write a longer letter; but it is a sad and wearisome thing to aim at playfulness where the hand is palsied by affliction. Be well; and all is well: be happy; and Athens rises up again, alert, and blooming, and vigorous, from between war and pestilence. Love me: for love cures all but love. How can we fear to die, how can we die, while we cling or are clung to the beloved?

CCXXXIV. PERICLES TO ASPASIA.

The pestilence has taken from me both my sons, You, who were ever so kind and affectionate to them, will receive a tardy recompense, in hearing that the least gentle and the least grateful did acknowledge it.

I mourn for Paralos, because he loved me; for Xanthippos, because he loved me not.

Preserve with all your maternal care our little Pericles. I cannot be fonder of him than I have always been; I can only fear more for him.

Is he not with my Aspasia? What fears then are so irrational as mine? But oh! I am living in a widowed house, a house of desolation; I am living in a city of tombs and torches; and the last I saw before me were for my children.

CCXXXV. PERICLES TO ASPASIA.

It is right and orderly, that he who has partaken so largely in the prosperity of the Athenians, should close the procession of their calamities. The fever that has depopulated our city, returned upon me last night, and Hippocrates and Acron tell me that my end is near.

When we agreed, O Aspasia! in the beginning of our loves, to communicate our thoughts by writing, even while we were both in Athens, and when we had many reasons for it, we little foresaw the more powerful one that has rendered it necessary of late. We never can meet again: the laws forbid it, and love itself enforces them. Let wisdom be heard by you as imperturbably, and affection as authoritatively, as ever; and remember that the sorrow of Pericles can arise but from the bosom of Aspasia. There is only one word of tenderness we could say, which we have not said oftentimes before; and there is no consolation in it. The happy never say, and never hear said, farewell.

Reviewing the course of my life, it appears to me at one moment as if we met but yesterday; at another as if centuries had passed within it; for within it have existed the greater part of those who, since the origin of the world, have been the luminaries of the human race. Damon called me from my music to look at Aristides on his way to exile; and my father pressed the wrist by which he was leading me along, and whispered in my ear:

"Walk quickly by; glance cautiously; it is there Miltiades is in prison."

In my boyhood Pindar took me up in his arms, when he brought to our house the dirge he had composed for the funeral of my grandfather; in my adolescence I offered the rites of hospitality to Empedocles; not long afterward I embraced the neck of Æschylus, about to abandon his country. With Sophocles I have argued on eloquence; with Euripides on policy and ethics; I have discoursed, as became an inquirer, with Protagoras and Democritus, with Anaxagoras and Meton. From Herodotus I have listened to the most instructive history, conveyed in a language the most copious and the most harmonious ; a man worthy to carry away the collected suffrages of universal Greece ; a man worthy to throw open the temples of Egypt, and to celebrate the exploits of Cyrus. And from Thucydides, who alone can succeed to him, how recently did my Aspasia hear with me the energetic praises of his just supremacy !

As if the festival of life were incomplete, and wanted one great ornament to crown it, Phidias placed before us, in ivory and gold, the tutelary deity of this land, and the Zeus of Homer and Olympus.

To have lived with such men, to have enjoyed their familiarity and esteem, overpays all labors and anxieties. I were unworthy of the friendships I have commemorated, were I forgetful of the latest. Sacred it ought to be, formed as it was under the portico of Death, my friendship with the most sagacious, the most scientific, the most beneficent of philosophers, Acron and Hippocrates. If mortal could war against Pestilence and Destiny, they had been victorious. I leave them in the field : unfortunate he who finds them among the fallen !

And now, at the close of my day, when every light is dim and every guest departed, let me own that these wane before me, remembering, as I do in the pride and fulness of my heart, that Athens confided her glory, and Aspasia her happiness, to me.

Have I been a faithful guardian? do I resign them to the custody of the gods undiminished and unimpaired? Welcome then, welcome, my last hour ! After enjoying for so great a number of years, in my public and my private life, what I believe has never been the lot of any other, I now extend my hand to the urn, and take without reluctance or hesitation what is the lot of all.

CCXXXVI. ALCIBIADES TO ASPASIA.

I returned to Athens in time to receive the last injunctions of my guardian. What I promised him, to comfort

him in his departure, I dare not promise his Aspasia, lest
I fail in the engagement ; nevertheless I will hope that my
natural unsteadiness may sometimes settle on his fixed
principles.   But what am I, what are all my hopes, in
comparison with the last few words of this great man,
surely the greatest that earth has ever seen, or ever will
see hereafter ! Let me repeat them to you, for they are
more than consolation, and better. If on such a loss I
or any one could console you, I should abominate you
eternally.

I found him surrounded by those few friends whom
pestilence and despair had left in the city. They had
entered but a little while before me ; and it appears that
one or other of them had been praising him for his
exploits.

" In these," replied he, " Fortune hath had her share ;
tell me rather, if you wish to gratify me, that never have
I caused an Athenian to put on mourning."

I burst forward from the door-way, and threw my arms
around his neck.

"O Pericles ! my first, last, only friend ! afar be that
hour yet ! " cried I, and my tears rolled abundantly on
his cheeks. Either he felt them not, or dissembled, or
disregarded them ; for, seeing his visitors go away, he
began with perfect calmness to give me such advice as
would be the best to follow in every occurrence, and
chiefly in every difficulty. When he had ended, and I
was raising my head from above his pillow (for I continued in that posture, ashamed that he, who spake so
composedly, should perceive my uncontrollable emotion),
I remarked I knew not what upon his bosom. He smiled
faintly, and said, "Alcibiades ! I need not warn you
against superstition ; it never was among your weaknesses. Do not wonder at these amulets ; above all, do
not order them to be removed. The kind old nurses, who
had been carefully watching over me day and night, are
persuaded that these will save my life. Superstition is
rarely so kind-hearted ; whenever she is, unable as we
are to reverence, let us at least respect her. After the
good, patient creatures have found, as they must soon, all

their traditional charms unavailing, they will surely grieve enough, and perhaps from some other motive than their fallibility in science. Inflict not, O Alcibiades! a fresh wound upon their grief, by throwing aside the tokens of their affection. In hours like these we are the most indifferent to opinion, and greatly the most sensible to kindness."

The statesman, the orator, the conqueror, the protector, had died away; the philosopher, the humane man, yet was living . . alas! few moments more.

CCXXXVII. ALCIBIADES TO ASPASIA.

Must I again, Aspasia, torment my soul? again must I trouble yours? Has the pestilence then seized me, that I want hardihood, strength, understanding, to begin my labor? No; I walk through the house of mourning, firmly, swiftly, incessantly; my limbs are alert as ever.

Write it I must. Somebody was at the house-door; admittance was, it seems, not granted readily. I heard a voice, feeble and hoarse, and, looking forth, saw two women who leaned against the lintels.

"Let her enter, let her enter; look at her; she is one of us."

These words were spoken by the younger; and maliciously. Scarcely had she uttered them when her head dropped forward. The stranger caught and supported her, and cried *help! help!* and rubbed her temples, and, gazing on her with an intensity of compassion, closed her eyelids; for death had come over them. In my horror (my fright and dastardly cowardice I should rather call it), I failed to prevent or check her.

Aspasia has, then, her equal on the earth!

Aspasia is all that women in their wildest wishes can desire to be; Cleone, all that the Immortals are. But she has friendship, she has sympathy; have those?

She *has*, did I say? And can nothing then bring me back my recollection? not even she! I want it not; those moments are present yet, and will never pass away.

She asked for you.

"Aspasia," answered I, " is absent."

"Not with her husband? not with her husband?"
cried she.

"Pericles," I replied, "is gone to the Blessed."

"She was with him then, while hope remained for her!
I knew she would be.   Tell me she was."

And saying it, she grasped my arm and looked earnestly
in my face.   Suddenly, as it appeared to me, she blushed
slightly; on her countenance there was, momentarily,
somewhat less of its paleness.   She walked into the
aviary; the lattice stood open; the birds were not flown,
but dead.   She drew back; she hesitated; she departed.
I followed her; for now, and not earlier, I bethought me
it was Cleone.   Before I came up to her, she had asked
a question of an elderly man, who opened his lips, but
could not answer her, and whose arm, raised with difficulty from the pavement, when it would have directed her
to the object of her inquiry, dropped upon his breast.   A
boy was with him, gazing in wonder at the elegance and
composure of her attire, such as, in these years of
calamity and of indifference to seemliness, can nowhere
be found in Athens.   He roused himself from his listless
posture, beckoned, and walked before us.   Reaching the
garden of Epimedea, we entered it through the house;
silent, vacant, the doors broken down.   Sure sign that
some family, perhaps many, had, but few days since,
utterly died off within its chambers; for nearly all the
habitations, in all quarters of the city, are crowded with
emigrants from the burghs of Attica.   The pestilence is
now the least appalling where it has made the most havoc.
But how hideous, how disheartening, is the sudden stride
before our eyes, from health and beauty to deformity and
death!   In this waste and desolation there was more
peacefulness, I believe, than anywhere else beyond, in the
whole extent of our dominions.   It was not to last.

A tomb stood opposite the entrance: Cleone rushed
toward it, reposed her brow against it, and said at
intervals:

"I am weary; I ache throughout; I thirst bitterly; I cannot read the epitaph."

The boy advanced, drew his finger slowly along, at the bottom of the letters, and said :

"Surely they are plain enough.

"'*Xeniades son of Charondas.*'"

He turned round and looked at me, well satisfied. Cleone lowered her cheek to the inscription; but her knees bent under her, and she was fain to be seated ou the basement.

"Cleone!" said I . . she started at the name . . "Come, I beseech you, from that sepulchre."

"The reproof is just!" she replied . . "Here too, even here I am an alien!"

Aspasia! she will gladden your memory no more; never more will she heave your bosom with fond expectancy. There is none to whom, in the pride of your soul, you will run with her letters in your hand. He, upon whose shoulder you have read them in my presence lies also in the grave. The last of them is written.

ANNOUNCEMENTS FOR THE FALL OF 1894.

MOLIÈRE (J. Bapt. Poquelin).
A new edition of MOLIÈRE'S DRAMATIC WORKS. Translated by Katharine Prescott Wormeley, the translator of Balzac's Novels.

This edition will include a preface to Molière's works by H. de Balzac, criticisms on the author by C. A. Sainte-Beuve, portraits by Coypel and Mignard, and decorative titlepages by Updike, and will be issued at short intervals in duodecimo volumes, leather backs. Price, $1.50 per volume.

Now Ready.
Vol. I. THE MISANTHROPE; LE BOURGEOIS GENTILHOMME.
Vol. II. TARTUFFE; LES PRÉCIEUSES RIDICULES; GEORGE DANDIN.

In Press.
Vol. III. LES FEMMES SAVANTES; LE MALADE IMAGINAIRE.
Vol. IV. L'AVARE; DON JUAN; LES FACHEUX.

BALZAC (H. de).
CATHERINE DE MEDICI. Translated by Katharine Prescott Wormeley. 12mo. Half Russia. Price, $1.50.

BOURGET (Paul)
A SAINT. From the "Pastels of Men." Translated by Katharine Prescott Wormeley. With 12 illustrations by Paul Chabas. Square 12mo. Parchment paper covers. Price, $1.00.
"A Saint" takes us to higher and healthier levels of life. The central incident is indeed a miracle, — the eternal miracle of a soul's regeneration by Christ's own method, as new and wonderful now as by the well of Sychar or on the road to Damascus. — *The Spectator*.

YOUNG (Franklin K.) and HOWELL (Edwin C.).
THE MINOR TACTICS OF CHESS: A Treatise on the Deployment of the Forces in Obedience to Strategic Principle. 16mo. Cloth. Price, $1.00.
The student of chess will find in this book an altogether original treatment of the opening or "development" of the game. Avoiding the cumbersome and frequently misleading analysis of which chess manuals have hitherto been composed, the authors have elaborated the known principles of development, have discovered and enunciated others of manifestly great value, and have built upon this theoretical foundation a practical method, or series of methods, of deploying the chess pieces so that they shall individually and collectively exercise their normal functions in the most effective and consistent manner.

WHITING (Lilian).
THE WORLD BEAUTIFUL. 16mo. Cloth. Price, $1.00; white and gold, $1.25.

HOSMER (F. L.) and GANNETT (W. C.).
THE THOUGHT OF GOD IN HYMNS AND POEMS. Second Series. 16mo. Cloth. $1.00. Paper covers, 50 cents.

HARNACK (Adolf).
THE HISTORY OF DOGMA. Vol. I. (*In press.*)

RENAN (Ernest).
HISTORY OF THE PEOPLE OF ISRAEL. Vols. IV. and V. (*In press.*)

CALL (Annie Payson).
AS A MATTER OF COURSE. 16mo. Cloth. Price, $1.00.

ECKSTEIN (Ernst).
A MONK OF THE AVENTINE. A Novel. Translated from the German by Helen Hunt Johnson. 16mo. Cloth. Price, $1.00.

DICKINSON (Emily).
LETTERS. From 1847 to 1886. Edited by Mabel Loomis TODD. With a portrait of Miss Dickinson and a view of her home in Amherst, and three fac-similes of her handwriting at different periods of her life. 2 vols. 16mo. Price, $2.00.

ADAMS (Francis).
A CHILD OF THE AGE. A Novel. With titlepage designed by Aubrey Beardsley. American copyright edition. 16mo. Price, $1.00.

COOLIDGE (Susan).
NOT QUITE EIGHTEEN. A volume of Stories, with illustrations by Jessie McDermott. 16mo, cloth, uniform with "What Katy Did," etc. Price, $1.25.

SMITH (Mary P. Wells).
JOLLY GOOD TIMES TO-DAY. A continuation of the "Jolly Good Times Series." Two illustrations by Jessie McDermott. 16mo. Cloth. Price, $1.25.

WEBSTER (Leigh).
ANOTHER GIRL'S EXPERIENCE. A Story for Girls. With illustrations by Jessie McDermott. 16mo. Cloth. Price, $1.25.

PLYMPTON (A. G.).
PENELOPE PRIG AND OTHER STORIES. Illustrated by the author. Small 4to. Cloth. Price, $1.00.
RAGS AND VELVET GOWNS. Illustrated by the author. Square 12mo. Cloth back, paper sides. Price, 50 cents.

RAYMOND (Evelyn.)
THE LITTLE LADY OF THE HORSE. With 21 illustrations by Frank T. Merrill. Small 4to. Cloth. Price, $1.50.

SLOCUM (Captain Joshua).
VOYAGE OF THE LIBERDADE. Small 4to. Illustrated. Cloth. Price, $1.00.

SAMUELS (Adelaide F.). FATHER GANDER'S MELODIES. Illustrated by Lillian Trask Harlow. Small 4to. Cloth. Price, $1.25.

EWING (Mrs. J. H.).
LAST WORDS. A Final Collection of Stories. With illustrations by H. D. Murphy. A new and cheaper edition, uniform with our edition of Mrs. Ewing's Books. Price, 50 cents.

GILMAN (John Bradley).
THE KINGDOM OF COINS. A Tale for Children of all Ages. Illustrated by F. T. Merrill. A new and improved edition. Small 4to. Price, 60 cents.

Latest Publications.

COLUMBIAN KNOWLEDGE SERIES.

Edited by Professor Todd, of Amherst College. A series of timely, readable, and authoritative monographs on subjects of wide and permanent interest and significance. Each work is intended to be complete in itself. The treatment will be scientific where best suited to the purpose; but the language will be untechnical, and illustrations freely used when appropriate. Issued in 16mo volumes, neatly and uniformly bound in cloth.

No. 1. Total Eclipses of the Sun. By MABEL LOOMIS TODD. With numerous illustrations. 16mo. Cloth. Gilt. $1.00.

The great eclipse of 1842 marked the dawn of a golden age of physical research upon the Sun, and the conclusion of a half-century of significant research forms a fitting epoch for summarizing salient results in review. Advantage has been taken of this opportunity to present the attractive features of remote eclipses; and the connection of those in early, mediæval, and later centuries with contemporary history will, it is hoped, add new interest to astronomical events already widely celebrated. Ample illustrations have been chosen from a wide field, and include a collection of the coronas of the different eclipses. The present volume is not written for astronomers, much less for eclipse experts, but to give very unprofessional information to those without technical knowledge who are yet curious as to these strangely impressive phenomena, — and with the hope, too, of creating further intelligent interest.

No. 2. Public Libraries in America. By WILLIAM I. FLETCHER, M.A., Librarian of Amherst College. With illustrations of noted Libraries and Librarians. 16mo. Cloth. Gilt. $1.00.

Mr. Fletcher first sketches the history and significance of the public library movement, — a movement in which public school teachers have the closest interest, — and then takes up the various details of administering an efficient library. The building, classification, catalogues, selection and purchase of books, the work and the training necessary for the librarian, and the many details which only one who has had long and intimate experience in management and administration can know and understand, are treated with discriminating explicitness. Chapters on the Library Association and on the representative libraries of the United States and Canada, illustrated with views of their houses and of men who are foremost in the library work help to make this an invaluable volume for any one who desires to engage in library work, or to know what this work means. In an appendix Mr. Fletcher gives a scheme of classification, a list of special collections in American Libraries, some facts in regard to Sunday opening, a list of the more important gifts to public libraries, and some statistics in regard to the one hundred largest free public libraries in the United States. A set of library rules, as used in Newark, N. J., is given. — *N. E. Journal of Education.*

No. 3. Stars and Telescopes. A Handybook of Astronomy. By DAVID P. TODD, M.A., PH.D., and WILLIAM T. LYNN, F.R.A.S. *In Press.*

A compendium of the astronomy of all times; the story of the large observatories, the great telescopes, and the important work done with them; together with numerous portraits and biographic sketches of eminent astronomers. Fully illustrated.

Other volumes in preparation.

THE TORCH-BEARERS.

By ARLO BATES. A Poem. Delivered at the centennial of the establishment of Bowdoin College, June 28, 1894. 8vo. Limp covers. 50 cents.

It is worthy a wide reading, and is a credit to the author, the college it particularly speaks to, and to the age. — *Boston Times.*

POOR FOLK.

A Novel translated from the Russian of FEDOR DOSTOIEVSKY, by Lena Milman, with decorative titlepage and a critical introduction by George Moore. American Copyright Edition. 16mo. Cloth. $1.00.

A capable critic writes : "One of the most beautiful, touching stories I have ever read. The character of the old clerk is a masterpiece,—a kind of Russian Charles Lamb. He reminds me, too, of Anatole France's 'Sylvestre Bonnard,' but it is a more puignant, moving figure. How wonderfully, too, the sad little strokes of humor are blended into the pathos in his characterization, and how fascinating all the naïve self-revelations of his poverty become,—all his many ups and downs and hopes and fear. His unsuccessful visit to the money-lender, his despair at the office, — unexpectedly ending in a sudden burst of good fortune, — the final despairing cry of his love for Varvara,—these hold one breathless. One can hardly read them without tears. . . . But there is no need to say all that could be said about the book. It is enough to say that it is over powerful and beautiful.

BROTHERS AND STRANGERS.

A Novel. By AGNES BLAKE POOR. 16mo. Cloth. $1.00.

A very pleasant story, in a natural key, and in a thoroughly healthful tone. The author of this story is not unused to the writing of short stories, but this is, if we are not mistaken, her first long novel. If so, it is an unusually successful first effort ; for it is admirably put together in the matter of construction, and it is written in a quiet and attractive style, free from extravagance, verbosity, and over-elaboration. The story is laid in Boston and central New York, and the contrast between the different kinds of society in the two places is very successfully drawn. The quality of the book promises well for books of the future from the same hand. *The Outlook.*

SUCH AS THEY ARE.

Poems by THOMAS WENTWORTH HIGGINSON and MARY THACHER HIGGINSON. Illustrated by E. H. Garrett. Small quarto. Cloth. $1.00.

Thoughtful, musical, and beautifully finished, these verses appeal to the best taste. The first part, containing about a score of short pieces, is by Colonel Higginson. The scholarly touch prevails here without pedantry. In the second part, which is by Mrs. Higginson, a very sweet and womanly spirit holds the pen and controls the strokes. It is a little volume to be kept as an embodiment of the gentlest influences of cultured life. The illustrations are beautiful. — *The Independent.*

THE WEDDING GARMENT.

A Tale of the Life to Come. By LOUIS PENDLETON. 16mo. Cloth, $1.00. White and Gold, $1.25.

"The Wedding Garment" tells the story of the continued existence of a young man after his death, or departure from the natural world. Awakening in the other world,— in an intermediate region between Heaven and Hell, where the good and the evil live together temporarily commingled,—he is astonished and delighted to find himself the same man in all respects as to every characteristic of his mind and ultimate of the body. So closely does everything about him resemble the world he has left behind that he believes he is still in the latter until convinced of the error. The young man has good impulses, but is no saint, and he listens to the persuasions of certain persons who were his friends in the world, but who are now numbered among the evil, even to the extent of following them downward to the very confines of Hell. Resisting at last and saving himself, later on, and after many remarkable experiences, he gradually makes his way through the intermediate region to the gateways of Heaven (which can be found only by those prepared to enter), where he is left with the prospect before him of a blessed eternity in the company of the woman he loves.

The book is written in a reverential spirit ; it is unique and quite unlike any story of the same type heretofore published, full of telling incidents and dramatic situations, and not merely a record of the doings of sexless " shades," but of *living* human beings.

THE DANCING FAUN.

A Novel. By FLORENCE FARR. With title-page by Aubrey Beardsley. American Copyright Edition. 16mo. Cloth. $1.00.

A clever and original story, evidently based on original observation of life. The surprise at the end is admirably managed, and the daring philosophy of murder which Miss Farr thus indicates makes a striking moral for the book, which is sure to attract notice and criticism

KEYNOTES.

A volume of stories. By GEORGE EGERTON. With title-page by Aubrey Beardsley. 16mo. Cloth. $1.00.

Not since "The Story of an African Farm" was written has any woman delivered herself of so strong, so forcible a book. — *Queen.*

Knotty questions in sex problems are dealt with in these brief sketches. They are treated boldly, fearlessly, perhaps we may say forcefully, with a deep plunge into the realities of life. — *Public Opinion.*

Indeed, we do not hesitate to say that "Keynotes" is the strongest volume of short stories that the year has produced. Further, we would wager a good deal, were it necessary, that George Egerton is a *nom de plume,* and of a woman too.

The characters are intense, yet not overdrawn; the experiences are dramatic, in one sense or another, and yet are never hyper-emotional. And all is told with a power of concentration that is simply astonishing. A sentence does duty for a chapter, a paragraph for a picture of years of experience. — *Times,* Boston.

DREAM LIFE AND REAL LIFE.

A Little African Story. By OLIVE SCHREINER, author of "Dreams," "The Story of an African Farm." 16mo. Half cloth. 60 cents.

"Dream Life and Real Life" is the title of the first story in a tiny volume by Olive Schreiner, containing ninety-one pages of perfect workmanship and unutterable pathos. She takes the vital elements of life, love, trust, and self-sacrifice, and weaves them into tales bristling with action. When the deed is done, the tale ends. Neither word of explanation nor thinly covered moral mars their dramatic force. Each reader must find out these stories for himself; but he should not read the first to a child, for his heart would beat too fast under the woe of it. Every selfish woman might take home the third sketch unto herself, in daily penance for want of insight into another's misery. — *Literary World.*

THE AIM OF LIFE.

Plain Talks to Young Men and Women. By Rev. PHILIP STAFFORD MOXOM. 16mo. Cloth. $1.00.

Of this book, the *New England Journal of Education* says: "Under the title of 'The Aim of Life,' Rev. Philip S. Moxom addresses to young people a series of plain, practical talks upon influences that are to be met, contended, or redeemed every day. The essays evince a keen yet sympathetic observation of young manhood and womanhood, and an appreciative regard for its foibles, the force of its environments, and, above all, of its possibilities of achievement. That possibility of achievement and the means thereto derives a forceful significance from being made the subject of the first essay and the title of the book. Having thus laid stress on his principle, the author forbears to lift up beautiful ideals in the hope that their intrinsic merit shall draw all men unto them, but rather he endeavors to incite the noble instincts that practical every-day life must either foster or annul. Such titles as Character, Companionship, Temperance, Debt, The True Aristocracy, Education, Saving Time, Ethics of Amusement, Reading, Orthodoxy, show the scope of the theme, which, if varied in expression, is one throughout all. The essays are not sermonic; they emphasize the power of Christianity; they recognize at the same time the power of personality. Christian ethics expressed in plain, forcible language, and innocent of didacticism, young people always appreciate. Such are Dr. Moxom's essays, originally given to the public as addresses to young people in Boston and Cleveland. Now their publication, in convenient form, it is to be hoped, seals their value with permanency."

BY MOORLAND AND SEA.

By FRANCIS A. KNIGHT, author of "By Leafy Ways," "Idylls of the Field," etc. Illustrated by the author. 12mo. Cloth. $1.50.

There is a vein of genuine poetry in Mr. Knight, and in his wanderings "By Moorland and Sea" it finds graceful expression. These fifteen descriptive essays are filled with close but never paraded observation of Nature in sunshine and storm, and each little delicate picture is firmly drawn, and has in it just the requisite amount of local color. He takes us to the stormy waters of the Hebrides, and in his company we sail up narrow Loch Dunvegan and climb the rock on which stands the gray stronghold of the Macleods,— a fortress that for ten centuries has remained in the family of its founders, and stands on its sea-washed reef today apparently untouched by time, in spite of the hurricanes and the sieges of a thousand years. Then we find ourselves far away to the south on Sedgmoor, thinking of Monmouth and of what Macaulay has termed "the last fight deserving of the name of 'battle' that has been fought on English ground." Once more — to pick another scene at random — we are in the midsummer fields in the dewy dawn, listening as the shadows vanish for the musical carol of the thrush, whose joyous prelude quickly awakens the invisible choir of the neighboring woodlands. The breath of the country is in these sketches, and that fact in part explains their spell, and the rest of the secret stands revealed in the brilliant descriptive gift of the writer. — *The Speaker.*

ART FOR AMERICA.

By WILLIAM ORDWAY PARTRIDGE. 16mo. Cloth. $1.00. A strong plea for the elevation of American Art to its rightful place in the scheme of general education.

CONTENTS: — The True Education and the False, An American School of Sculpture, The Outlook for Sculpture in America, Manhood in Art, The Relation of the Drama to Education. Goethe as a Dramatist.

Mr. Partridge is thoughtful, forceful, and sincere, and he has put his thoughtfulness, forcefulness, and sincerity into this book, and for this reason the essays it contains are interesting as discourses and valuable as arguments. The book is a plea for a more general art culture, for a higher refinement, and for a bringing out of that which is noblest in our people, trusting and believing that the outcome will be an American school of art that will express the highest and noblest life and spirit, as did the grand art of the Greeks during the era of their highest culture, refinement, and nobility. — *Boston Traveller.*

LIBRARY CLASSIFICATION.

By W. I FLETCHER, A.M., Librarian of Amherst College. Reprinted with alterations, additions, and an index from his "Public Libraries in America." One volume, thin 8vo, limp covers. $1.00.

There are already in the field many rival schemes of classification for libraries. The present publication is not intended to add one to the number, but rather to offer a way of escape for those who shrink from the intricacies and difficulties of the elaborate systems, and to substitute for painstaking analytical classification a simple arrangement which it is believed is better adapted to be practically useful in a library, while doing away with most of the work involved in carrying out one of these schemes.

WAYSIDE SKETCHES.

By EBEN J. LOOMIS. 16mo. Cloth. $1.00.

A pleasing out-of-door book, embodying essays on : The Advance of the Seasons, The Coming and Going of the Birds, Searching for the First Flowers of Spring, and Observations of the Processes of Nature during Quiet Walks in the Country.

Here are twenty essays, a few of them in verse, all breathing the love of Nature, and pervaded by a sweetness, restfulness, and simplicity, that make them very attractive. The author recommends quiet walks in the country, and a loving observation of the processes of Nature, as a cure for unhealthy introspection, to say nothing of ennui and dyspepsia. Next to taking such walks, we should say, would be the reading of such essays as this. — *Portland Transcript.*

www.ingramcontent.com/pod-product-compliance
Lightning Source LLC
Chambersburg PA
CBHW030622030726
47497CB00006B/1603